I0811808

CASEBOOK
Developmentally Appropriate Practice in Early Childhood Programs

Serving Children from Birth Through Age 8

EDITED BY

Pamela Brillante, Jennifer J. Chen, Stephany Cuevas, Christyn Dundorf, Emily Brown Hoffman, Daniel R. Meier, Gayle Mindes, & Lisa R. Roy

National Association for the Education of Young Children

Washington, DC

naeyc®

National Association for the Education of Young Children

1401 H Street NW, Suite 600
Washington, DC 20005
202-232-8777 • 800-424-2460
NAEYC.org

NAEYC Books
Senior Director, Publishing & Content Development
Susan Friedman

Director, Books
Dana Battaglia

Senior Editor
Holly Bohart

Editor II
Rossella Procopio

Senior Creative Design Manager
Charity Coleman

Senior Creative Design Specialist
Gillian Frank

Publishing Business Operations Manager
Francine Markowitz

Photo Credits

Courtesy of Olabisi Adesuyi-Fasuyi: 111

Courtesy of Alicia Alvarez: 122

Courtesy of Brandon L. Gilbert: 59

Courtesy of Larissa Hsia-Wong: 126

Courtesy of Sueli Nunes: 119

Courtesy of Guadalupe Rivas: 105

Courtesy of Angela Vargas: 137

Casebook: Developmentally Appropriate Practice in Early Childhood Programs Serving Children from Birth Through Age 8.

Library of Congress Control Number: 2022935933

ISBN: 978-1-952331-12-1

Item: 1163

Contents

Editors, Contributors, and Reviewers

Part Editors

Pamela Brillante, EdD, is professor in the Department of Special Education, Professional Counseling and Disability Studies, at William Paterson University. She has worked as an early childhood special educator, administrator, and New Jersey state specialist in early childhood special education. She is the author of the NAEYC book *The Essentials: Supporting Young Children with Disabilities in the Classroom*. Dr. Brillante continues to work with schools to develop high-quality inclusive early childhood programs.

Jennifer J. Chen, EdD, is professor of early childhood and family studies at Kean University. She earned her doctorate from Harvard University. She has authored or coauthored more than 60 publications in early childhood education. Dr. Chen has received several awards, including the 2020 NAECTE Foundation Established Career Award for Research on ECTE, the 2021 Kean Presidential Excellence Award for Distinguished Scholarship, and the 2022 NJAECTE's Distinguished Scholarship in ECTE/ECE Award.

Stephany Cuevas, EdD, is assistant professor of education in the Attallah College of Educational Studies at Chapman University. Dr. Cuevas is an interdisciplinary education scholar whose research focuses on family engagement, Latinx families, and the postsecondary trajectories of first-generation students. She is the author of *Apoyo Sacrifical, Sacrificial Support: How Undocumented Parents Get Their Children to College* (Teachers College Press).

Christyn Dundorf, PhD, has more than 30 years of experience in the early learning field as a teacher, administrator, and adult educator. She serves as codirector of Teaching Preschool Partners, a nonprofit organization working to grow playful learning and inquiry practices in school-based pre-K programs and infuse those practices up into the early grades.

Emily Brown Hoffman, PhD, is assistant professor in early childhood education at National Louis University in Chicago. She received her PhD from the University of Illinois at Chicago in Curriculum & Instruction, Literacy, Language, & Culture. Her focuses include emergent literacy, leadership, play and creativity, and school, family, and community partnerships.

Daniel R. Meier, PhD, is professor of elementary education at San Francisco State University. His publications include *Critical Issues in Infant-Toddler Language Development: Connecting Theory to Practice* (editor), *Supporting Literacies for Children of Color: A Strength-Based Approach to Preschool Literacy* (author), and *Learning Stories and Teacher Inquiry Groups: Reimagining Teaching and Assessment in Early Childhood Education* (coauthor).

Gayle Mindes, EdD, is professor emerita, DePaul University. She is the author of *Assessing Young Children*, fifth edition (with Lee Ann Jung), and *Social Studies for Young Children: Preschool and Primary Curriculum Anchor,* third edition (with Mark Newman). Dr. Mindes is also the editor of *Teaching Young Children with Challenging Behaviors: Practical Strategies for Early Childhood Educators* and *Contemporary Challenges in Teaching Young Children: Meeting the Needs of All Students.*

Lisa R. Roy, EdD, is executive director for the Colorado Department of Early Childhood. Dr. Roy has supported families with young children for over 30 years, serving as the director of program development for the Buffett Early Childhood Institute, as the executive director of early childhood education for Denver Public Schools, and in various nonprofit and government roles.

Casebook Contributors

Barbara Abel, PhD, visiting clinical lecturer, University of Illinois at Chicago

Olabisi Adesuyi-Fasuyi, MA, doctoral student in educational leadership, San Francisco State University

Josephine Ahmadein, BA, IMH-E, early childhood quality improvement specialist, CCCC of Union County, New Jersey

Bridget Amory, EdD, director of student learning, Milford, Delaware, S.D. 12

Marcela Andrés, EdM, CEO and president, designEDengagement, PBC

Jovanna Archuleta, early childhood community outreach director, Los Alamos National Laboratory (LANL) Foundation

Erika Bocknek, PhD, LMFT, associate professor of educational psychology, Wayne State University

Ellie Bold, MA, doctoral student, University of Denver

Lauren Bond, BA, president and early childhood education specialist, Bond Education Services & Training

Alyssa Brillante, MEd, kindergarten teacher, Haledon Public School, Haledon, New Jersey

Kameron C. Carden, MA, CCC/SLP, LSLS cert., doctoral candidate, University of Alabama

Leah Catching, MA, doctoral student, San Francisco State University

Jennifer J. Chen, EdD, professor of early childhood and family studies, Kean University, Union New Jersey

Lea Ann Christenson, PhD, associate professor in early childhood education, Towson University

Marie Ann Donovan, EdD, associate professor and program director for early childhood, DePaul University, Chicago

Addison Duane, PhD, postdoctoral research fellow, Innovations for Youth, University of California, Berkeley

Valeria Erdosi, MS, executive director emerita, The King's Daughters Day School, New Jersey

Isauro M. Escamilla, EdD, early childhood educator, San Francisco Unified School District

Suzanna Ewert, EdM, CalFresh Healthy Living, University of California Cooperative Extension

Sarah Rendón García, PhD, NSF SBE & HGSE dean's postdoctoral fellow, Harvard Graduate School of Education, Cambridge, Massachusetts

Esther Garza, PhD, associate professor of bilingual and ESL education, Texas A&M University–San Antonio

Brandon L. Gilbert, EdD, assistant professor, Metropolitan State University, Denver

Jennifer Gonzalez, MA, infant-toddler program coordinator, Early Childhood Lab School, University of California, Davis

Michelle Gonzalez, PhD, associate professor, William Paterson University of New Jersey, Wayne

Ron Grady, MSEd, doctoral student in education, Harvard University; former teacher, NOLA Nature School

Marsha Shigeyo Hawley, MEd, Early Childhood Consortium Project associate director, Illinois State Board of Higher Education, Chicago

Meghann Hickey, MS, senior manager of professional development, Hatch Early Learning Inc.

Abby Hodges, PhD, BCBA, postdoctoral resident, Emory School of Medicine, Marcus Autism Center, Atlanta

Nicola Holdman, master's degree candidate, San José State University

Larissa Hsia-Wong, EdD, lead kindergarten teacher, Presidio Hill School, San Francisco

Zeynep Isik-Ercan, PhD, professor of early childhood education, Rowan University, Glassboro, New Jersey

LaKenya Johnson, MA, TLLP, doctoral candidate, educational psychology, Wayne State University, Detroit, Michigan

Lee Ann Jung, PhD, founder and director of Lead Inclusion and clinical professor, San Diego State University

Cierra Kaler-Jones, PhD, director of storytelling, Communities for Just Schools Fund

Sunyoung Kim, PhD, BCBA-D, associate professor, University of Illinois at Chicago

Donna Kirkwood, PhD, program project coordinator, Arkansas State University Childhood Services

Saili S. Kulkarni, PhD, associate professor, San José State University

Racheal Kuperus, BA, pre-K teacher, Franklin Lakes Board of Education, New Jersey

Marie L. Masterson, PhD, senior director of quality assessment, McCormick Center for Early Childhood Leadership, National Louis University, Chicago

Kevin McGowan, PhD, associate professor, Bridgewater State University, Massachusetts

Martha Melgoza, EdD, director, Skytown Cooperative Preschool, Richmond, California

Lauren C. Mims, PhD, assistant professor, Department of Applied Psychology, New York University Steinhardt School of Culture, Education, and Human Development

Leah Schoenberg Muccio, PhD, associate professor of early childhood education, University of Hawai'i at Mānoa

Karen Nemeth, consultant, Language Castle LLC

Sueli Nunes, MA, coeducation director, Felton Early Care and Education Programs, San Francisco

Desarae Orgo, BA, inclusion pre-K teacher, Franklin Lakes Board of Education, New Jersey

Guadalupe Rivas, MA, interim assistant director, Children's Campus at San Francisco State University

Amy Schmidtke, EdD, director of program development, Buffett Early Childhood Institute, University of Nebraska

Megan Schumaker-Murphy, EdD, assistant professor, Department of Early Childhood and Care, Salem State University, Massachusetts

Janis Strasser, EdD, professor emerita of early childhood education, William Paterson University, Wayne, New Jersey

Germaine Kaleilehua Tauati, early literacy coordinator, Institute of Native Pacific Education and Culture, Hawai'i

Janet Thompson, MA, director (retired), Early Childhood Lab School, Center for Child and Family Studies, University of California, Davis

Julia Torquati, PhD, professor and interim chairperson, Department of Child, Youth and Family Studies, University of Nebraska

Angela Vargas, MEd, early learning teacher on special assignment/coach, Beaverton School District, Oregon

Renee B. Whelan, EdD, early childhood instructional coach, Belmar Elementary School District and Matawan-Aberdeen Regional School District, New Jersey

Colleen E. Whittingham, PhD, clinical assistant professor, Loyola University, Chicago

Eleni Zgourou, PhD, assistant professor of early childhood and family studies, Kean University, Union, New Jersey

Reviewers

Camille Catlett, MA, senior technical assistance specialist, Frank Porter Graham Child Development Institute, University of North Carolina, Chapel Hill

Christan Coogle, PhD, associate professor of early childhood special education and board-certified behavior analyst, George Mason University, Fairfax, Virginia

Ivana Espinet, PhD, assistant professor, The City University of New York, Kingsborough Community College, Brooklyn

Nora Krieger, PhD, associate professor emerita, Bloomfield College, Bloomfield, New Jersey

Jane Lannak, PhD, clinical associate professor, Boston University, Boston, Massachusetts

Alissa Rausch, EdD, assistant research faculty, University of Denver, Denver, Colorado

Holly Seplocha, EdD, professor emeritus, William Paterson University, Wayne, New Jersey

Introduction and Book Overview

Jennifer J. Chen and Dana Battaglia

Why a Casebook on Developmentally Appropriate Practice?

As a resource for the early childhood profession, the text *Developmentally Appropriate Practice in Early Childhood Programs Serving Children from Birth Through Age 8* (hereafter called *Developmentally Appropriate Practice*) continues to evolve to meet the needs of teachers and teacher educators who must navigate a constantly shifting early childhood education landscape. Previous versions of NAEYC's position statement on developmentally appropriate practice, upon which *Developmentally Appropriate Practice* is based, sought to provide a framework for "best practice." Over time the position statement has been expanded to reflect advanced knowledge of child development and learning and of multiple appropriate and effective approaches to teaching children. For example, as reiterated in the fourth edition of *Developmentally Appropriate Practice*, developmentally appropriate practice does not mean a single "best" practice. Rather, it emphasizes a dynamic and complex set of practices that respect, value, and build on the varied strengths children and their families bring to the educational process. It encompasses the understanding that the social, cultural, linguistic, and historical contexts in which children, their families, and teachers live and work have a tremendous influence on these children's development and learning. Likewise, the supporting resources and the ways faculty teach developmentally appropriate practice to the early childhood educators of the future have had to change and adapt to facilitate educators' understanding that the unique and vital work of educating and caring for children must reflect our current knowledge of child development and learning as situated within diverse social, cultural, linguistic, and historical contexts.

With the publication of the fourth edition of *Developmentally Appropriate Practice*, NAEYC (2022) introduced new resources to support faculty in the teaching of developmentally appropriate practice (see NAEYC.org/dap/faculty-resources). A casebook as a companion to the fourth edition presented additional opportunities for further study and engagement with developmentally appropriate practice in new ways.

Case study methodology serves as an informative and transformative framework for teachers, teacher educators, and teacher candidates to engage in critical analysis and discussion of and reflection on how a teaching practice might or might not be developmentally appropriate practice, a process through which they can grow professionally. Importantly, professional growth is both a process and a product of lifelong learning that may resonate with educators and teacher educators. The case studies in this book present authentic classroom scenarios that reflect real-life challenges and opportunities facing educators. The cases encourage educators and teacher educators to engage in further study, reflection, and discourse to deepen their understanding of developmentally appropriate practice. In doing so, each may become a "reflective practitioner" (Schön 1983, 1987) and, in turn, become more knowledgeable and skillful at developing and implementing contextually adaptive strategies and approaches to working with children to optimize their developmental and learning potentials.

For example, key to developmentally appropriate practice is the intentional teaching and decision making that occur when educators consider specific developmental and learning needs in terms of the three core considerations: (1) commonality—understanding the general processes of children's development and learning at different ages; (2) individuality—seeing each child as an individual with unique characteristics and experiences; and (3) context—acknowledging and understanding the diverse social, cultural, linguistic, and historical contexts within which children, their families, and teachers construct their experiences. These considerations help educators not only adapt but also *become adept at adapting* their teaching to common and individual characteristics and contextual circumstances, enabling educators to thrive at implementing developmentally appropriate practice. In addition, as stated by NAEYC's (2020) most recent position statement on developmentally appropriate practice, "Educators make decisions that result in developmentally appropriate practice within the context of their specific program setting, a larger early childhood sector, and extended systems with institutionalized policies and practices" (29). All of these contextual factors suggest that the complex navigation and negotiation among various terrains require educators' intentional efforts to engage in developmentally appropriate practice.

The cases in this book promote critical thinking of creative, flexible, and reflective pedagogical solutions that align with the developmentally appropriate practice framework. Informed by developmentally appropriate practice, effective educators use the aforementioned core considerations to intentionally scaffold children's learning so that each child may achieve their potential. Vygotsky (1978) suggested that the most potent scaffoldings occur within the child's "zone of proximal development," defined as the difference between what a child can achieve with assistance (for example, from the educator) and what they can achieve unassisted. The case examples in this volume demonstrate how appropriate teacher scaffoldings of children's development and learning optimally operate within the three core considerations, their associated nine principles of child development and learning, and the six guidelines for developmentally appropriate practice in action. They also demonstrate teacher reflections on the unexpected teachable moments, challenges that arise, and emerging ideas and opportunities for future practice, highlighting the complexity and intentionality of educators' decision-making process in real-life teaching situations.

Instruction using the case analysis model in teacher education programs offers indirect firsthand experiences and possibilities for preservice teachers to develop strong content and pedagogical knowledge, skills, and positive dispositions to make informed decisions about effective solutions involving developmentally appropriate practice. Thus, case study instruction should occupy an important place in teacher preparation programs (Heitzmann 2008). Yet, this case study pedagogy has not been widely applied in early childhood teacher preparation. This book seeks to fill this gap in the teaching and teacher education literature and hopes to inspire the integration of case studies in teacher education programs.

About this Book

The cases are organized into eight parts, each of which is edited by an early childhood education professional who has extensive expertise in the topic. The case writers likewise have an abundance of diverse experience in working directly or indirectly with children through their various professional capacities and bring their authentic voices to the case studies. While cases vary in their usage of first or third person, all are inspired by actual events that have occurred in early childhood programs or families' homes, and many are the firsthand experiences of the authors.

The first six parts mirror the six guidelines for developmentally appropriate practice in action, as shown in the graphic below.

1 Creating a Caring, Equitable Community of Learners

2 Engaging in Reciprocal Partnerships with Families and Fostering Community Connections

3 Observing, Documenting, and Assessing Children's Development and Learning

4 Teaching to Enhance Each Child's Development and Learning

5 Planning and Implementing an Engaging Curriculum to Achieve Meaningful Goals

6 Demonstrating Professionalism as an Early Childhood Educator

Parts 7 and 8 provide additional focus on two important groups of learners who have unique developmental and learning needs and are increasingly present in classrooms throughout the country:

- Part 7: Supporting Children with Disabilities and Implementing Inclusive Practices
- Part 8: Supporting Dual Language Learners and Respecting Cultural and Linguistic Diversity

Individually and collectively, these parts revolve around the three core considerations, nine principles, and six guidelines. They also reflect current knowledge in (1) pedagogy, curriculum, and assessment, (2) ethical professional practices, (3) the importance of considering the contexts of children and families from diverse social, cultural, and linguistic backgrounds, and (4) effective practices for supporting children with disabilities and/or dual language learners in early childhood programs and classrooms.

Each case follows the same basic structure:

Connections to *Developmentally Appropriate Practice*: This section outlines the specific chapters and content in the fourth edition of the book and the position statement that the case illustrates. The case may describe a scenario in which developmentally appropriate practice is evident, or it may show a situation in which the teacher is not applying the guidelines and principles effectively. In either scenario, it is the accompanying critical, "reflection-in-action" (making decisions on teaching while it is occurring [Schön, 1983, 1987]), "reflection-on-action" (thinking back on an action that has already occurred [Dewey, 1910, 1933; Schön, 1983, 1987]), and/or "reflection-for-action" (thinking about and planning for future actions [Killion & Todnem 1991]) that make a difference in educators' professional growth. This is because educators' reflections (whether about a past, present, or future action) are conducted with the intention of improving their teaching practices to ultimately benefit children's learning and development.

Case Overview: This section includes a brief description of the purpose of the case and provides background information for context.

Learning Objectives: This section offers concrete, defined learning objectives to be achieved upon reading and evaluating the case.

Case Narrative: The details of the case are set forth in this section.

Takeaways and Next Steps: The section includes reflections from the educators in the case scenario and invites readers to think about next steps, forecasting based on the study of the case—what dilemmas may be ongoing, what challenges and opportunities need monitoring, and what next-level solutions might be, all of which reflect the educators' role as important decision makers in their vital work with children.

Case Discussion Questions: This section includes targeted questions on case specifics related to developmentally appropriate practice.

Some cases also provide general discussion questions, which pertain to the topic of the case but are not specific to it, and/or suggested resources for additional study.

Online Resources

Additional material, including tips and resources for faculty and discussion questions for teacher inquiry groups, can be found online at NAEYC.org/dap-casebook.

Note on Terminology

You will see both *dual language learner* and *emergent bilingual* used in this book to refer to young children who are learning English while simultaneously mastering proficiency in their home language.

Integrating this Casebook in Teacher Education Programs

This casebook can be easily integrated into teacher education. For instance, teacher preparation programs can incorporate it in both their teaching methods and fieldwork courses to engage preservice teachers in critical thinking and perspective taking about the pedagogical challenges and opportunities embedded in the cases (for example, solving ethical dilemmas; facing limited resource affordance; teaching children of different age groups, developmental characteristics, and social and cultural backgrounds). Thus, these cases can be instrumental in introducing preservice teachers to real-life classroom scenarios they may similarly encounter in their fieldwork.

Furthermore, teacher education course instructors can use the critical thinking questions that are case specific and general topic questions for in-class discussions, online discussion boards, and assignments. These questions can serve as starters for preservice teachers to (1) reflect on their own experience observing classroom teaching; (2) foster respect for diverse viewpoints and multiple approaches to solving pedagogical challenges; (3) develop analytic, problem-solving, critical thinking, and perspective-taking skills; and (4) identify opportunities for improving practice.

Course instructors may use specific cases to spark conversations about developmentally appropriate practice with preservice teachers. For example, discussion and analysis of cases may start individually, then continue in small groups, and finally occur with the whole group. Instructors may also provide opportunities to foster a discourse on developmentally appropriate practice inside the classroom and extend it outside the classroom with intentional assignments, such as individual or collaborative inquiry-based analytic projects and reflective writing. These assignments may encourage preservice teachers to individually and collaboratively identify key issues and brainstorm practical solutions. The process can promote both individual construction (Piaget 1963) and collaborative co-construction of knowledge (Vygotsky 1978). A variety of opportunities for learning about developmentally appropriate practice can foster a community of educators who appreciate the pedagogical challenges and innovative possibilities of working with children who have diverse social and cultural identities and developmental characteristics.

In addition, an early childhood teacher curriculum may be designed in a way that allows preservice teachers to revisit case studies at different points in their coursework and fieldwork. Over time, as their practical experience and knowledge increase, these preservice teachers may offer varying analyses and perspectives that reflect their own professional growth. For instance, as preservice teachers learn more about family engagement, they may apply such knowledge to analyzing a case from a family engagement perspective.

Integrating this Casebook in Professional Development

While *Developmentally Appropriate Practice* and this companion casebook can effectively introduce preservice teachers to the field of early childhood education and the vital yet complex work with children, they also serve as equally effective mechanisms to reinforce and remind in-service teachers who are knowledgeable about developmentally appropriate practice of the dynamic and intricate complexities of putting various aspects of developmentally appropriate practice into action. Furthermore, the casebook may motivate in-service teachers to reflect on their own engagement with developmentally appropriate practice and ways in which they can strengthen their own practices. Professional development presents itself as such an opportunity for fostering lifelong learning in educators. While educators may seek resources on their own, such as using this casebook, to continue developing their teaching craft, they should also be well supported with opportunities (for example, workshops and seminars from their school districts or early learning programs) to engage in continuous professional development to further establish themselves as professionals and advance their teaching expertise. For instance, school districts may leverage and incorporate both *Developmentally Appropriate Practice* and this casebook in professional development activities for in-service teachers, especially those who have had little or no exposure to the developmentally appropriate practice framework. In this way, professional development is a critical means through which educators grow and become better at the critical yet complex art of implementing developmentally appropriate practice with intentionality.

Ongoing Learning

The work of putting developmentally appropriate practice into action starts with understanding the richness and complexity of the processes of child development and learning and the educational practices that best support this development and learning in all areas. Each interaction with children, families, and other early childhood professionals is an opportunity for educators to learn and grow. Thus, it is imperative that educators understand that learning about developmentally appropriate practice is an ongoing process as demonstrated by the case studies.

There are many options for using and engaging with the cases in this book. Each offers a jumping-off point for more discussion and learning. For example, to become actively immersed in the stories of the educators, the children, and the families; to consider the questions and takeaways carefully; and then to engage in meaningful analysis and discussion with fellow students and colleagues is to begin to understand what these narrative accounts reveal to us about why developmentally appropriate practice is so important in nurturing child development and learning. The cases offer glimpses and insights into the everyday and the unique, the challenging and the surprising, the revelatory, the stressful, and the joyful—everything that is involved in becoming and being an effective early childhood educator.

References

Dewey, J. 1910. *How We Think*. Boston: D.C. Heath.

Dewey, J. 1933. *How We Think: A Restatement of the Relation of Reflective Thinking to the Educative Process*. Rev. ed. Boston: D.C. Heath.

Heitzmann, R. 2008. "Case Study Instruction in Teacher Education: Opportunity to Develop Students' Critical Thinking, School Smarts and Decision Making." *Education* 128 (4): 523–42.

Killion, J.P., & G.R. Todnem. 1991. "A Process for Personal Theory Building." *Educational Leadership* 48 (6): 14–16.

NAEYC. 2020. "Developmentally Appropriate Practice." Position statement. Washington, DC: NAEYC. www.naeyc.org/resources/position-statements/dap.

NAEYC. 2022. *Developmentally Appropriate Practice in Early Childhood Programs Serving Children from Birth Through Age 8*. 4th ed. Washington, DC: NAEYC.

Piaget, J. 1963. *The Origins of Intelligence in Children*. New York: Norton.

Schön, D.A. 1983. *The Reflective Practitioner: How Professionals Think in Action*. New York: Basic Books.

Schön, D.A. 1987. *Educating the Reflective Practitioner: Toward a New Design for Teaching and Learning in the Professions*. San Francisco: Jossey-Bass.

Vygotsky, L.S. 1978. *Mind and Society: The Development of Higher Mental Processes*. Cambridge, MA: Harvard University Press.

PART 1

Creating a Caring, Equitable Community of Learners

Lisa R. Roy

Creating a caring, equitable community is foundational to children's development and their future success as lifelong learners. As a mother and a grandmother, I can attest to how important it is that early childhood environments (children's homes, early learning programs, schools, and communities) promote equity and nurture the mind, body, and soul of all children, families, and educators.

Educators and advocates commit to culturally responsible and responsive pedagogies to ensure that children have the social and emotional competence and security they need, facilitating young children's regard and respect for other children and adults and ensuring a safe environment for learning. Educators address these complexities through modeling and intentionality. They model their commitment to equity by embracing beliefs, attitudes, and perceptions around gender, economic status, race, ethnicity, and ability that support practices benefiting all children, families, and communities. They are intentional in building supportive, positive relationships where children feel seen and heard and their identities are honored and welcomed. What could be more foundational?

In Part 1, the case authors explore ways to support diversity, equity, and inclusion while putting relationships front and center. The cases are strengths based and highlight the joy of learning and the development and nurturance of relationships among children, early childhood professionals, and families.

Topics include the following:

- Identifying opportunities to build friendships and a sense of belonging among a toddler with a disability and her peers
- Valuing and respecting all children and families by pronouncing and spelling each child's name according to child and family preference
- Leveraging lessons learned from virtual teaching to serve children and families upon returning to in-person learning
- Fostering child–child relationships across the daily schedule, including during academic learning and teacher-directed collaborative work
- Supporting caring connections among children by celebrating the many different ways they show kindness to each other
- Building on positive relationships with families by fostering stronger connections and deeper understandings

The authors of these cases include professors of early education whose research focuses on play, attachment security, natural environments, parent–child relationships, children's social processes, early literacy, English as a second language, STEAM teaching and learning, equity pedagogy, early childhood curriculum, teacher education and professional development, and birth-to-third-grade school district partnerships. All have experience working in the policy, practitioner, and researcher arenas as well as in addressing the needs of children and families who have been historically marginalized.

1.1 Missed Opportunities: Relationship Building in Inclusive Classrooms

Julia Torquati

Connections to *Developmentally Appropriate Practice*

- Chapter 6: Creating a Caring, Equitable Community of Learners

Case Overview

This case explores the importance of identifying and using opportunities to help a child with a disability gain a sense of belonging among peers and build friendships. In this example, a teacher is sitting with a toddler, Bella, who is being fed with a feeding tube. The other children are playing in the room, and a couple of them come over to where Bella is being fed. This case illustrates guideline 1 of the position statement on developmentally appropriate practice and how it relates to providing equitable learning experiences for children, with special emphasis on 1A ("Each member of the community is valued by the others and is recognized for the strengths they bring") and 1B ("Relationships are nurtured with each child, and educators facilitate development of positive relationships among children"). The case also highlights the importance of principle 6 ("Children's motivation to learn is increased when their learning environment fosters their sense of belonging, purpose, and agency").

Learning Objectives

1. Examine how fostering development of relationships among children with and without disabilities relates to providing equitable learning experiences, with special emphasis on valuing each member of the community and their strengths.
2. Identify opportunities for relationship building, including peer relationships, among infants and toddlers.

Case Narrative

Bella is a 15-month-old who requires a nasogastric feeding tube because she has difficulty swallowing. Ms. Sophia sits with Bella until she is finished with the feeding tube. Bella has a special chair with a tray that she uses when she is fed so that she can play with something on the tray and to keep her from moving too much while the feeding tube is connected. She begins her feeding at the same time other children are eating breakfast, but it sometimes takes up to 45 minutes to complete the feeding, so the other children usually finish breakfast and transition to other activities before Bella. Today, the other children have finished their breakfast and are scooping seeds out of a pumpkin or playing in different areas of the classroom.

Ms. Sophia has placed a ziplock plastic bag of goop (a cornstarch and water mixture for sensory exploration) on the tray for Bella to explore. Ms. Sophia shows Bella how the goop moves around inside the bag when she taps on it. Bella taps on the bag and manipulates the goop inside it for about a minute, then throws it on the floor. Ms. Sophia picks up the bag and demonstrates again how to move the goop in the bag by pressing on it. Bella pats the bag a few times, picks it up and squishes it between her hands, and then throws it on the floor.

Ahmed, who has finished scooping seeds out of the pumpkin, walks past Bella on his way to the sink to wash his hands. He stops to pick up the bag of goop and places it on her tray. Ms. Sophia says, "Thank you, Ahmed," as he walks to the sink. Ms. Sophia pats the bag on the tray, and Bella picks up the bag and throws it on the floor.

Ms. Sophia turns away from Bella to ask Lily, who is pushing a fire truck, "Where is the fire?" Lily smiles and keeps pushing the fire truck past Bella's chair. Lily stops, stands up, smiles at Bella, and then continues pushing the fire truck to the other side of the room. Ms. Sophia picks up the bag of goop and places it on Bella's tray. When Bella is done with her feeding, Ms. Sophia asks, "Are you all done and ready to play?" Ms. Sophia helps Bella out of the chair and seats her on the floor. Bella looks around at children playing in different areas of the room, then rocks forward onto her hands and knees and slowly crawls toward the children scooping seeds out of the pumpkin.

Takeaways and Next Steps

Later that day, Ms. Sophia meets with her coteachers and coach to review their documentation of the children's learning and development, identify emerging skills they've observed, and select individual learning objectives for each child. When the discussion turns to Bella's social and emotional development and specifically her ability to enter play and interact positively with peers, Ms. Sophia reflects on how the length of Bella's feedings limits her opportunities for interacting with peers. Ms. Sophia and her colleagues discuss Bella's strengths, including her interest in other children; her expressive communication skills, such as making eye contact and smiling, showing curiosity, and using gestures like pointing and nodding her head; and her calm, nonreactive temperament. Wondering if she is underestimating Bella's interest in her peers and her ability to engage with them, Ms. Sophia sets a goal to observe Bella's behaviors around the other children so she can more intentionally plan opportunities for Bella to engage with her peers. Early peer relationships are important because they help children to feel a sense of belonging to a group, and they are also a context for learning social and emotional skills that are critical for making friends and sustaining friendships.

Bella was using her strengths to exercise her agency and communicate with Ms. Sophia through her behavior. However, Ms. Sophia did not seem to check her assumptions about what Bella may have been communicating. Asking Bella a question—and waiting for a response—would have allowed Ms. Sophia to check her understanding as well as scaffold Bella's language development. A behavior reflection such as this would also communicate to Bella that she is valued and that what she is trying to communicate is important, a reflection of guideline 1 of the position statement on developmentally appropriate practice.

Case Discussion Questions

1. How do you think Ms. Sophia interpreted Bella's behavior of throwing the bag of goop on the floor? Why do you think she interpreted the behavior this way?
2. What do *you* think Bella was trying to communicate when she repeatedly threw the bag of goop on the floor? How would you have responded to confirm and then support Bella's intention?
3. Noticing opportunities to support a child's learning and development takes practice and intentionality. What strategies could Ms. Sophia use to sharpen her observation skills?
4. What are peer relationships typically like among young toddlers? How could Ms. Sophia have facilitated positive relationships between Bella and the other children who approached her during this feeding?
5. How could Ms. Sophia have supported Bella's motivation to learn by facilitating a sense of belonging, purpose, and agency (principle 6 of the position statement on developmentally appropriate practice)?

General Discussion Questions

1. It can be challenging for educators to be fully present and attentive to the needs of individual children and to the whole group. What are some strategies that can help educators to be fully present and attentive?
2. How can children who gravitate toward solitary play be supported to engage in play with their peers? How about children who are sometimes excluded from group play or have difficulty entering play with others? How does support in each of these situations change for children of different ages?
3. Entering and sustaining play can be more challenging for children with disabilities. What are some strategies educators can use to help children with disabilities play with their peers?

1.2 "My Name Is Not a Shame"

Kevin McGowan

Connections to *Developmentally Appropriate Practice*

- Chapter 6: Creating a Caring, Equitable Community of Learners
- Chapter 7: Engaging in Reciprocal Partnerships with Families and Fostering Community Connections

Case Overview

One of the first steps in terms of connecting with and respecting children and their families is to learn and pronounce children's names. Some early childhood educators may find it challenging to pronounce children's names that are not Eurocentric, such as DeShondre, Shondredelia, Maemi, Keun Suk, or Eyad. In this case study, Mr. O'Sullivan, a pre-K teacher, has developed strategies for learning and using the correct pronunciation of each child's name.

Learning Objectives

1. Explain the importance of pronouncing a child's entire name based on guidance from the child and family.
2. Identify strategies for pronouncing a child's entire name.

Case Narrative

Mr. Declan O'Sullivan is an African American, heterosexual, cisgender man who works in a public elementary school located in an urban middle-class neighborhood where 93 percent of the residents identify as African American. The school serves children in pre-K through grade 3. All 523 students enrolled in the school identify as African American. On average, Mr. O'Sullivan has 20 students enrolled in his pre-K class each year. Mr. O'Sullivan started teaching at this school right out of college and has been there for the last 20 years. He loves being a pre-K teacher and gets a great deal of personal and professional satisfaction as he goes about his day working with the 4- and 5-year-olds in his class. Mr. O'Sullivan is well regarded by families, school administrators, and peers. He is especially known for authentically connecting to all children and their families.

Before the first day of school, Mr. O'Sullivan reviews his class roster and verbally says each child's name and notes names that he may not be pronouncing correctly. For example, he highlights the names DeShondre and Shondredelia. The next step is for Mr. O'Sullivan to call each child's family. After an initial introduction, Mr. O'Sullivan asks family members if he is pronouncing the child's name correctly. If the family confirms that Mr. O'Sullivan is pronouncing the name correctly, he places a check mark by that name on his class roster. If he is not pronouncing the name correctly, he writes the name out phonetically or in a way that helps him to remember how to correctly pronounce that name. For example, after talking to DeShondre's family, this is the note that Mr. O'Sullivan writes on his class roster: DeShondre (Day Shawn Drah). Mr. O'Sullivan reviews his roster and continues to practice this name to be sure he is pronouncing it correctly.

Mr. O'Sullivan uses exploration of names to make initial connections to families. Over the years, he has learned some interesting facts about families this way. When Mr. O'Sullivan talks to families about the children's names, families will often share why they selected that name for their child. Mr. O'Sullivan also uses this as an opportunity to talk about his own name. Both names have Irish origins. Mr. O'Sullivan explains that he is an African American man from Houston, Texas, with an Irish surname because he is a proud descendant of enslaved people. His family provided free labor to the White O'Sullivan family until their release on June 19, 1865.

Mr. O'Sullivan calls Mrs. Jackson, Shondredelia's mother. "Good morning, Mrs. Jackson. I am Mr. O'Sullivan. I am your daughter's teacher for the upcoming school year. I am calling to introduce myself and get to know you and your child a little bit. Tell me if I am pronouncing Shondredelia's name correctly?"

Mrs. Jackson says warmly, "You almost got it! Here is the correct pronunciation." Mr. O'Sullivan writes it out phonetically on his class roster (Shondredelia [Shawn Dray Da Leah]) and says it back to Mrs. Jackson. Mrs. Jackson says, "You got it." Mr. O'Sullivan tells her, "I adapt the 'Name Game' song by Shirley Ellis as a way to introduce all of the children's names to the class." Mrs. Jackson says that her grandmother used to play that song all the time.

As he does with all families, Mr. O'Sullivan asks Mrs. Jackson how they selected Shondredelia's name. Mrs. Jackson explains, "Shondredelia's name is a combination between my name, Shonda—it rhymes with Rhonda—and my mother's name DeLia." Mr. O'Sullivan goes on to talk about the history of his own name connected to his enslaved ancestors. Mrs. Jackson notes, "I do not know the history of the Jackson family name since I married into the family five years ago. I will have to talk to my husband to see what he knows about our family name."

In class, Mr. O'Sullivan uses rhyming name songs that incorporate all of the children's names. He especially likes adapting the "Name Game" song, as he explained to Mrs. Jackson. For example, "Shirley Shirley, Shirley Bo-ber-ley Bo-na-na fanna Fo-fer-ley Fee-fi-mo-mer-ley Shirley!" During circle time, Mr. O'Sullivan uses opening songs and chants where he pronounces the child's name. The children enjoy the songs incorporating their names. All of the children participate in singing and chanting each other's names. For example, "DeShondre is here today, DeShondre is here today, let's all clap our hands, DeShondre is here today!"

Takeaways and Next Steps

Families often express their appreciation to Mr. O'Sullivan for his attention to the pronunciation of their children's names. Like many early childhood teachers, Mr. O'Sullivan connects children's names to concepts the class is learning, such as the alphabet, phonological awareness, and emergent writing. For example, he uses songs that incorporate rhyme, a building block for phonological awareness.

You may like your own name or not. You may not have thought about it one way or another. You may not have liked your name because when you were a child, your teachers didn't pronounce it correctly. Perhaps the mispronunciation of your name continued into your adult life where colleagues constantly shorten your name after you have told them on numerous occasions what your name is and how to pronounce it. As you reflect on your own name, think about the importance of pronouncing each child's name, and those of their family members, correctly.

Case Discussion Questions

1. How does Mr. O'Sullivan use name exploration as a strategy for connecting to families? What could Mr. O'Sullivan do if a family is reluctant to share more information about their child's name?
2. What does Mr. O'Sullivan do to demonstrate that he understands the importance of pronouncing all children's names correctly?
3. What strategies is Mr. O'Sullivan using to ensure that he pronounces names correctly? What other strategies could be used?
4. What do you know about the story of your own name? How can you use the story of your name to connect to children's name stories?

General Discussion Questions

1. Why is it important that educators pronounce and spell all children's names correctly? Is it acceptable to shorten or adapt a child's name or use a more Eurocentric nickname because the educator finds it easier? Why or why not? How might doing so affect a child and family?
2. Vignette 1.1 on page 6 in *Developmentally Appropriate Practice* and the discussion that follows it offer some examples of learning experiences around children's names. What other name games or activities could be used to help children learn about and respect each other's cultures and uniqueness? How might the classroom environment be used to feature children's names?

1.3 Fostering Developmentally Appropriate Practice Through Virtual Family Connections

Lea Ann Christenson

Connections to *Developmentally Appropriate Practice*

- Chapter 6: Creating a Caring, Equitable Community of Learners
- Chapter 7: Engaging in Reciprocal Relationships with Families and Fostering Community Connections

Case Overview

This case describes how a pre-K teacher in a suburban, public elementary school pivots to virtual learning during the 2020 pandemic and leverages what she learns to serve her young children and families once the school is back to in-person learning. She continues virtual meetings with children and families as part of a comprehensive plan of communication.

Learning Objectives

1. Identify strategies to connect and support families in virtual settings.
2. Explain the basic concepts of leveraging virtual events to support young children and their families and apply these concepts in diverse settings.

Case Narrative

The elementary school in which Ms. Emma's pre-K class is located is in a densely populated suburban area with many small manufacturing plants and warehouses nearby. Many of the families work either the swing shift or overnight shifts in these businesses. Most students are bused to school. Ms. Emma and her fellow teachers have tried different ideas for connecting with families, including family–teacher conferences; science and literacy evenings; an afternoon for make-and-take literacy projects; and World Earth Day, a schoolwide, community-wide cleanup day to beautify the building grounds. However, many families have found it difficult to participate due to their work schedules.

Then comes the COVID-19 pandemic, and Ms. Emma's public pre-K class pivots to virtual learning overnight, which results in many challenges. The first is to make sure all of her young students have the technology and connectivity to attend virtual sessions. Another is to collaborate with families so they can facilitate virtual learning for their children and help them navigate the hands-on learning at home. While Ms. Emma has gained a deep understanding of and experience in early childhood theory and practice and feels prepared to teach all children and to work with all families, she wonders how she is to leverage what she knows to a virtual setting. How can she continue to build relationships with families and support them during this stressful time?

Family Engagement Sessions

Before the virtual lessons begin, Ms. Emma communicates with the families via the schoolwide online management system, email, texts, and phone calls. She finds that some families respond better to certain forms of communication, so she employs all of these tools. After she makes sure that each family can connect to the lessons, she encourages them to attend the lessons if they can. Ms. Emma thinks this is necessary to keep the children engaged in virtual lessons, particularly to assist with the hands-on activities she is planning. This is a challenge as many of the family members are working from home while caring for their children. However, nearly every child has someone to sit with them and engage in the lessons. Sometimes it is a parent, a grandparent, or an older child in the home. Sometimes younger children and even pets join in and participate in the lessons. Instead of treating these as unwanted interruptions, Ms. Emma seamlessly works the extra visitors into the lessons and forms a welcoming, inclusive community of learners.

Ms. Emma plans her virtual lessons around themes chosen from the district curriculum and ones she created that children can relate to while spending time at home. For example, she creates measurement lessons by having the children record how many spoonfuls of cereal it takes to fill their bowl or how many bites it takes to make a piece of toast disappear, and a mapping lesson where children map their kitchen and measure the length and width by using a nonstandard measurement tool—the shoes of the family members. She includes directions for the families to guide these activities, along with targeted academic vocabulary and sample questions. She sends home learning materials for each child to make sure they have the tools they need, such as a whiteboard, markers, blank journals, pencils and crayons, and math manipulatives. Each lesson addresses the required learning standards and includes a read-aloud of an e-book with the link provided and a hands-on follow-up activity that the multigenerational adults in the household can participate in.

At first, Ms. Emma does not see evidence that the follow-up learning activities are being supported or that there is synergy from one lesson to the next. Several families ask for more information on the lessons, so she creates a lesson information guide. She finds that if families know what is being taught each week and are given a few suggestions for supporting this learning, they are better equipped to support their child with the follow-up learning activities. In addition, this resource seems to foster connections between lessons, and group discussions during virtual lessons with the children become richer.

Because Ms. Emma has a window into each family's life during the virtual lessons, she learns more about the children and families over the year of online teaching than she ever has before. For example, she has not known that one of her students is living in an apartment with her family of five, as well as her aunt and three teenage cousins, because they experienced a house fire six months earlier and are living there until their house is rebuilt. No wonder this child has often fallen asleep in class; she is sleeping in the living room. In addition, Ms. Emma gains a deeper understanding of the families' diverse cultures and customs. She leverages this understanding by weaving what she learns in her lessons. Her typical unit on spring, for example, takes on a new depth when she has the children share from their own homes their favorite traditions and foods.

Continuing to Support Families

While Ms. Emma is very relieved when the school returns to in-person learning, she wants to continue to create these close connections with families that she has fostered during virtual learning. Ms. Emma decides to add a few elements to her in-person learning:

1. **Virtual conferences.** As a follow-up to the in-person Back to School Night at the beginning of the year, Ms. Emma schedules virtual conferences with each family and child, providing extra time for families who were unable to attend Back to School Night. These conferences give her a glimpse into the families' lives early in the year and enable her to build relationships by starting with a positive introduction. She finds that she receives a higher rate of return and much more detail on the interest surveys—about children's interests and aptitudes and a description of their home environment—that she sends out after the virtual conferences in comparison to the interest surveys she sent out before the pandemic.
2. **Family engagement planning guide.** Prior to the pandemic, Ms. Emma gave the families only a broad overview of the units and lessons their children were studying. Now, each week Ms. Emma shares a planning guide for major units and three to four key lessons with the families. Families can use the information in the guide to create meaningful extensions at home because they know exactly what their child is learning and because Ms. Emma offers specific suggestions for reinforcing at home what is being learned at school.
3. **Family feedback.** Prior to the pandemic, Ms. Emma relied on the regularly scheduled family–teacher conferences to obtain feedback from families. During the virtual sessions, she received ongoing feedback from various family members that was valuable for planning future lessons. Now, Ms. Emma sends out a survey to families quarterly via the schoolwide online management system. Their feedback is substantive because the families are more knowledgeable of day-to-day lessons.

Takeaways and Next Steps

Ms. Emma enjoys the new level of connection with her families that she is experiencing. The strategies she has developed fosters deeper connections with families, which is especially important when she needs to address a child's learning struggles or challenging behavior with the family. As a next step, Ms. Emma is thinking about including some of the learning specialists (reading, dual language learning, behavior, and so on) who work with the children in her classroom in some of her virtual meetings. This will help families better understand how the specialists collaborate with Ms. Emma and contribute to their children's learning.

Case Discussion Questions

1. What benefits did Ms. Emma discover about virtual learning? How did it provide her with a greater depth of understanding of children and families?
2. What evidence is there that the tools that evolved from Ms. Emma's virtual teaching experiences strengthened the children's in-person learning?
3. How might virtual meetings with families and a tool such as the family engagement planning guide be adapted for your setting or one you are familiar with?
4. How did Ms. Emma ensure that the learning activities aligned with developmentally appropriate practice?
5. What evidence do you see that Ms. Emma engaged in building reciprocal relationships with families? What other strategies might she consider?

General Discussion Questions

1. What are some benefits of virtual learning to children? To families? What are the drawbacks to virtual learning?
2. How can the logistics of periodic virtual sessions with children and families be accommodated? What steps would you need to take to make sure that such sessions align with developmentally appropriate practice guidelines?
3. In what ways can educators partner with families to support children's learning both in the classroom and at home?

1.4 Counting Collections in Community

Amy Schmidtke

Connections to *Developmentally Appropriate Practice*

- Chapter 6: Creating a Caring, Equitable Community of Learners
- Chapter 9: Teaching to Enhance Each Child's Development and Learning

Case Overview

This case explores how a kindergarten teacher makes intentional efforts to foster child-to-child relationships across the daily schedule, including during academic learning and teacher-directed collaborative work. He integrates social and emotional goals with math goals by explicitly guiding the children to engage in positive interactions with one another while counting collections of objects. In doing this, he fosters a caring, equitable community of learners and explicitly teaches social skills during academic instructional time.

Learning Objectives

1. Identify the value of explicit attention to fostering child-to-child interactions in support of creating a caring, equitable community of learners.
2. Describe how relationship building and collaboration among children is supportive of children's academic, social, and emotional development.
3. Identify opportunities to integrate academic instruction with social engagement.

Case Narrative

Mr. Jon is a kindergarten teacher in a culturally and racially diverse urban public school. He enjoys building strong relationships with the children in his class and their families. He is regarded as a highly effective teacher and is actively engaged in his own continuing education and professional development. The school in which Mr. Jon teaches created a school improvement plan that includes the schoolwide goal of increasing positive interactions between staff and children, children and children, and staff and families.

Mr. Jon recently learned about the benefits of a math approach known as counting collections from the school district's math coach assigned to his building. It involves a structured activity in which children work in pairs to cooperatively select, plan, count, and record—through illustration—a collection of objects, such as stones, buttons, keys, and paper clips. The school's kindergarten math curriculum focuses units of study on number sense and counting, gradually requiring increasing amounts with partners. The math coach provides guidance on how to utilize counting collections to enhance children's learning of expected concepts and skills. Mr. Jon realizes that this approach could be a great instructional fit and helpful for guiding children to reach both their math goals and their schoolwide goal of increasing positive interactions between children.

To help his kindergartners successfully engage in the counting collections activity, Mr. Jon recognizes that, at this developmental stage, children need guidance and scaffolding support for positive interactions and collaboration with each other. The school counselor uses the Second Step social and emotional curriculum during weekly counseling lessons with all children beginning in kindergarten and continuing through sixth grade (Second Step 2011). Mr. Jon intentionally connects these lessons throughout the school day by referring to strategies and displaying visual cues in the classroom. For example, during the children's study of Second Step's problem-solving unit, Mr. Jon prompts children to utilize the problem-solving strategies while counting collections, including deciding on fair ways to play together. He sustains children's attention to these explicit strategies by introducing them at the beginning of the lesson and providing scaffolding support while they engage with their partners.

While teaching a counting collections lesson, Mr. Jon follows a gradual release of responsibility approach. He draws children's attention to lesson objectives, piques children's interest, models procedures, provides explicit directions, invites children to engage in independent work with a partner, sustains observation, provides scaffolded support as needed, and summarizes the lesson experience with the whole group. Today, his procedures include the following:

1. **Attention to lesson objectives.** Mr. Jon draws children's attention to a chart paper in the front of the room listing two objectives. He reads the objectives aloud while tracking the print: (1) Engage in positive interactions with a partner, and (2) count objects up to 30. He reminds children that they have been working on positive interactions in the classroom and prompts children to share examples of times they have seen classmates engaging in positive interactions with one another. Children are familiar with this objective. Two children share examples.

2. **Pique children's interest.** Mr. Jon leads the children in singing "Five Little Monkeys," which they all enjoy. He models and encourages children to sing along, use their fingers to show the number of monkeys, and act out the song. He explains that this is a counting song, and today they will engage in positive interactions while counting collections with a partner.
3. **Model procedures and provide explicit directions.** Mr. Jon draws children's attention to an anchor chart in the classroom with the steps children will engage in while counting collections. He selects a child to model with him for the class on how to follow the steps. They role-play and use explicit language to find a partner; agree upon a selected collection; and plan, count, and draw their collection together.
4. **Invite children to engage in independent work with a partner.** Mr. Jon prompts children to follow the steps outlined on the anchor chart. Children begin following the steps, regularly referring to the anchor chart to remember next steps.
5. **Sustain observation and provide scaffolded support as needed.** Mr. Jon observes the children throughout the lesson. He provides support as needed for the partners to follow directions and stay on task. He continually reminds children of the lesson objectives to engage in positive interactions with their partner and count their collections. The classroom is filled with the joyful noise of children's voices. Children engage in talk about math. They solve social problems by agreeing on which collection of objects to count and what their counting plan involves, taking turns, and drawing together on the same piece of paper to document their collection. They act as "mini teachers" by helping their peers understand their thinking.
6. **Summarize the lesson experience.** After completing their partner work, children clean up and return their selected collections to the shelf. Partners sit together in the whole group area holding their papers documenting their collections. Mr. Jon again refers to the objectives on the chart paper. He selects three partners to share about their counting and explain what was positive about their interactions as partners. Mr. Jon says, "This is great! We can learn math and practice positive interactions. Our class is both smart and kind. We work and learn together." He next facilitates a group conversation, prompting children to share how working with a partner has helped them learn.

Takeaways and Next Steps

Mr. Jon's counting collections approach evolves over time. He doesn't expect children to engage in these multistep directions all at once. He supports children to build capacity one step at a time over the period of two weeks. He focuses on the goal of positive child-to-child interactions across the full schedule every day. Because of this, children are accustomed to talking about the characteristics of positive interactions and identifying them in action. Building this social practice into academic instruction is a perfect fit because it provides the children with real-world experiences and social challenges. Mr. Jon shares, "My students really enjoy participating in counting collections, and I enjoy hearing their conversations during the process. Not only are they reviewing core math skills including place value, adding, skip-counting, and sorting, but they are also working on their positive interactions. They are encouraged to share and count materials with their partner. However, they are also encouraged to help their peers understand their thinking." He notes that occasionally, students will engage in disagreements about their collection, and this creates new challenges that tie to their everyday lives: What can we do to solve this problem peacefully? How can we change our way of thinking so we can all understand? Do we have to think of this differently? If so, what else can we do?

Mr. Jon shares that intentionally integrating academic and social and emotional learning during instruction requires a lot of work preplanning, preparing, and actively providing scaffolded support for both children's learning and social skill development. It is a work in progress as the complex skills children are required to utilize can be challenging even for adults. Mr. Jon feels that the efforts involved are worth it because he sees great reward for children. He is continuing to refine his processes in teaching math, reading, and other subject areas so that children regularly experience interactive lessons that are engaging and joyful and that enable them to reach their academic goals. He is supporting his colleagues to integrate social and emotional learning with academic learning in their classrooms. He is hopeful that engaging with colleagues in a caring, equitable community of learners will help him learn more strategies to foster a caring, equitable community of learners for the children in his classroom.

Case Discussion Questions

1. How did Mr. Jon's explicit attention to social and emotional learning before and during the lesson guide children to effectively engage in counting collections with a partner?
2. What do you think Mr. Jon did before this lesson to help children understand and identify characteristics of a positive child-to-child interaction?
3. Why was it important to explicitly draw children's attention to both the academic and social objectives of the lesson? Why is Mr. Jon's attention to social objectives important for the children's academic learning?
4. What impact do approaches like Mr. Jon's have on creating a caring, equitable community of learners?

General Discussion Questions

1. Describe a child-to-child positive interaction. What might this look like during child-initiated play?
2. What challenges and barriers do teachers face when organizing interactive and collaborative work with young children?

Suggested Resources

Meaningful Math Moments: www.meaningfulmathmoments.com/counting-collections.html.

Teacher Education by Design: https://tedd.org/counting-collections.

References

Second Step for Elementary Classroom Kit. 2011. Seattle, WA: Committee for Children.

Wright, B.L. 2022. "Creating a Caring, Equitable Community of Learners." In *Developmentally Appropriate Practice in Early Childhood Programs Serving Children from Birth Through Age 8*, 4th ed., NAEYC, 111–44. Washington, DC: NAEYC.

1.5 The Joy Jar: Celebrating Kindness

Leah Schoenberg Muccio

Connections to *Developmentally Appropriate Practice*

- Chapter 6: Creating a Caring, Equitable Community of Learners

Case Overview

This case provides an example of how a kindergarten teacher intentionally facilitates positive relationships among children. She builds a loving and supportive classroom community. In particular, she uses a joy jar to build the children's strengths to support caring connections among them and to celebrate the many ways the children show kindness to each other.

Learning Objectives

1. Identify the strategies the teacher uses to create a caring community of learners at the beginning of the school year.
2. Describe the ways a focus on empathy and kindness in the classroom supports joyful learning and the well-being of all children.
3. Describe the impact of the teacher fostering the development of relationships among the children.

Case Narrative

At the beginning of the school year, Ms. Alegria, a veteran kindergarten teacher in a public school in a community with many recent immigrants, prioritizes building a nurturing social climate in her classroom as a foundation for joyful learning and development. For the majority of the children and families, this is their first experience with the school system. She wants the children to not only feel welcome but also feel a sense of belonging as a member of the Alegria Arctic Foxes, the class name the children voted on during their circle time the first week of school. From her experiences with the Alegria Airplanes, Alegria Alligators, and many other groups of children over the years, Ms. Alegria believes that children learn best when they are treated as cherished members of the community. She and her coteacher, Mrs. Castellanos, seek to connect with the 22 new children in their classroom this year and support them to build connections with each other. They create classroom agreements together and practice classroom routines. By the end of the first week, the children are proud to share with their fifth grade buddies the classroom quilt where each child contributed a square they made from construction paper showing what makes them unique. Ms. Alegria leads a discussion with the children, using the quilt to explore how the children are similar and different from others in their classroom community.

Besides completing the kindergarten entry assessment with each child, Ms. Alegria also observes the ways the children interact with their teachers and peers as they explore the classroom environment. Through observation and conversations, she learns the languages the children speak, their favorite superheroes, the adults they care about, and the songs they love to dance to. Ms. Alegria forms hypotheses about the children's strengths and develops an initial plan for the best ways to support each child's learning and development, mastery of the state standards, and Individualized Education Program (IEP) goals for the children with disabilities. In addition to focusing on children's academic development, she values their social and emotional development. In their weekly planning meetings, she and Mrs. Castellanos discuss their observations related to the children's social and emotional well-being. Mrs. Castellanos notes that during recess, one child was teasing another for not yet being able to cross the monkey bars. She recalls, "Anna called Sebastian a baby at recess and Sebastian was really upset." Mrs. Castellanos tells Ms. Alegria how she had pulled the children aside to talk about it at the time, telling Anna about the importance of using kind words and asking her to think about how Sebastian might have felt when she called him a baby. Although they plan to address typical situations like this as they come up, they wonder if there is a way to further support the children to engage in positive social interactions. They decide to set up expectations for kindness in the classroom by supporting and encouraging the children to engage in empathetic interactions.

Ms. Alegria builds in many activities during the next few weeks to model and emphasize the importance of empathetic interactions and support a classroom culture of respect. During a lesson to introduce reading strategies, they read children's books about kindness and empathy and the children write about how they can show that they care in their writing journals. At circle time, she introduces the children to the joy jar. This is a more positive variation on the marble jar reward system that some teachers use. The focus of the joy jar is on the positive contributions children make to the well-being of others rather than a focus on compliance with rules. Puffballs (small pom-poms) are added to the jar when children say or do something kind for others, but children are never penalized for unkind behavior because they are still learning about how to interact with their peers.

Ms. Alegria and Mrs. Castellanos wear funny glasses when they introduce the joy jar and tell the children they will be watching closely for acts of kindness that add to the sense of comfort and joy in the classroom. When they observe a child being caring, or when the children notice an act of kindness, the teachers will add a puffball to the joy jar and post a joy note to a bulletin board. They talk about how they can all authentically interact with each other in joyful ways and act out examples and non-examples. Ms. Alegria illustrates that if she fell down in the hallway and Mrs. Castellanos helped her up or asked her if she was okay, that would be an act of kindness that would earn a puffball, but teasing her about falling would be unkind and not earn a puffball. Mrs. Castellanos tells the children that since both she and Ms. Alegria speak Spanish, if she understands a direction in English but Ms. Alegria doesn't, she could tell Ms. Alegria the directions in Spanish and this would be an act of kindness that would earn a puffball. The children vote on the type of celebration they would like to have when they fill up the joy jar and select a dance party. The children excitedly brainstorm a list of ways they might be kind to each other, and each child illustrates a page that goes into their book, "Kind Alegria Arctic Foxes." When the children share their book pages, Anna compliments Sebastian by saying, "You worked really hard on your book page." Mrs. Castellanos asks all the children to freeze and excitedly declares, "Anna used kind words to compliment Sebastian. Hooray for an act of kindness!" She drops the first puffball into the joy jar, records "Anna complimented Sebastian" on the joy note and draws a thumbs-up next to it, then posts the note. The children are on their way to filling the jar.

Takeaways and Next Steps

After implementing the joy jar in the classroom, Ms. Alegria and Mrs. Castellanos see the children engage with each other with kindness in expected and unexpected ways. There is an increase in compliments, encouragement, and other helpful forms of support for each other, as they expected. Less expected, the children begin to think about fairness and inclusion. After Ms. Alegria adds a puffball in the joy jar when Sebastian invites Ji-Hoon, who usually elects to engage in learning centers by himself, to play a counting game with him, the children begin talking about how they might work with others they don't usually work with. In expanding the positive ways they can treat others, and especially with people who are different from themselves, the children quickly fill their joy jar. For example, a child whose home language is Korean teaches the other children the Korean variant of rock, paper, scissors, and soon all the children play it, especially on the playground, regardless of their home languages. In another instance, Enrique asks Mrs. Castellanos if he and Daniel (a child with autism spectrum disorder) might be able to eat in the classroom since the noisy cafeteria bothers Daniel. After Ms. Alegria and Mrs. Castellanos fill the joy jar, the Alegria Arctic Foxes celebrate the many ways they filled their classroom with joy through kindness during the dance party.

Case Discussion Questions

1. Which aspects of guideline 1 of the position statement on developmentally appropriate practice are evident in this case?
2. Imagine you are walking into Ms. Alegria and Mrs. Castellanos's classroom. What might you see, hear, and feel in the learning environment? How do you think the learning environment would impact the learners?
3. What potential benefits are there from the teachers using children's books about kindness and empathy for a reading strategies lesson?
4. What might happen after the children fill the joy jar and have their long-anticipated class dance? Should the teachers continue to use the joy jar? What other strategies might they use to continue to support the children to interact with each other with empathy?
5. Compare and contrast Ms. Alegria's and Mrs. Castellanos's classroom with kindergarten teacher Amy Blessing's classroom (described in vignettes in *Developmentally Appropriate Practice,* Appendix A, pp. 281–85). What are the teachers' priorities in each of the classrooms? What else would you like to know about these classrooms? How can you use the strategies the teachers use in both classrooms in your own?
6. Explore NAEYC's resources on children's social and emotional development at NAEYC.org/resources/topics/social-and-emotional-development. How do the strategies you read about in these resources compare with the strategies in this case?

General Discussion Questions

1. How effective do you think something like the joy jar is? What downsides might there be to using this type of reward system with young children?
2. What are other ways that a class rewards system can be adapted as it was with the joy jar?

1.6 Prioritizing Listening to and Learning from Families

Amy Schmidtke

Connections to *Developmentally Appropriate Practice*

- Chapter 6: Creating a Caring, Equitable Community of Learners
- Chapter 7: Engaging in Reciprocal Partnerships with Families and Fostering Community Connections
- Chapter 9: Teaching to Enhance Each Child's Development and Learning

Case Overview

This case explores how a third grade teacher, Ms. Cindy, makes intentional efforts to take the friendly relationships she typically experiences with families to the next level by fostering stronger connections and deeper understanding. She is inspired to do so after engaging in professional learning focused on why and how to listen to families during family–teacher conferences and subsequently participating in a book study with colleagues around the book *Creating Welcoming Schools: A Practical Guide to Home-School Partners with Diverse Families* by JoBeth Allen (2007). Ms. Cindy has not previously used families' funds of knowledge to strengthen her teaching practices and children's learning experiences in the classroom. With her new inspiration, she decides to take a different approach to engaging in meaningful conversations with families where she can learn from them and use their assets in the classroom.

Funds of knowledge refers to the collection of knowledge and practices children gain through their personal experiences in their households, communities, and cultures through interactions with their family, peers, and neighbors (Moll et al. 1992). Young children's learning is enhanced when they have opportunities to learn and develop through experiences that connect new ideas and concepts to their existing knowledge, interests, and cultural values.

Learning Objectives

1. Describe how partnerships with children's families contribute to the development of a caring and equitable community of learners in the classroom.
2. Identify opportunities to develop positive, ongoing, and goal-oriented relationships with families.

Case Narrative

Ms. Cindy is a White third grade teacher in a school community serving a large Latinx population. She speaks Spanish fluently and values frequent opportunities to communicate with children in their home language. She enjoys and appreciates the children and their families in the school community, and she is skilled at and committed to developing friendly relationships with families. She loves teaching in her school and is highly regarded as an effective teacher.

At family–teacher conferences in previous years, Ms. Cindy has focused on telling the families about their child's academic progress and behavior at school. Most families are quiet during conferences, and Ms. Cindy feels this is because they don't have a lot to say and that, as a colleague told her, families are intimidated at school. After asking the families more open-ended questions and listening with more intention, however, she realizes that while some families may indeed feel intimidated both because of their own experiences as students and because of the way they are treated by some educators, her assumptions are not necessarily correct and possibly represent an implicit bias on her part. With her newfound understanding of the importance of building reciprocal partnerships, she prioritizes listening to families, intentionally balancing the amount of time she spends talking with the amount of time they spend talking. She prepares open-ended questions so she can learn about the family's culture and values, their hopes for their child's education, and their insights about their child's interests and background. Providing more space to talk about the child and family leads to a more mutual and reciprocal conversation.

After this initial shift, Ms. Cindy continues to reflect on how to engage in reciprocal partnerships with families to benefit children's learning. She is inspired by a chapter from the book study about home visiting, and her principal agrees to support her in giving home visiting a try. During the school year, many families welcome her to their homes. She again prioritizes spending the time at their homes listening to and learning from each family. With their permission, she takes pictures during the home visit of what is meaningful to the child.

Ms. Cindy incorporates the pictures into a writing activity for language arts. She provides materials for children to make a book about themselves, their home, and their family using the pictures and notes collected during the visit. She supports the children in composing paragraphs with grammatically correct sentences of varying length and complexity appropriate for third grade curriculum expectations. Children apply the writing process to plan, draft, revise, edit, and publish their writing using correct spelling, grammar, punctuation, and other standard conventions appropriate for the grade level. To further support children's development as writers in parallel with their development as a caring and equitable community of learners, Ms. Cindy asks the children to share their writing with a partner and provide both oral and written feedback to their partner. Upon completing their books, children can choose to keep them at home or include them in the classroom library. This writing activity leads to the highest quality writing the children have produced, and it also leads to long-term writing progress. Ms. Cindy's weekly writing conferences with individual children become more effective. The insights into children's interests that she has gained from her stronger relationships with their families help her ask better questions and give more meaningful feedback.

Ms. Cindy is amazed at how much she learns through this new approach. She develops stronger relationships with families than she has ever had before. She feels she has a deeper understanding of each child and gains new insights about how she can connect learning in the classroom to what is culturally and personally relevant to her students. For example, Jasmine is hesitant to read at the table during small group reading time. Ms. Cindy assumes she lacks proficiency in reading, but at the home visit Jasmine shows her all the books she reads aloud to her mom at night before bed. Ms. Cindy asks why she hesitates to read at school. Jasmine's mom explains that she likes to read in quiet with her mom away from her siblings. After the visit, Ms. Cindy asks Jasmine to read to her alone without other children at the table. Jasmine is able to demonstrate stronger reading skills than Ms. Cindy could have imagined. With this better understanding of Jasmine's ability, Ms. Cindy adjusts her instruction to support Jasmine more appropriately and provides more challenge. Ms. Cindy also learns that Jose keeps chickens in his backyard. She invites Jose's family to teach the class about the life cycle of a chicken during their life cycle unit in science, which includes analyzing and interpreting data.

Ms. Cindy conducts a survey to collect feedback from families about their experiences with her approach to family–teacher conferences and home visiting. The survey responses indicate that families feel more empowered to advocate for their child than in years past and feel more valued as true partners in their child's learning. For example, one parent responds, "I feel she listened to me more than other teachers. She wanted to hear what I had to say." Because of Ms. Cindy's success in partnering with families to learn from them, Ms. Cindy's principal asks her to act as a mentor and facilitate professional learning for her colleagues. The training and mentorships center on connecting with families to make learning relevant for children and on gaining the skills needed to take on this approach to family partnerships.

Takeaways and Next Steps

Chapter 6 in *Developmentally Appropriate Practice* highlights the importance of relationship building with children and their families in an effort to create a caring community of learners. This case study offers an example of how a teacher takes action to make connections with families so she can learn about the children in her classroom and deepen her relationships with them. Ms. Cindy takes great steps toward valuing and establishing meaningful partnerships. She learns what is personally relevant to the families and intentionally incorporates these connections into the curriculum. She learns about children's strengths and shifts her approaches so the children can effectively demonstrate their skills and engage in learning. She builds a foundation of positive relationships and takes this to a higher level by incorporating what she learns through family partnerships to enhance her teaching and children's learning. Relationships and intentional partnerships with families are essential in making the concept of developmentally appropriate practice a reality for children.

Ms. Cindy can celebrate her hard work and build on it to effectively support children's learning. She can continue to learn individualized instructional strategies like she does with Jasmine and incorporate family assets into the curriculum like she does with Jose. These actions have great value in enhancing children's learning experiences in the classroom and helping children feel like they belong and are valued at school. As she shares her experiences and strategies with her colleagues, Ms. Cindy's skill and expertise in instructional practices, family partnerships, and leadership are making a difference not just in her own classroom but also in her school overall.

Case Discussion Questions

1. Ms. Cindy made a few assumptions about her students and her families that changed as part of the home visiting process. What is an example of an assumption Ms. Cindy made, and how was clearing it up important to the children's learning?
2. How can Ms. Cindy use what she learns from families to ensure children have opportunities to learn in ways that are culturally, linguistically, and personally relevant to them?
3. What is an example of how Ms. Cindy tapped into children's funds of knowledge to better understand and promote their academic, social, emotional, and/or cognitive development?
4. Ms. Cindy was intentional about learning from families. How did she integrate what she learned into her curriculum and instruction in literacy, math, science, and other content areas? How could Ms. Cindy expand on what was discussed in this case to provide more academic connections for children?

General Discussion Questions

1. What challenges and barriers do teachers face in their attempts to intentionally listen to families about their children, their family's interests, and their preferred ways of engaging with school?
2. How do teachers establish a personalized relationship with each individual family? How can home visits fit into these efforts? What are some considerations for setting up home visits?
3. How can educators integrate families' cultures, languages, and values into the classroom in support of children's sense of dignity and belonging?
4. Share an example of how teachers can use insights provided by families to enhance children's learning of curriculum content.

References

Allen, J. 2007. *Creating Welcoming Schools: A Practical Guide to Home-School Partners with Diverse Families*. New York: Teachers College Press.

Moll, L.C., C. Amanti, D. Neff, & N. Gonzalez. 1992. "Funds of Knowledge for Teaching: Using a Qualitative Approach to Connect Homes and Classrooms." *Theory into Practice* 31 (2): 132–41.

PART 2

Engaging in Reciprocal Partnerships with Families and Fostering Community Connections

Stephany Cuevas

Respectful, reciprocal partnerships between families and educators are essential for children's social and emotional well-being and academic success. When families, educators, and other adults involved in children's upbringing and education have strong relationships, children thrive; decades of research has documented higher grades and test scores, greater literacy and numeracy skills, and healthy social and emotional regulation, just to name a few outcomes. Collaborative partnerships allow educators to learn more about individual children, their particular likes and dislikes, and how their home contexts impact their development. As families and educators develop and maintain open lines of communication and trust, they are able to work together in the children's best interests.

The case studies in Part 2 illustrate the importance of strong family–educator relationships. While each case scenario is unique, addressing different perspectives and outcomes, the scenarios represent the many challenges involved in establishing and building successful and fruitful partnerships. Through discussion questions and analysis, the cases offer thoughts on ways educators can navigate these challenges.

Topics covered in these cases include reconsidering what effective family engagement looks like, looking at the entirety of children's ecosystem of supports, and understanding how families' life contexts shape their engagement in their children's education. Cases also explore classroom practices embracing the assets of children's families. Furthermore, these cases demonstrate how building reciprocal partnerships with families is related to intentional teaching; helps to create a caring, equitable community of learners; and impacts broader communities.

Specific questions covered in these cases include the following:

- How does a school leader balance families' preferences with institutional realities and respectfully communicate unpopular decisions to families?
- How can early childhood education spaces support teen parents and their children?
- How can educators include children's families in the classroom and curriculum in ways that honor and support families?
- How can teachers help families feel empowered in their role in their children's development and education?
- How can educators and families work together to appreciate and support children's unique characteristics?

The authors of these case studies have many years of experience in family engagement as professional development providers, leaders in state departments of education, consultants, researchers, teacher educators, and advocates. Their areas of expertise include early childhood development, asset-based approaches to early education, and education in rural communities. Three cases are written from the viewpoint of parents, providing readers an opportunity to consider the perspective of families and how doing so can enhance educators' understanding of children and facilitate improvement of educators' practice.

2.1 **Julio's Village: Early Childhood Education Supports for Teen Parents**

Donna Kirkwood

Connections to *Developmentally Appropriate Practice*

- Chapter 7: Engaging in Reciprocal Partnerships with Families and Fostering Community Connections

Case Overview

This case explores the day of a young couple as they navigate high school and their infant's care and education with the help of the nurturing adults in their environment. Their infant's teacher helps build their confidence and competence as parents, connecting their child's development and well-being to elements the young couple are familiar with.

Delia and Marco, who each live with their respective parents, are enrolled in an alternative high school program for students who struggle with a typical school day because of personal, work, or family conflicts. The school has an early learning center, which was added in response to the need for reliable child care services for young parents. Finding that teen parents who had high-quality, convenient care for their babies were more likely to attend school and graduate, the school district partnered with local businesses to develop an NAEYC-accredited center adjacent to a centrally located high school in the district. The district provides transportation for teen parents and their children to and from school and also accommodates alternative schedules for students who work or have other obligations during a typical school day. This works well for Delia and Marco because they can spend time with each other and with their baby while they finish high school.

Learning Objectives

1. Explain the importance of educators showing that they genuinely care about circumstances and events affecting families and communities, and identify ways they might adjust their practices to better support the immediate needs of children and families.
2. Identify strategies educators can use to better understand the cultural and linguistic practices of the families and communities they serve.
3. Discuss ways for educators to communicate with families and build mutual understanding and trust and explain the importance of this in resolving issues that arise.

Case Narrative

Beep, beep, beep! The alarm isn't going to stop ringing, so Delia gets out of bed and starts to get herself and her 6-month-old baby Julio ready for their day. Julio was fussy last night, and they are both tired. After she gets dressed, Delia changes Julio's diaper and sits down in the rocker to feed him. She knows that rocking and nursing him before school will be the calmest part of her day. The school bus will arrive soon and she needs to get him dressed and out the door.

After a short feeding, Delia hears the bus approaching and runs out the door with her backpack, Julio's bag, and Julio in his baby carrier. They get on the bus and ride to school like they have since he was 6 weeks old. After a few more stops, Julio's dad Marco boards the bus and sits in the same row as Delia and Julio.

Seeing that Julio is fussy, Marco speaks to him in a calm voice and gently rubs his tummy. This seems to help. When they get to school, Marco picks up the carrier and walks with Delia inside the early learning center. Delia signs Julio in, and they take him to his classroom together.

Ms. Tracy's face lights up when she sees them approaching. She smiles and asks, "How's our sweet boy this morning?" Delia tells her that they had a rough night and are a little tired and rushed this morning. Ms. Tracy assures both parents that sometimes babies have restless nights and she will watch Julio closely all day to make sure nothing is wrong. "You know I will come get you if there is a problem. And you can come check on him anytime," she reminds them.

As Delia and Marco get Julio out of his carrier, Ms. Tracy gently rubs Julio's tummy and asks them about his evening. "Did he eat well last night? Was anything different than usual?"

Delia and Marco think about how their evening with Julio had gone. Nothing was really unusual. But then Delia remembers that she had to study for a test last night and rushed through Julio's bedtime routines. Marco says, "Delia, next time you need to study, let me know and I'll stay and put Julio to bed." Before Julio was born, Delia and Marco agreed that they would do everything they could to graduate from high school and raise Julio together. They took a class for young parents that emphasized sharing responsibilities, especially when things are stressful. Marco can tell that Delia might need some extra help, so he reminds her that he is available to help if she needs it.

Ms. Tracy looks at the young parents and says, "Your baby is so loved. Remember that your parents are all there to help too. They say it takes a village to raise a child, and you have a very supportive village."

Ms. Tracy mentions that Julio really likes music and seems to calm down more easily at nap time when they sing to him. Delia shares that she doesn't sing to Julio much because all of the lullabies she knows are in Spanish and they want Julio to speak English. Ms. Tracy tells the young parents about an article she read about the benefits of dual language environments for young children. "I'll print the article and put it in Julio's bag for you to read," she says.

Ms. Tracy assures Delia and Marco that she will keep a close eye on Julio and give him extra love during the day. The parents kiss Julio goodbye and walk down the hall to the high school adjacent to the center. "Good luck on your test!" Ms. Tracy calls out as they leave.

After Julio gets settled in for the day, Ms. Tracy sends a few pictures of him to Delia and Marco so that they can see he is okay. After his morning nap, Delia goes back to Julio's classroom and feeds him. He is smiling and cooing like normal. Later, Marco stops by to check on Julio and he is happily playing next to Ms. Tracy on the floor. Ms. Tracy holds up Julio's hand to wave at Marco and says, "Hi, Dada!"

After school, Ms. Tracy give Delia and Marco a full report about Julio's day and ask if they would like a copy of the playlist of songs and lullabies that they played in the classroom. It has songs in several languages that the children love. Ms. Tracy laughs. "I try to sing along with the words even when I don't know what they mean—the babies don't seem to mind. They love to dance and move to the fast songs and the lullabies help them drift off to sleep."

Ms. Tracy knows that every interaction she has with the children in her class are important, but her interactions with the babies' parents are just as important. She models gentle nurturing, open communication, and kindness so that these teen parents can learn to do the same.

Delia, Marco, and Julio get on the bus to go home. They listen to the playlist on Marco's phone. One song reminds Marco of a song his dad used to play for him on the guitar when he was younger.

Marco goes home with Delia and Julio so he can spend more time with them. Delia makes a snack, and they do their homework while taking turns playing with Julio. They listen to the songs that Ms. Tracy gave them and dance and giggle as a family. When Delia's mother gets home, they eat dinner and give Julio a bath.

A little later, Marco's dad comes to pick him up. Marco runs out to the car and plays the lullaby that he remembered for his dad. Marco's dad tears up and says, "You remember that song? I used to play for you all the time. Tomorrow, when I pick you up I will bring my guitar and play for Julio, Delia, and her family."

As Marco leaves, Delia holds up Julio's hand to wave and says, "Bye, Dada!" Delia reads a book to Julio and sings him a lullaby from the playlist Ms. Tracy had given them. She falls asleep humming the lullaby.

Takeaways and Next Steps

This case demonstrates how a community positively affects a child and his family's first experiences. By noticing a dropout pattern that could be addressed by adding extra resources for young parents, the school district creates a support system for Julio and his parents that will help them to build a stable home for their family once they graduate from high school. Delia's and Marco's parents and teachers are part of a system that helps them to take care of their child and develop the skills needed to nurture him as he grows.

Ms. Tracy nurtures Julio, Delia, and Marco as they navigate their new family unit. She also guides them with her knowledge of best practices and models for them the nurturing interactions that Julio needs.

Case Discussion Questions

1. Think about the direct and indirect supports that were in place for Julio. How had the school district, local businesses, teachers, and other adults adjusted their practices to create a nurturing village for him? What might happen if one of the supports in this narrative were removed?
2. Ms. Tracy showed that she cared about Delia, Marco, and Julio through verbal and nonverbal communication. Describe a few things she did to relay warmth, honesty, and respect to them.
3. How could Ms. Tracy use the information that she learned from Delia and Marco to support the cultural diversity in her infant class?

General Discussion Questions

1. What kind of supports are available for teen parents and their children in your community?
2. What happens if the type of supports shown in this case are not in place? How might educators address that with the families with whom they work?
3. How would other parents benefit from the type of mentoring or modeling illustrated in this case?
4. The NAEYC (2019) position statement on advancing equity stresses the importance of early childhood educators "support[ing] the development of children's first languages while simultaneously promoting proficiency in English" (7). Where might educators find information about evidence-based practices for supporting young children who are dual language learners and their families?

Reference

NAEYC. 2019. "Advancing Equity in Early Childhood Education." Position statement. Washington, DC: NAEYC. www.naeyc.org/resources/position-statements/equity.

2.2 Healthy Boundaries: Listening to Children and Learning from Families

Jovanna Archuleta

Connections to *Developmentally Appropriate Practice*

- Chapter 7: Engaging in Reciprocal Partnerships with Families and Fostering Community Connections

Case Overview

Toddlers have already learned what they like and don't like and express this in their own individual ways. Yet adults often consider toddlers to have little understanding of personal boundaries, and they expect toddlers to be socially adaptive to the world and the people around them, accepting that adults have the right to, for example, pinch their cheeks and tickle their stomachs. This case relates the journey of one toddler's mother to respect and support the boundaries her child expressed from a very early age without feeling the need to apologize to other adults, and how the support of the child's teacher was a pivotal point for the child's mother.

Learning Objectives

1. Describe the importance of understanding parents' perspectives of their children's behavior.
2. Analyze effects of individual child temperament and preferences on a child's development and interaction with other people.

Case Narrative

At a very early age, my daughter Lily would pull away when people would lean in to say how cute she was or want to touch her face. Before she was old enough to vocally express her dislike, she would yell or scoot away; now 3 years old, she is more vocal with her boundaries. From the start, however, I found myself, as the parent, often apologizing for her behavior; at one point I isolated myself and her from being around people to avoid feeling guilty for constantly apologizing. At around age 1, Lily would tell people no or stop if they came near her. I felt as if I always had to display a warning label, saying things like "Just to warn you, she doesn't like to be touched." Still, I would get comments about my daughter being a brat, mean, or unfriendly.

Most children express their discomfort with other people or situations by hiding behind Mom or Dad, wanting to be held, holding back from engaging in the interaction, having a meltdown, or displaying similar behaviors. Most often, it happens with people children are not familiar with. Lily's behavior, however, is the same with people who are unfamiliar to her and those she is comfortable being around. She will say something like "I don't want to talk right now, I am feeling sad" or "No, I am not ready for a hug." Many of these statements start with "I am not ready," but family members are more likely to take offense at this than respect it.

Lily is enrolled at our local tribal Head Start. In a conference I had with her teachers, they told me how impressed they were that when she needs a moment to regulate, she will tell them so, using those exact words. As we talked, I realized that the teachers viewed this not as a problem, not something to apologize for, but as a *strength*. From that point on, my response and support shifted to advocate for Lily's requests rather than be concerned that she might hurt someone's feelings. As adults, how nice would it be to be able to say those things out loud without people taking offense! Encouraging children to express their emotions and wishes and giving them tools to stand up for themselves are all part of supporting strong social and emotional development. It is the mindset of *adults* that needs to shift in order to recognize and honor these behaviors rather than label them "unfriendly" and "problematic."

Even with the support of Lily's teachers and my new perspective, it has taken some time for me to adjust to Lily's expression of her feelings and behavior. It has taken time to realize that I need to support her rather than discipline her for not wanting to be affectionate with people she does not know or knows very little. It has taken time to stop comparing her with other children who welcome those embraces or who are demanded by their parents to give embraces. I believe that the support I give her today will lead her to be a strong, confident woman who will be able to say no when in uncomfortable situations; it will allow her to protect her physical, mental, and spiritual well-being and her body when she ventures out into our world and, hopefully, prevent her from being a statistic in a #MeToo movement.

Takeaways and Next Steps

As you continue in your early childhood profession, it is important to have conversations with parents and assist families in recognizing and advocating for their children's preferences and boundaries that they themselves have set. Children know their own feelings, so listening to them *and* their families is the first important step to understanding each child as an individual.

Case Discussion Questions

1. Explain how this case presents an opportunity for the teacher to implement DAP guideline 2E of the position statement on developmentally appropriate practice: Educators and the family share with each other their knowledge of the particular child and understanding of child development and learning as part of day-to-day and other forms of communication (e.g., family get-togethers, meetings, support groups).
2. How could Lily's initial behavior and then her ability to self-regulate be discussed in terms of principle 4 of the position statement on developmentally appropriate practice: Although general progressions of development and learning can be identified, variations due to cultural contexts, experiences, and individual differences must also be considered?
3. What can an educator learn about patience and perseverance from Lily's mother?
4. How can teachers support children's expression of emotions and wishes?
5. Lily's mother felt she had to learn to stop comparing her daughter with other children. What role does an educator play in assisting parents who struggle with comparing their child to other children?
6. What other encouragement, advice, and/or resources would you share with Lily's mother?

2.3 Roadmap of Family Engagement to Kindergarten: An Ecological Systems Approach

Marcela Andrés

Connections to *Developmentally Appropriate Practice*

- Chapter 2: The Principles in Practice: Understanding Child Development and Learning in Context
- Chapter 6: Creating a Caring, Equitable Community of Learners
- Chapter 7: Engaging in Reciprocal Partnerships with Families and Fostering Community Connections

Case Overview

This case study provides a glimpse into the yearlong journey of one family from an underresourced community who is planning to enroll their child in kindergarten. The perspective is that of the parents and community. Drawing from Urie Bronfenbrenner's (1979) ecological systems theory, this case highlights some of the many relationships that support children in their academic and social development. The case provides a scenario to discuss the assets families possess that may be overlooked or not valued by the education system, explore preconceived ideas educators may hold about families, and consider the work educators may need to do to build partnerships with families.

Learning Objectives

1. Discuss the ecosystem of support this child has in her life.
2. Identify assets in the child's ecosystem to support with kindergarten readiness.
3. Explain ways teachers can prepare for meaningful partnerships with families.

Case Narrative

Gabriela and her husband, Daniel, have just moved from Austin, Texas, to Dallas with their nearly 4-year-old daughter, Lucia, to seek new job opportunities. Before the family moved, Gabriela and Daniel both worked full time, and Gabriela's sister and mom watched Lucia because of the high cost of child care. Although Gabriela's and Daniel's jobs in Austin provided for their family's needs and a little more, their combined income was considered at the bottom of the middle-class income bracket. While Daniel makes $20,000 more than he had in his previous job, Gabriela hasn't yet found a job after several months. Daniel's income is just above the middle-class income bracket, making them ineligible for state-subsidized child care.

Despite their financial challenges, Gabriela and Daniel are determined to celebrate Lucia's fourth birthday with family and neighbors in their new townhouse. Everyone is looking forward to the party and the carne asada!

"It's so good to see you, Gabriela. Thank you so much for inviting us to Lucia's party," says Victoria, their new neighbor. "Living in the US can sometimes be challenging because people don't speak with one another, so I was very excited about your invitation."

"We understand how hard it can be to come to a new place and want to build a community with our neighbors," Gabriela shares.

“Well, hopefully, you’ll have many more of these parties now that the girls will go to kindergarten next year. What have you been doing to prepare?” Victoria asks.

“We have made sure that Lucia knows how to count to 100 in both English and Spanish and can read, write, and recite at least 100 words,” Daniel says proudly. “We read every night before bed. One night we read an English book and the next night we read a Spanish book.”

“That’s wonderful. We are teaching Julieta how to read, write, and recite in Spanish too!” Victoria says excitedly. “What other activities are you doing to prepare Lucia for kindergarten?”

Gabriela and Daniel look at each other. “What do you mean by other activities?” Gabriela asks hesitantly.

Victoria starts firing off questions. “Do you have Lucia enrolled in an enrichment program at her child care? How does she get along with other children? Does she feel ready to start school?”

With looks of concern, Gabriela and Daniel shake their heads. “No, we really haven’t engaged in many other activities and, unfortunately, are unable to afford child care right now,” Gabriela says. “I am staying home until I find a new job.”

Realizing that her questions have caused discomfort, Victoria chuckles nervously. “Oh my, I am keeping you from the other guests.”

As the party progresses, Gabriela’s mind keeps replaying this conversation. She wonders if she and Daniel have failed their daughter. Will Lucia be behind the other students in kindergarten or, worse yet, not be able to reach her full potential? Gabriela wants to find answers to what now seems like a big problem, but a wave of guests arriving keep her from giving the conversation much more thought. Instead, Gabriela finds joy in Lucia’s happiness as Lucia runs around with new friends and opens her gifts.

The next day at church, Gabriela and Daniel are in the parking lot securing Lucia in the back seat of their car. Gabriela is about to bring up the conversation they’d had with Victoria when they hear someone call out to Daniel.

“Hey, Daniel!” Gustavo yells again across the parking lot as he jogs toward the vehicle. “I’m sorry that I missed Lucia’s party yesterday and your carne asada! We had family come in unexpectedly, and well, you know how that goes, hermano.”

“Don’t worry about it, Gustavo, we will have more get-togethers. I love grilling!” says Daniel.

“Perfect. So how did everything go?” asks Gustavo.

“Everything was great, man. Lucia had a nice time and received some great gifts,” replies Daniel.

“Cool. So why the frown today, hermano?” Gustavo probes.

Daniel gives a heavy sigh. “Man, I was just thinking about something we talked about with one of our neighbors. She asked us what we were doing to prepare Lucia for kindergarten. And hermano, I think we are letting our little girl down. We don’t have the money to pay for child care, and we are afraid our daughter will not be ready to start school next year.”

“Hermano, I understand what you are going through, and I will tell you right now that Lucia is going to be just fine,” Gustavo says as he pats Daniel on the shoulder. Gustavo, a third grade teacher, has recently enrolled in a master’s program to pursue his goal of becoming a superintendent one day. “Working on my master’s, for the first time I have the language to explain what I know to be true in our community, hermano. We don’t have a lot of money in our community, and many people consider us low income with a lot of disadvantages, and it’s true there are a lot of things we don’t have. But we have a lot of resources and assets that can’t be measured with dollars,” Gustavo continues.

Daniel crosses his arms and listens as Gustavo goes on.

“Look, this next year that you and Gabriela are preparing Lucia for kindergarten, I want you to remember two things. First, the ecosystem of support that Lucia has—”

“Ecosystem? Like in science with frogs and tadpoles?” Daniel laughs.

"Sort of, but with children in the center. Think of it as the connections that enrich and support life options and opportunities. The idea comes from Urie Bronfenbrenner's ecological systems theory," Gustavo says, getting excited. "There are different categories—systems—of relationships that people have within their community and society. Every child has a variety of relationships that support them with their development. Think about Lucia. Before attending school, she'll interact with your family, other kids in the neighborhood, kids and families at our church, and lots of other people in other places such as the doctor's office, the grocery store, her child care program, or even the library. Every time you interact with folks from these groups, there is an opportunity to support Lucia's learning and development."

"This totally makes sense, but, like I said, we can't afford child care. I think that would really help Lucia," Daniel says.

"Don't beat yourself up, hermano. Many of the families in our community can't afford child care. It's ridiculously expensive. So we take advantage of the assets we have in our community. Take, for example, Sunday school. Lucia is reading and learning Bible stories and learning values. Or, when y'all take her to the park with other kids, Lucia is developing social skills to interact and play with other children. And when you take her to the library and check out both English and Spanish books to read to her every night, she is developing her identity as a multicultural learner. Lucia has community child care, bro." Gustavo laughs encouragingly.

"You are right. Looking at it that way, we have so many relationships and opportunities to leverage as we prepare Lucia for kindergarten! Thanks, hermano," Daniel says gratefully. "Wait, you said two things? What is the other one?"

"That's the opportunity for Lucia's teachers to partner with you through her journey to support you in championing, fighting, and advocating for her hopes and dreams," Gustavo says. "Begin a relationship with her new teachers. Share with them what Lucia has learned and the ways you and Gabriela—and the other people in her ecosystem—support her learning and development. Ask what children her age are learning and for ideas on how you can continue her learning at home or in other places in the community. The great teachers will have ideas to extend her learning—they will encourage you to make everything a teachable moment." Gustavo smiles. "I have to run, but let's continue talking later this week at the gym or find a time to grab coffee."

"Definitely! Thank you, hermano. Your perspective really gives me comfort. I was feeling pretty down on myself and now I can't wait to share with Gabriela everything you said." Daniel shakes Gustavo's hand and hugs him.

Takeaways and Next Steps

The case example reflects the lived experience of a family from an underresourced community and taps into the idea that there are assets in every community to leverage for a child's growth and development. It demonstrates how thoughtfully and authentically learning about a family's ecosystem (that is, people, connections, relationships) can offer insights to build reciprocal connections between families and educators. Because schools in the United States tend to value certain types of resources and experiences over others as important for children's learning and readiness for school (consider Victoria's comments to Gabriela), both families and educators may overlook all the resources families have around them even when circumstances are difficult. Educators can seek to deeply understand the community they are working in by becoming familiar with the area the children and families live in and the rich cultures represented and by identifying community resources they can partner with to support children and families. When a child enters a program, educators can conduct an eco-map, a graphic representation of a family's formal and informal supports within the larger social system (McCormick et al. 2008), with the family to coidentify the rich assets within their community. Educators also have a responsibility to reflect on any biases they may have and how these might affect their work with families and children, and then work to change their perceptions.

Case Discussion Questions

1. What do you remember about your own kindergarten readiness experience, either as a child or as a parent? How does it compare with the experience Gabriela and Daniel are providing their daughter?
2. What reaction did you have hearing this Latino father's perspective?
3. What, if any, assumptions came up for you before the conversation with Gustavo? Were your thoughts deficit or asset based? Why? What actions can you take to explore your thinking?

General Discussion Questions

1. How can educators learn about each family's system of support? In what ways can educators proactively help parents and families to recognize and leverage the ecosystem of support they have in their communities?
2. What are practical ways you can leverage your expertise as an educator and honor parents' and families' expertise as a child's first teacher to support and extend their learning at home?
3. Learning about a family's ecosystem can be a point on the journey toward family engagement, but some families may have fewer connections on which to build. What might be additional strategies for fostering community connections in ways that are respectful and responsive? For example, if Lucia's family asked for specific resources for supporting her school readiness, how might you respond?

References

Bronfenbrenner, U. 1979. *The Ecology of Human Development: Experiments by Nature and Design.* Cambridge, MA: Harvard University Press.

McCormick, K.M., S. Stricklin, T.M. Nowak, & B. Rous. 2008. "Using Eco-Mapping to Understand Family Strengths and Resources." *Young Exceptional Children* 11 (2): 17–28. https://doi.org/10.1177/1096250607311932.

2.4 Taking Trust for Granted? The Importance of Communication and Outreach in Family Partnerships

Suzanna Ewert

Connections to *Developmentally Appropriate Practice*

- Chapter 1: Intentional Teaching: Complex Decision Making and the Core Considerations
- Chapter 2: The Principles in Practice: Understanding Child Development and Learning in Context
- Chapter 3: Context Matters: Reframing Teaching in Early Childhood Education
- Chapter 7: Engaging in Reciprocal Partnerships with Families and Fostering Community Connections

Case Overview

This case explores the dynamics between school staff and families of young children in a rural school district. While rural schools share similar challenges to engaging families as in other contexts, the strategies and resources available to do so often differ. In this particular case, community ties between school staff and families are already strong, but a situation arises that highlights the need for trust and two-way communication to continually be strengthened. Within the context of teacher shortages and resource scarcity, the principal of a rural Texas school hires an uncertified, "homegrown" teacher to fill a kindergarten vacancy, triggering a backlash from the families of the incoming class.

The purpose of this case is to lay out a problem for readers to consider by applying their knowledge of developmentally appropriate practice to engage families in reciprocal partnerships. The open-ended conclusion of the narrative sets the stage for discussion of what practices could be used to build relationships with the families as the school year begins, based on the perspectives and community context outlined.

Learning Objectives

1. Identify how context shapes and affects family engagement and community partnership work.
2. Apply the core concepts of developmentally appropriate family and community partnerships to a specific problem and context.
3. Explain ways family partnerships are fostered and maintained at the administrative level in addition to the classroom level.

Case Narrative

The Context

This case takes place in Ceniza, a rural unincorporated community in West Texas. Residents, approximately half of whom are White and half of whom are Latinx, typically work as ranch hands or in service or skilled labor jobs in the nearby county seat. The majority of students in the Ceniza Independent School District (ISD) receive free or reduced-price lunch. The district is the economic driver of its community as it is the largest employer. This is the situation for many similar small towns in the region—without the school, there would not be a community. This means that the district—which houses approximately 200 students, pre-K through 12th grade, in two adjacent buildings—is the center of its community. School sports competitions double as social gatherings, and school buildings are regularly used for community events.

The school benefits from close community ties and good relationships with students' families. Many parents donate their time to volunteering at extracurricular events and in the classroom. These relationships between school staff and community members further benefit from a lack of class divides—economically, school staff are at about the same level as their fellow residents. Families are typically comfortable meeting with teachers and administrators, as most have been area residents for most, if not all, of their lives.

Many districts nationwide are facing a teacher shortage, particularly those in rural communities, where schools struggle to attract outside hires to remote areas. To curtail this, Texas offers Districts of Innovation designation, which allows eligible districts to be exempt from certain sections of the Texas Education Code to meet their goals. This designation is contingent on the district maintaining high academic performance and locally adopting an Innovation Plan (TEA 2022). Among other flexibilities, Districts of Innovation can hire teachers before they receive certification. These new staff teach in the classroom while pursuing their certification, as well as their bachelor's degree if they do not already have one. They receive both professional development and financial assistance in obtaining their certification and degree. This route to hiring and certification often applies to homegrown teachers, or those who already live in the community. Ceniza ISD is a District of Innovation.

The Challenge

A longtime third grade teacher has just retired from Ceniza ISD. After struggling to recruit a new teacher, particularly from nearby universities where teaching programs have seen shrinking enrollments over the past decade, the principal, Mr. Márquez, decides to move the district's highly effective kindergarten teacher into the vacant position. This way, an experienced teacher is placed in a grade with a state standardized-tested subject. Unlike third grade, student performance in kindergarten does not factor into state report cards for districts. For the kindergarten vacancy, Principal Márquez recruits Ms. Dreschner to fill the position. She graduated from Ceniza High School three years prior and has since continued to live and work in the community where she was raised. For the past year, she has worked part time at a grocery store in the county seat and part time as a paraprofessional at Ceniza ISD. Besides her experience as a paraprofessional, she earned career and technical education (CTE) credits in the education and training career cluster during high school, which means she completed courses in teacher education.

However, families of incoming kindergartners are upset with the decision to hire an uncertified teacher, even if she is one from their community. Rather than come to Principal Márquez directly, they have taken to social media to air their concerns.

The Perspectives

The principal: Mr. Márquez feels the pressure of family expectations and the tight budgetary constraints of a rural district. He cannot offer a salary high enough to attract outside hires to live in a remote community, and recent vacancies have only received one or two applicants, if any at all. He is an avid proponent of homegrown teacher initiatives, seeing them as a way to build the professional and economic capacity of people in their community. This is particularly true of potential teachers like Ms. Dreschner, who has worked so diligently as a paraprofessional in the school. As Ms. Dreschner works toward her certification, Mr. Márquez will devote time to getting her the professional development she needs to succeed as a first-year teacher. He is frustrated with families who take their concerns to social media rather than to him directly, as these same families were invited to and did not attend the District of Innovation meetings that explain the district's growth plan and its budget. He sent home letters explaining these as well.

The kindergarten families: Ceniza families understand the importance of early childhood education—that a child's learning experience in kindergarten is the foundation for the rest of their schooling. They were looking forward to their children learning from the veteran kindergarten teacher, who has now been moved to a grade level in which there is a state-standardized test subject. They are confused and upset as to why Principal Márquez would hire someone without certification or teaching experience instead. It's true that Ms. Dreschner is from the community, sharing the same values and social circles as the families she'll be working with. However, they remember her as a mid-performing high school student who caused trouble with teenage antics just a few short years before. She did not go on to college, and they do not trust her to be an effective teacher.

The teacher: Ms. Dreschner is excited about her new position and all the learning opportunities she'll receive both in the classroom and through college and certification courses. This includes getting to use the knowledge and skills she gained from CTE courses in high school and from her time as a paraprofessional in the district. She is eager to continue to turn her life around from her high school reputation that brought the scrutiny of her close-knit community. She is hurt that families are disappointed in her hire. She wants to do whatever she can to gain their trust and do the best by their children but is already feeling defensive about communicating with them. She had planned to schedule one-on-one conferences with families at the beginning of the year, but now she wonders whether she would be able to hold her own during those meetings. She is leaning toward just sending the families welcome letters.

Takeaways and Next Steps

Even if community ties are strong and there is a general feeling of trust, knowing *of* families and community members is not the same as *knowing* them. As the school year begins, Ms. Dreschner has several opportunities to begin building partnerships with the kindergarten families. Principal Márquez can further strengthen his two-way lines of communication with families, as well as make district decisions more transparent by adopting ways to better meet families where they are.

Case Discussion Questions

1. What aspects of this community's specific context facilitate or hinder family–school partnerships? Based on this community's context and its relationship with the school, how are families already engaged, and where is there room for improvement?
2. What biases or assumptions is each perspective bringing to the situation?
3. Of the seven areas of the position statement on developmentally appropriate practice on engaging in reciprocal partnerships with families and fostering community connections (guidelines 2A–2G), which do the educators in this case already follow? Which are areas for improvement and opportunity?
4. What initial steps can Ms. Dreschner take to build relationships with her new students' families? What should she consider in making her decision to either have meetings with families or send welcome letters?
5. In what ways could Principal Márquez have better communicated the reasons for his decision to hire Ms. Dreschner to families? What steps can he take now to have more collaborative relationships with families through this rough patch and into the future?
6. If you were Principal Márquez, what practices would you have implemented before putting this plan in place?
7. How is the context of this case different or similar to the context of your own practice?

Reference

TEA (Texas Education Agency). 2022. "Districts of Innovation." Accessed August 2. https://tea.texas.gov/texas-schools/district-initiatives/districts-of-innovation.

2.5 Book Reading: Learning About Migration and Our Family Stories

Sarah Rendón García

Connections to *Developmentally Appropriate Practice*

- Chapter 6: Creating a Caring, Equitable Community of Learners
- Chapter 7: Engaging in Reciprocal Partnerships with Families and Fostering Community Connections

Case Overview

This case describes a classroom experience in which the teacher acknowledges and engages her learners' social identities, home languages, cultures, and family experiences to help each child "feel psychologically safe and able to focus on being and learning" (NAEYC 2020, 17). The teacher also seeks to "learn about the community in which they work, and . . . use the community as a resource across all aspects of program delivery" (18). In this case, an elementary school teacher focuses on guideline 2G of the position statement on developmentally appropriate practice to plan and implement a two-part classroom activity. This educator places particular emphasis on using the families as a resource for her curriculum development to find ways to incorporate students' families into their learning without the families needing to be physically present in the classroom.

Learning Objectives

1. Identify ways of honoring and centering students' family experiences as a resource for curriculum development.
2. Demonstrate understanding of the importance of incorporating families' expertise and experiences in creating safe learning environments for students.

Case Narrative

The Plan

Many students in Ms. Martinez's third grade classroom are multilingual learners whose families immigrated to the United States. Ms. Martinez draws on this fact as a strength of her classroom community: she wants to offer her students a positive contrast to what they may hear outside of school about this aspect of their family's experience. She develops a lesson plan centering the importance of immigration and family histories. The activity takes some planning ahead to provide ample time for families to participate—there is an at-home family component with options for participation with different degrees of time and mode of commitment. Before the classroom component, Ms. Martinez sends out a communication to families to explain the activity and provide guidance for participating.

For the family component, Ms. Martinez requests that each child and a family member read the book *Dreamers* by Yuyi Morales ahead of time. Following the reading, families are asked to cocreate a piece of art (for example, drawing, video, and so on) about their own family's origin story at home that their child will share with the class. Ms. Martinez also invites families to choose an artifact to send from home about their family's story or history (for example, a photograph or an item from their country of origin) to share.

Ms. Martinez explains to students that even if their families have lived in the same place all their life, they can choose to tell a story of a family member who has moved away or a family story from generations before. Ms. Martinez shares all this information to students' families two to three weeks in advance.

Discussing Families in the Classroom

After Ms. Martinez has provided ample time and scaffolded support for the family component of the activity, her class reads *Dreamers* together. Her students take turns reading each page, which has short sentences with beautiful illustrations. In the book, a mother tells the story of migrating to the United States with her child. The mother shares examples of the challenges they face as they navigate a new language and ways of life. Ultimately, the mother and her child find libraries, which become their safe place where they learn to dream and achieve a better future.

During the book reading, Ms. Martinez encourages students to comment on the illustrations and what is happening to the mother and child in the story. Some students comment on the bridge the mom crosses with her baby as they travel to the United States. Others are captivated by the mother having trouble navigating the subway map and offer similar stories of confusion and misunderstanding. In all these cases, Ms. Martinez validates the students' observations and expresses gratitude for sharing their associations to the story.

After the story, Ms. Martinez has a short discussion with her students about the book that incorporates reading comprehension skills and largely focuses on the theme of migration and family traditions. She asks students the following questions:

1. What were your favorite parts of the book?
2. In the book, the mom says she and her baby are immigrants. Do you know what an immigrant is? (During the conversation, Ms. Martinez clarifies that an immigrant is someone who moves from one place to another to live.)
3. For the mother and the baby, libraries became their safe place in their new country, and it was a place they always went to together. What are some places where you feel safe?
4. What are some traditions you have with your family?

During the class discussion, Ms. Martinez notices that students are excited to share their safe spaces and family traditions. Some students share pictures of their grandparents in different countries, with their parents as younger children. As students share their family art (done at home), artifacts (brought in from home), and reflections on the book (done in class), Ms. Martinez draws attention to cultural differences and similarities. For instance, families are similar in the way they like to eat meals together and different in the types of foods they like to eat.

Week-Long Project

After students share about their safe spaces and family traditions, Ms. Martinez tells them that as a classroom community, or "family," it is important for all to learn about each other's home family. During the upcoming week, she informs them, they will work on another project to include an important part of their families in their classroom. Ms. Martinez tells students that they can chose between these two options:

1. Interview a family member about a time when they had to move to a new place.
2. Find an artifact from home with the help of their family (picture, souvenir, drawing, short video clip, and so on) that represents a family trip or tradition.

Ms. Martinez also tells her students that they will have selected time each day of the week to work on their family project (family story and family artifact), draft their interview questions and receive feedback, and compose narratives to present to the class about their chosen activity (interview or artifact). At the end of the week, the class will have a celebration where students present their work. The presentations will be recorded and shared with their families.

Takeaways and Next Steps

This case study shows how an educator acknowledges learners' family history, traditions, and culture in a positive and strengths-based manner. By incorporating book reading both at home and as part of a classroom activity, Ms. Martinez is also able to intertwine family engagement, reading comprehension, and interpersonal skill development. At the same time, she can begin helping her students make sense of the conversations about immigration or migration they might be hearing outside of school without delving into the larger debates but focusing on the simple definition of migration as an act of movement of peoples. For some children, especially multilingual learners, this provides an acknowledgment of their reality and their identities without any negative connotations. Instead, it offers an avenue through which all students in a classroom can see how they are connected around the theme of migration—everyone has a connection to someone who has traveled, migrated, or shared family traditions. Rendón García (2022) shows that children as young as 7 years old have begun developing knowledge of migration as a concept, and the activities in this classroom provide children with appropriate scaffolding to encourage their learning in this area.

Case Discussion Questions

1. How did the teacher's choice of book and follow-up activities support her goal for her students and for engaging families?
2. How does this classroom activity use the family as a resource for classroom learning?
3. How might the teacher and students explore things they have heard or experienced about immigration outside the classroom?
4. How might this classroom activity help educators achieve guidelines 2A and 2C of the position statement on developmentally appropriate practice?
5. How might the children relate differently to the story in the book, and what might this mean for how the teacher engages with their families in the future?
6. How else might the teacher engage with the families in meaningful ways? How might this be different for families of varying cultures or life circumstances?

General Discussion Questions

1. What potential challenges or concerns might this experience present for an educator of different age groups in a primary setting? Different geographical contexts?
2. What other books may serve as a conversation starter for young children learning about migration?
3. How might educators leverage their colleagues for advice or to find resources in preparing for implementing this type of classroom activity?

Suggested Resource

Colorín Colorado. n.d. "Parent Tips: Reading with Your Child." Accessed August 2, 2022. www.colorincolorado.org/parent-tips-reading-your-child.

References

NAEYC. 2020. "Developmentally Appropriate Practice." Position statement. Washington, DC: NAEYC. www.naeyc.org/resources/position-statements/dap/contents.

Rendón García, S. 2022. "Navigating Immigration Status en Familia: An Exploration of Caregiver Understanding, Caregiver-Child Attachment Quality, and Child Knowledge in Latine Mixed-Status Families." PhD diss., Harvard University. https://nrs.harvard.edu/URN-3:HUL.INSTREPOS:37372098.

PART 3

Observing, Documenting, and Assessing Children's Development and Learning

Gayle Mindes

Assessment can be one of the most mysterious aspects of teaching for an early childhood educator. Beyond numbers and tests, it requires educators to thoughtfully watch, listen to, reflect on, and document young children's play and learning. Authentic assessment is a dynamic and reciprocal process between educator and child. Through conversations and interactions, observational notes and recordings of children's conversations and activities, work samples, checklists, and formal assessments, educators compile a holistic picture of a child's progress toward developmental and educational goals to share with families, children, and other stakeholders. At each age, the key ingredients in developmentally appropriate assessment are observations paired with a keen knowledge of child development and an appreciation of each child's health, cultural, linguistic, and family dynamics, including environmental influences such as poverty, personal tragedies, access to basic human resources, and life history. Each of these factors can affect growth and development starting from birth.

Critically, as a first educator in a young child's life, the teacher's role is to share with the family multiple forms of assessment documentation. Each form—such as notes from conversations with individuals and groups as well as work products like drawings, writings, posters, and videos—shows a snapshot in time documenting the child's progress. Although the products of observation vary by age, growth and development cannot be converted to numbers and letter grades. Checklists assess whether critical skill dimensions are progressing, but qualitative information creates a more complete picture of learning and development. Children of all ages can engage in self-evaluation through teachers' prompts and discussion of their products and performance; this process facilitates their understanding of their own learning.

Underlying all teacher observation and assessment is a teacher's reflection upon practice, necessary to assure equity and fairness, avoid bias, and inform instruction. For a particular curricular decision, teachers ask:

- What worked for all the children?
- Can I track what each child learned?
- Did I miss the mark with one or more of the children?
- How can I modify the experience so all will be successful?
- How can I involve families, supervisors, and consultants for puzzling situations?

In this way, teachers can adapt curriculum to support assessment in a continuous cycle to ensure culturally, linguistically responsive, and authentic learning experiences for every child.

The writers of the cases in Part 3 share complex snapshots of formal and informal assessment, standards, and standardized measures, illustrating a number of tools in a practitioner's toolbox for effective observation and assessment practice. Settings are geographically and culturally diverse, chosen to show how practitioners can involve families and other stakeholders, make sense of assessment data, and promote learning. The cases illustrate developmentally appropriate practice for

- Capturing learning for children with complex developmental needs
- Collaborating with families to gain insight into children's behaviors
- Sharing information with families on learning and assessment in a play-based program
- Making sense of in-depth child conversations to promote literacy and connect evidence for a published and required assessment system
- Identifying alternative ways to assess emergent bilinguals' learning
- Documenting language and literacy progress in Spanish and English
- Using formative assessment during whole group learning
- Documenting children's content learning with alternative methods

The writers of these cases, located across the United States, are teacher educators, child development directors, infant practitioners, Head Start teachers, early intervention specialists, and special educators. Each brings a breadth of professional experience and together reflect the cultural diversity of our world. As field-experienced scholars knowledgeable of the nitty-gritty of daily problem solving and intentional teaching, they deftly illustrate the cycle of observation, curricular implementation, documentation, and reflection in action.

3.1 Pairing Standardized Scale with Observation

Megan Schumaker-Murphy

Connections to *Developmentally Appropriate Practice*

- Chapter 7: Engaging in Reciprocal Partnerships with Families and Fostering Community Connections
- Chapter 8: Observing, Documenting, and Assessing Children's Development and Learning

Case Overview

Jaime, a 12-month-old baby with an adjusted age of 8 months, was a micropreemie with a complex medical history. Sarah, the early interventionist who works with Jaime and his family, is struggling to write a six-month update accurately capturing Jaime's progress. Although his developmental age on the Hawaii Early Learning Profile (HELP; Warshaw 2006) has not improved significantly to show any quantitative progress, Jaime has gained new skills. This progress makes a big difference in his interactions with the world. Sarah and Jaime's mother work together to capture his achievement in a narrative describing Jaime's skills.

Learning Objectives

1. Articulate the importance of multiple methods of assessing and describing developmental progress.
2. Identify the challenges of using standardized assessment tools to capture developmental progress of infants with developmental delays.
3. Identify alternative methods of assessment and reporting to augment children's quantitative developmental profiles.

Case Narrative

Jaime is a 12-month-old baby with an adjusted age of 8 months. He was born at 24 weeks gestation, weighing 580 grams (roughly 1 pound 4 ounces). Jaime spent his first six months in the neonatal intensive care unit (NICU). At the NICU, Jaime underwent multiple surgical procedures to prevent fluid from building up in his brain, correct a condition that impacts vision, and remove part of his intestine. Brain scans showed that Jaime experienced brain bleeding during or shortly after birth. During his stay in the NICU, his mother, Ariana, was not able to spend much time holding him due to his medical conditions. By the time Jaime was discharged home from the hospital, he had established a clear preference for lying on his back and didn't like to be touched. Jaime fussed and cried when Ariana or his grandmother picked him up or tried to hold him. Jaime was easily calmed by laying him down on his back and giving him a pacifier.

As soon as Jaime got home from the NICU, the family started working with early intervention (EI) services. Sarah, the early interventionist, came weekly. When she first reviewed Jaime's Individualized Family Service Plan (IFSP), Sarah thought the initial IFSP outcome, "We want Jaime to be more playful so that he can learn more skills," was vague. Similarly, the goals included strategies that were very broad, such as "promoting visual attention," "encouraging play in a variety of positions," and "parent education." Sarah asked Ariana what she and the evaluation team were thinking about when they wrote the goals. Initial evaluation happened in the hospital shortly before Jaime was discharged home, when Ariana was feeling overwhelmed. She didn't really remember contributing to the conversation for the IFSP outcome. When Sarah asked Ariana what she was hoping to achieve in early intervention, Ariana tearfully said, "I just want to be able to hold him without him screaming and for him to do more than lay in his crib and look at the ceiling. Right now, I have to lean over the side of his crib to give him a bottle because when I try to hold him, he just screams and won't even eat."

Sarah and Ariana spent the next several months addressing this goal. Sarah taught Ariana how to use infant massage to help Jaime learn that being touched could be pleasant. They experimented with Ariana wearing a cloth wrap to hold Jaime close to her and using a combination of bouncing and rocking side to side while holding him to see if this input would help Jaime tolerate being held. After the first month, Jaime stopped crying when his mother touched or held him. After about two months, Ariana could hold Jaime to feed him. After the third month, Ariana said that "Jaime turned into a snuggle monster." He started to make more eye contact. Now, when Ariana comes into a room, Jaime turns his head toward her. Last week, he started to laugh.

The IFSP team also worked on engaging Jaime in play in supported sitting, prone (on his tummy), and in supine (on his back) positions. Jaime has shown a preference for looking at the book *Brown Bear, Brown Bear, What Do You See?* and a light-up toy turtle. He looks at these things and turns his head to follow them when they move. Sometimes, Jaime will reach out to try to touch the light-up turtle toy. When someone places a toy in his hands, he will grasp it briefly. Ariana hopes now that Jaime isn't so fussy and is starting to play, perhaps she can find an early learning program that will accept him so that she can go back to work.

Now that Jaime's been in EI for six months, it's time for the IFSP team to review progress. Besides Ariana and Sarah, the IFSP team includes Latrisha, the EI service coordinator; Louann, a physical therapist; Malia, a nutritionist; and Curtis, a speech and feeding therapist. The team is waiting for an occupational therapist to become available to work with Jaime. Each provider is required to write a report detailing Jaime's six-months progress. Ariana said she is excited for the team to get together to talk about how far she knows Jaime has come since coming home from the NICU.

When Sarah begins to administer the HELP during a home visit, she quickly realizes that Jaime's progress isn't going to show significant progress. According to the HELP, Jaime's score is 4 months, which is only one month beyond his developmental age when he was first assessed six months ago. Ariana asks how Jaime scored on the assessment. Sarah isn't sure how to respond. She feels strongly that the progress Jaime's made over the last six months is really significant for his quality of life, and she is crushed that this progress isn't showing up in his developmental age. Before Sarah can decide how best to respond, Jaime starts to fuss for his mother to pick him up. Sarah comments, "I am so happy to see him demanding that you hold him. This is such a big change from the baby I met six months ago!" Sarah then excuses herself to go to her next appointment.

Sarah knows that she must include the results from the HELP assessment but also knows that she needs to honor the significance of Jaime's progress, however small it may appear quantitatively. Sarah reviews the IFSP goal to see if she can frame the descriptions around progress toward the outcome of Jaime being more playful. Sarah thinks she can write a little about how Jaime is now engaging in some visual attention and playing in supported sitting, but these just don't seem to be the progress areas that are most important to Ariana.

Feeling frustrated and a little stumped, Sarah calls Jaime's physical therapist, Louann, to talk about how she feels at the seeming lack of progress in the numbers. Sarah and Louann spend several minutes talking about how Jaime becoming a "snuggle monster," looking intentionally at people and objects, and starting to laugh has made such a huge change in relationship with his family and his ability to engage with the world around him. Sarah and Louann devise a plan to make sure that they both address these perceptions in their reports and verbally at the IFSP review meeting.

Sarah thinks a lot about how to talk to Ariana about the assessment numbers. She decides it's best to meet with Ariana before the IFSP review instead of breaking the news to her in a room full of other service providers. Sarah calls Ariana to schedule a call for sharing in the joy of all the behaviors Jaime gained the last few months. She explains how the standardized HELP is just one tool and numbers can't fully describe the impact of Jaime's changes on his daily life. Ariana is disappointed to hear Jaime's developmental age, but the news doesn't change how excited she is about all the ways their relationship and lives improved over the last six months.

Takeaways and Next Steps

After the team completes the IFSP meeting, Sarah meets with Louann to reflect on their experience. Sarah doesn't want any other families she works with feeling surprised by formal annual assessments. She and Louann discuss strategies to avoid this in the future, including avoiding vague statements about progress like "He's doing great!" and instead being very specific about developmental progress. Sarah decides that she will talk with families often about the different kinds of assessments and assessment data that she and the IFSP team use when measuring progress so that families understand that a formal assessment like the HELP is only a part of the holistic picture. Sarah and Louann decide that they will also start framing developmental progress conversations with families around the IFSP outcomes and family priorities and include how even small developmental gains or newly introduced strategies relate to the family's larger outcomes and priorities. Sarah also begins to look for professional development trainings about holistic assessment.

Case Discussion Questions

Developmentally appropriate practice guidelines recommend that families and educators engage in frequent, two-way communication to share information about children. While Sarah and Ariana appeared to have a reciprocal partnership, Sarah was initially reticent to share the standardized assessment results with Ariana.

1. During the session when Sarah completed Jaime's HELP assessment, she took advantage of Ariana getting distracted so that she could take some additional time to process the results and confer with a trusted colleague before sharing assessment findings with Ariana.
    a. What is your reaction to how Sarah handled this?
    b. What do you think the outcome of the conversation may have been if Ariana hadn't gotten distracted by taking care of Jaime?
    c. Is there anything that Sarah should have done differently?

2. If you were writing Jaime's progress report, how would you craft an accurate narrative reflecting his small quantitative developmental progress and the significance of the developmental progress on his relationship with his mother, interaction with the environment, and overall quality of life?

Developmentally appropriate assessment supports attainable goals cocreated with families. Ariana doesn't remember being involved in identifying Jaime's initial IFSP goal.

1. What are some questions that Sarah, Louann, and the rest of the IFSP team should ask Ariana before the team writes an updated IFSP outcome?
2. What are some strategies they can employ before and during the meeting to make sure that Ariana doesn't feel overwhelmed by information or left out of goal setting?

Ariana would like Jaime to attend an early learning program.

1. Based on Jaime's current skill level and his mother's priorities, what are some IFSP outcomes that you could propose for Jaime's updated IFSP?
2. How would you help prepare for Jaime's transition from being home full time to starting at a program?
3. If you were Jaime's educator at his early learning program, what would be helpful for you to know about Jaime? What kinds of skills would you want his EI team to support so that he could fully engage with the other children and the environment?

General Discussion Questions

Guideline 3D of the DAP position statement states that methods of assessment should be responsive to the experiences of young children and recognize individual variation in learners. Most special education programs utilize assessment tools like the HELP or the Battelle Developmental Inventory (Newborg 2005), which are standardized based on typical development.

1. What are some of the challenges of using these kinds of assessments in assessing developmental progress for children with significant developmental delays?
2. What are the benefits of using these assessment tools?
3. What other tools or methods of assessment can be helpful when assessing children with developmental differences?

Suggested Resources

Early Intervention Training Program at the University of Illinois: https://eitp.education.illinois.edu/index.html.

EI on the Fly podcast: https://eionthefly.podbean.com.

Prematurity and NICU terms glossary: www.babyfirst.com/glossary-of-nicu-terms.

Virginia Early Intervention Professional Development Center: www.veipd.org/main/index.html.

References

Newborg, J. 2005. *Battelle Developmental Inventory: Examiner's Manual.* 2nd ed. Rolling Meadows, IL: Riverside Insights.

Warshaw, S.P. 2006. *Inside HELP 0–3 Administration and Reference Manual: For Using the Hawaii Early Learning Profile as a Birth to Three, Curriculum-Based Assessment.* Menlo Park, CA: VORT.

3.2 The Power of Observing Jordan

Marsha Shigeyo Hawley and Barbara Abel

Connections to *Developmentally Appropriate Practice*

- Chapter 7: Engaging in Reciprocal Partnerships with Families and Fostering Community Connections
- Chapter 8: Observing, Documenting, and Assessing Children's Development and Learning

Case Overview

This case occurs in a federally and state-funded early childhood program in a large city. Both the neighborhood and families served are culturally and linguistically diverse as are the center's staff. Jordan is a 21-month-old toddler who started walking at 9 months and is very physically active. In recent weeks Jordan cries, tantrums, and clings to Sheila, her mother, upon arrival at the center. At a family–teacher conference, Sheila expresses concerns about Jordan's behavior and lack of language. The teachers use observations and assessment to explore and address Sheila's worries, as well as some questions they themselves have.

Learning Objectives

1. Identify formal and informal ways to carry out observation, documentation, and assessment of toddlers' development and learning.
2. Explain how to observe toddlers' communication strategies to understand the multiple ways toddlers communicate their needs and thoughts.
3. Describe ways to use child observations to partner with families and devise plans for enhancing toddlers' development and learning both at home and in the early childhood program.

Case Narrative

Jordan is the youngest child in her family with two older brothers (5 and 8 years old). They live with Sheila, their mother, their grandmother (Sheila's mother), and Sheila's 22-year-old brother. Sheila works full time as a store manager of a large chain store and is the primary provider for the family.

Jordan has been with the same three caregivers at her early learning program since she was 6 weeks old. She has always been physically precocious (started walking at 9 months) with a great deal of energy. One of her favorite activities is putting the balls into a tube at the top of the classroom loft, finding them in the basket at the bottom, and bringing them one by one up the stairs to the top of the loft to watch them go down through the tube again.

Jordan often drools and has frequent ear infections, a constant runny nose, and difficulty settling at naptime. Her appetite is sporadic; she only wants to eat specific foods. She has verbal utterances and occasionally uses one or two words, mainly "ball" and "mama." She screams and tantrums each morning when Sheila brings her to the classroom, kicking and yelling "Mama!" as Sheila leaves the room. At day's end, she does not want to leave with Sheila, running away when Sheila enters the room. Sheila, who is increasingly frustrated with this behavior, sometimes tells Jordan, "You can have candy when you get to the car." On most days the candy bribe does not help her leave. Then Sheila picks Jordan up, kicking and screaming.

Family–Teacher Conference

In a recent family conference, Sheila shares her frustrations about Jordan's limited language and her behavior. She compares Jordan's language skills with her sons' when they were her age. Based on raising her two boys, who have always done well in school, Jordan's behavior and limited use of words are raising red flags for her.

In this conference, Seth, the lead teacher and Jordan's primary caregiver, shares observations of Jordan's ability to hop on one foot, run competently outside with some of the older children, and pick up a ball and throw it while retrieving another on the ground. Josie and Kia, assistants in the classroom, are thrilled with Jordan's ability to toss balls into a hoop and pour water into a funnel in the water table.

Though Sheila agrees that Jordan displays impressive physical abilities, she is worried about Jordan's language abilities and behavior. "My boys were talking in full sentences at this age," she says. "They never cried when I brought them to this school, nor did they ever kick and scream like she does."

Unsure of how to respond, Josie says, "Jordan said 'Bien' to me the other day when I said, 'Muy bien' to her." Kia says, "She definitely lets us know when she doesn't like something." Seth shares, "Many toddlers express their frustrations through physical actions. We are a little worried that Jordan is not eating as much as she used to and wondered if her runny nose and drooling are signs that she might need to see a doctor."

Staff Meeting to Plan Next Steps

While the teachers agree with Sheila's concerns, they also feel that Jordan's behavior is expected developmentally. At the next classroom team meeting, they plan additional observations by Seth at times when Jordan struggles and when Jordan is engaged in play with objects or with others. In particular, he'll look at how the transitions and environment in the classroom may affect Jordan's behavior. Each observation of Jordan, including observations from the family, are written, captured in photos, and stored in the daily notes and portfolio that the teachers keep for each child. The teachers also want to be sure Jordan participates in the upcoming audiology testing.

Preparing for the Next Family–Teacher Conference

To prepare for this conference, Seth reviews the Ages and Stages Questionnaires (ASQ; Squires, Bricker, & Twombly 2015) as well as the recent detailed written observations and child-produced drawings, pictures of Jordan's block structures, and other assessment documentation. When Seth pulls out the ASQ-SE (Social-Emotional) Questionnaire that Sheila completed with him during a home visit, he realizes that there had been no concerns about Jordan's eating and sleeping when she was 12 months old. As he thinks about the nine months since they had done the screening, he realizes that the problems they are having at snack, mealtimes, and naptime only recently started. In reviewing the quarterly assessment completed three months ago of Jordan's overall development, he confirms that Jordan was meeting or exceeding expectations in all developmental domains. His review does not indicate any areas of concern in either language or social and emotional development, but he also notices Jordan far exceeded expectations in large and small motor development. He notices that even though she was meeting expectations in language, she scored higher for receptive language. This helps to alleviate his fears about potential hearing loss from all of Jordan's ear infections.

Seth presents these findings at a team meeting. He also notes that Jordan's drop-off experience is different every day. Sometimes Jordan and her mother arrive when the center opens and other days they come in after breakfast is served. On some days Sheila is rushed, dragging Jordan into the classroom and running out in a hurry. On other days, Sheila carries Jordan in kicking, crying, screaming, "Mama!" Sheila seems reluctant to leave, sometimes leaving and coming back.

The team next considers transitions throughout the day. Seth notes that whenever he mentions it is almost time for cleanup, Jordan grabs whatever she is playing with and darts around the room, sometimes grabbing toys from other children or knocking over whatever others were building. Kia reports Jordan's tantrums before outdoor playtime. According to Josie, at snack and lunchtime, Jordan seems uninterested in food, ready to leave the table right away, but when she stands up, she grabs food off her plate and eats it. When reminded she needs to sit at the table to eat, Jordan drops the food and runs off to play.

The team agrees that some of what they are seeing is typical toddler behavior. Jordan is not the only child in the room who likes to eat on the run, though she is at this moment the only one who won't eat at the table. They also recognize that other children besides Jordan are struggling with transitions and separations.

Based on their more in-depth look at Jordan's language and behavior, the team agrees they need to do more planning around all transitions, including preparing each child individually for what would be happening next. Though they come up with this plan to help Jordan, they feel it would probably help all the children and themselves.

For the meeting with Sheila to discuss their findings, they plan to ask her if it is possible to be more consistent with drop-off and pickup times and to say goodbye the same way every day. They discuss ideas for goodbye rituals.

Seth's Meeting with Sheila

Seth arranges to meet Sheila at 8:00 a.m. In the meeting, Seth learns that Sheila is dealing with staff shortages at work, which is why drop-off and pickup times are so inconsistent. This work situation is also taking away time with Jordan, not to mention affecting how stressed Sheila feels. In addition, Sheila says that everyone at home treats Jordan like a princess, anticipating her every want and need, which Sheila believes is spoiling Jordan. Seth presents his findings of the data and recent observations. He provides dates for the hearing tests at the center. Seth appreciates that the work scheduling issues that Sheila is dealing with are not going to change right away. Given that the inconsistent arrival times would continue for a while, they discuss creating a goodbye ritual, so that no matter what time they arrive, the goodbye is the same every day. Sheila agrees to read one book to Jordan and then press her hand on the glass door when she leaves the room, while the caregivers help Jordan do the same.

Though Sheila is relieved to hear about Jordan's receptive language, she still has concerns about her language development. Seth agrees to continue observing and to meet again after her second birthday to talk about having Jordan evaluated if nothing changes. They also agree to keep each other informed if they notice any changes at home or school. Seth thanks Sheila for her trust in him and his team and reassures her that they are there to help her and Jordan with whatever is needed.

Three Months Later

On her second birthday, Jordan and Sheila bring cookies to the classroom to share. Jordan surprises everybody by singing the entire happy birthday song to herself out loud as they enter, without any prompting. Sheila, two of the teachers who are present, and another parent, stand in shock as she sings. Jordan carries the tune perfectly and smiles as she sings each word.

Takeaways and Next Steps

Although Jordan's behavior improves with the intervention strategies the team tries, she still has difficulty with transitions at naptime; Jordan has trouble resting, although she yawns and rubs her eyes. Coming inside after playing outdoors remains a challenge too. From outside she stands at the door and holds onto the door jambs as children try to enter the classroom.

Sheila creates a ritual for their transition in the morning, but there are still many challenging situations at the end of the day when Sheila returns. The teachers continue to try different strategies to address these transitions, including using language to describe angry feelings and a transitional object for Jordan to hold when she becomes overwhelmed.

Case Discussion Questions

1. How were observation, documentation, and assessment used at different points in this case? What is the difference between the ongoing observations and documentation gathered on Jordan for the purposes of assessment and those Seth and his team gathered to help address the specific issues raised?
2. The team first brought Jordan's strengths to the parent/teacher conference. How did the parent's concerns and information influence the team's decisions and the strategies they implemented?
3. What factors influenced the team's decision to begin to address Jordan's issues by looking at transitions?

4. How might the discovery that Jordan could sing the entire birthday song have led the teachers to change their approach to supporting her language needs?
5. What other approaches might you take to address Jordan's language and behavior needs?

Suggested Resources

Cohen, D.H., V. Stern, N. Balaban, & N. Gropper. 2016. *Observing and Recording the Behavior of Young Children*. New York: Teachers College Press.

Koplow, L. 2021. *Emotionally Responsive Practice: A Path for Schools That Heal, Infancy–Grade 6*. New York: Teachers College Press.

Lieberman, A.F. 2018. *The Emotional Life of the Toddler*. New York: Simon and Schuster.

Reference

Squires, J., D. Bricker, & E. Twombly. 2015. *Ages & Stages Questionnaires®: Social-Emotional (ASQ®:SE-2): A Parent-Completed Child Monitoring System for Social-Emotional Behaviors*. 2nd ed. Baltimore, MD: Brookes.

3.3 "But What Is My Child Learning?"

Janet Thompson and Jennifer Gonzalez

Connections to *Developmentally Appropriate Practice*

- Chapter 5: The Power of Playful Learning in the Early Childhood Setting (Learning Through Play: A Play Spectrum—pages 86–92)
- Chapter 7: Engaging in Reciprocal Partnerships with Families and Fostering Community Connections
- Chapter 8: Observing, Documenting, and Assessing Children's Development and Learning

Case Overview

In this case, the new teacher of a class of 3-year-olds has a conference with Mei's family. The teacher shares her observations of Mei's development and learning, which are based on an informal but systematic assessment method. She later realizes that she has neglected to first establish a reciprocal partnership with Mei's family by not including them in the assessment process. Through reflection with her mentor teacher, she rethinks how to explain to all families the role of assessment and to share assessment information in ways that respect the families' goals and expectations for their children's education. The teacher also considers how she might make the links between classroom learning experiences and skill development more obvious to families. The follow-up meeting between teacher and family provides an opportunity to plan ways they might collaborate and communicate regularly about Mei's learning, both at home and at school.

Learning Objectives

1. Identify the roles children's families can play in the assessment process and the benefits of their involvement.
2. Describe the role of teacher reflection at various points in the informal assessment process and the forms it can take.
3. Describe in what ways a playful learning program design can present both challenges and opportunities for the informal assessment process.

Case Narrative

Mei Lin begins preschool the day after her September birthday. She holds up three fingers to show Ms. Gonzalez, her new teacher, how old she is. During their December family conference, Ms. Gonzalez tells Mei's mother and grandmother all about the class's fall projects and the cooperative play skills Mei is using as she and her classmates explore together. She shares her anecdotal observation documentation notes and assures Mei's family that her assessment of Mei's progress shows growth in all developmental domains. When Ms. Gonzalez asks if they have any questions, Mei's mother shakes her head and thanks the teacher.

A week later, Mei's father calls her to request another meeting. Ms. Gonzalez, a bilingual (Spanish/English) second-year teacher, wonders why and begins to think the family conference may not have gone as smoothly as she'd thought. She decides to discuss this during her upcoming meeting with Mrs. Lopez, her mentor teacher.

At their meeting, Ms. Gonzalez describes briefly to Mrs. Lopez how she conducted the family conference and her resulting concerns. Her mentor begins their reflection session with a few questions.

Mrs. Lopez: We discussed family learning goals at a staff meeting earlier this year. Did the Lin family share with you any of their own learning goals for Mei?

Ms. Gonzalez: No, I guess we really haven't talked about it. I've mostly been trying to meet the goals I know are in the state guidelines.

Mrs. Lopez: I have a list of questions I usually ask my families at our first family visit. I am happy to share it with you. Also, I wonder whether they have a clear understanding of our program's approach to assessment. It can seem unusual to new preschool parents and may not provide the kind of information about traditional school subjects that families expect.

Ms. Gonzalez: That's a good point. I just assumed they knew what preschool was about, but I guess the ways we do everything would seem new if it's their child's first year in preschool.

Mrs. Lopez: Yes, that's often true, especially since our preschool's program is built around playful learning experiences. I wonder whether our newer families can really envision the ways it supports early learning. Do you think they may have expected a different-looking classroom experience?

Ms. Gonzalez: Yes, I need to remind myself that everyone has different expectations depending on what they grew up with.

Mrs. Lopez: And just one more thought. I wonder what languages Mei's family is most comfortable using. Could that have explained their silence during the conference?

Ms. Gonzalez: Hmm, well Mei's family is Chinese American, and I do know that Mei's grandmother, who lives in the household and drops off and picks her up from preschool, speaks only Cantonese. Her parents understand both languages, but now that I'm thinking about it, Mei's mother seems more self-conscious about speaking English than her father. (*Sighs.*) Thanks for helping me think through all this. I guess I need to do some more thinking between now and next week's conference with Mei's father. I'll check back in after it's over.

As part of her ongoing reflective practice, Ms. Gonzalez takes some time to journal about her experience with Mei's family and the questions Mrs. Lopez asked her to consider. It was true that she had not spent time explaining to families how she designs the learning environment so that all children have a variety of foundational experiences that enable them to develop the skills outlined in their states' early learning guidelines. And while she uses portfolios to keep a record of children's ongoing development and to inform her intentional curriculum planning, she hadn't thought to use them as a tool for communicating children's learning to families. She also acknowledges that she hasn't made much effort to include families in her informal assessment process or explicitly ask them about the experiences they hope their child has at school. To begin to establish a reciprocal relationship with Mei's family, and to learn more about their goals for her learning and development, she plans for her follow-up conversation with Mr. Lin. She review's Mei's portfolio and chooses a photo and writing sample that highlights a rich learning experience from the fall.

Mr. Lin: Thank you for taking the time to meet with me. I have some questions about what Mei is learning at school. Her mother passed along the story you told about Mei and her friends playing together in the in the block area. And her grandmother shares that she looks happy when she picks her up, but she doesn't have much information about her day. While we are of course glad Mei is making friends and having fun, we would like to know more about how, without many formal teaching and worksheet activities, she is learning the skills that will help her get ready for kindergarten.

Ms. Gonzalez: I appreciate you following up with me and certainly understand your wanting to know more about what Mei is learning at school. Our program design focuses on playful learning experiences that support children's social, emotional, physical, and cognitive development. I brought her portfolio with me to show you some of examples of how we document and assess children's learning and development and plan curriculum that builds on children's strengths and supports their growth. (*Opens Mei's portfolio, which includes anecdotal observation notes, photo documentation, writing samples, and artwork. Flips to a page that includes a photo of Mei playing in the dramatic play area with two other children.*)

Ms. Gonzalez: Here is Mei playing with her friends in our play kitchen. Mei was pretending to cook food and looked through the recipe book on the table. As she flipped through the pages, she pointed to some letters as she named them. She was particularly interested in the letter *M*. When she couldn't find anything she wanted to cook, I suggested she make her favorite food and that together, we write her own recipe. Here is a sample of her writing. You can see the shape of an *O* and an *L* that she wrote to stand for the word *noodles*, referencing the list of ingredients I had written as she dictated what we needed. I also took this photo to highlight her ability to count with one-to-one correspondence as she set the table with three plates and three cups. You can also see that she gave everyone matching colors; she put the red cup with the red plate, the blue with the blue, and green with green. This is an important early math skill.

Ms. Gonzalez continues the conversation by sharing a few more examples of the learning Mei is doing at school. Mr. Lin thanks her for the detailed information and shares the skills he sees his daughter exhibiting at home. He also asks that Ms. Gonzalez share more specific examples with them throughout the year.

Takeaways and Next Steps

While Ms. Gonzalez feels the second conference was a success, she still has a lot to think about. Having the portfolio at the meeting allowed her to highlight specific skill development and illustrate for the family how she plans for children's exploration and learning. She will continue to do that. In her next meeting with her mentor, she hopes to brainstorm ideas for involving families in the assessment process; after all, they have repeated opportunities to observe their child's activities and interactions over time and in a variety of situations. Their perspectives, combined with her observations, will provide a completer and more reliable picture of each child's knowledge, skills, and behaviors.

It is also clear to Ms. Gonzalez that she needs to find a way to pass on information to families about children's school experiences despite any language barriers that might exist. She realizes that she did not ask Mr. Lin about the family's goals for Mei's learning and development and decides to make a point to ask all families in the future about this. As a new teacher, she knows she has a lot to learn and is thankful for the mentorship of Mrs. Lopez and for families that challenge her to articulate her methods. She knows this will make her a better educator of young children.

This case illustrates several of the many challenges a new teacher encounters beyond planning curriculum and mastering effective teaching strategies. Developing a clear sense of the benefits of assessment, both for children and families and for herself, will strengthen Ms. Gonzalez's teaching practice. Building truly reciprocal partnerships with families around learning goals and their assessment will support children's learning in both home and school contexts. Thinking more about how playful learning approaches benefit children will help her learn how to describe them to others and ensure that they remain central to her teaching and to her authentic assessment of children's learning and development. Developing comfort and confidence with this process is crucial to Ms. Gonzalez's ability to be an effective early childhood educator.

Case Discussion Questions

1. Describe how building an ongoing, reciprocal partnership with the Lin family can enhance the future assessment of Mei's progress toward learning goals.
2. What approach did Mrs. Lopez use to assist Ms. Gonzalez (a beginning teacher), and how will it strengthen Ms. Gonzalez's future professionalism? What additional supports could build Ms. Gonzalez's future competence in the assessment process?
3. Considering what she learned through her experience with the Lin family, what steps can Ms. Gonzalez take to strengthen reciprocal partnerships with families of varying cultural and linguistic backgrounds?

General Discussion Questions

1. What routines, practices, and program supports are key to helping a teacher use formative assessment effectively to support each child's learning?
2. How can a teacher meaningfully involve a young preschooler's family in all three steps of the informal assessment process (gathering of information, documentation, and reflection; see Scott-Little, with Reschke 2022, 161)?
3. Cultural expectations affect what children are expected to learn and how they demonstrate their knowledge. How can a teacher address families' differing beliefs about how early learning programs should facilitate the acquisition of foundational knowledge and skills?
4. What language and examples might a teacher use to explain to families and others the advantages of a play-based program over a more direct instructional style? How can program leaders prepare and support teachers to do this effectively?

References

Scott-Little, C. With K.L. Reschke. 2022. "Observing, Documenting, and Assessing Children's Development and Learning." In *Developmentally Appropriate Practice in Early Childhood Programs Serving Children from Birth Through Age 8,* 4th ed., NAEYC, 159–80. Washington, DC: NAEYC.

3.4 Drawing and Dialogue: Using Authentic Assessment to Understand Children's Sense of Self and Observe Early Literacy Skills

Brandon L. Gilbert

Connections to *Developmentally Appropriate Practice*

- Chapter 8: Observing, Documenting, and Assessing Children's Development and Learning

Case Overview

Ms. Kim, a preschool teacher, invited me, Dr. Gilbert, an education researcher, to collaborate on assessment-related activities in the play-based curriculum she implements in her classroom. As part of this collaboration, I am working with children in small groups on drawing activities that explore how children develop a sense of their own artistic ability and whether they can be cognizant of themselves in their art—that is, what they know about who or what it is they are drawing, how they feel about it, and how they perceive their process of this drawing experience (Gilbert 2019). As I work with the children, I intentionally engage in dialogue with them as part of the observation and assessment process. This case shows how authentic dialogue with young children offers a glimpse into how they think of themselves and into their early literacy skills.

Learning Objectives

1. Identify ways to dialogue with children using authentic, responsive language, and explain the importance of this.
2. Explain how a rich, nuanced conversation with a child can elicit information that helps assess social, emotional, and literacy development.
3. Explain how a child's ideas and emotions can be recorded in artwork that can be used to assess their social and emotional development.
4. Describe ways assessment can be embedded in play-based activities.
5. Analyze data from participatory observations of language and emotions as described in this case.

Case Narrative

There are 12 children in Ms. Kim's preschool classroom. Ms. Kim maintains a warm, welcoming atmosphere in her class and embeds intentional assessment-related activities in the play-based curriculum by observing and documenting children's learning.

The classroom environment tells a narrative of multiculturalism, family, and learning through visual posters (one of which says "Family is the best team you could ever have") and includes a diverse display of puppets, process art, and gingerbread cutouts, including today's read-aloud, *The Gingerbread Man Loose in the School.* The interest areas are well designated and equipped, from the woodworking area to the science area with tropical fish. The classroom is decorated with the orange and blue sports memorabilia of the Denver Broncos. It's spirit week, so some children are wearing Disney character costumes.

On this particular day, the children move to their small group tables after circle time. I pass out construction paper while another child distributes the markers, crayons, and colored pencils. I ask the children to draw whatever they like in relation to their circle-time conversations in which they discussed their favorite shows. Cries of "Transformer!," "Hello Kitty!," "Football!," and even "My sister!" come from their small groups. Some children run to their cubbies for additional supplies. As the children settle in to work independently on their drawings, Ms. Kim goes around to each table, checking in with the children.

Jaime is wearing her turquoise fairy-tale costume dress. She is energetic and is sociable with her peers, teachers, and me. She claps in excitement when told the small groups will now start drawing.

Jaime pulls out a chair and asks me, "Do you want to join me? Here, sit down." The child next to her works quietly, shading in a picture. Jaime runs to her cubby and returns to the table with her markers. We have the following conversation.

Jaime: Do you like my *Frozen* dress?

Dr. Gilbert: I like your dress and this color blue.

Jaime: What's your favorite color? (*Opens her pink case of markers.*)

Dr. Gilbert: My favorite color is yellow. (*Selects a piece of paper to participate in the drawing while note-taking this observation.*)

Jaime: Have you seen *Frozen*? (*Selects a yellow piece of construction paper.*)

Dr. Gilbert: I have not.

Jaime: (*Shows surprise.*) So you don't know Elsa and her sister?

Dr. Gilbert: I'm afraid I don't know, but I would like to hear about her if you want to share.

Jaime: No, it's okay. Well, do you like Christmas? (*Begins drawing.*)

Dr. Gilbert: I think Christmas is exciting.

Jaime: Christmas is my favorite holiday and the snow and the presents. My daddy has a new dog, and I don't get to see my daddy. I don't get to see him all the time, at all. (*Stops drawing to look me in the eyes.*)

Dr. Gilbert: Well, I hope you get to see him soon and the new dog.

Jaime: Do you have a daddy? (*Places all her markers on the table.*)

Dr. Gilbert: Yes, his name is Melvin. (*I select the purple marker.*)

Jaime: Well, do you get to see him? (*Turns to look directly at me again.*)

Dr. Gilbert: I do remember seeing him often. (*Begins to draw clouds.*)

Jaime: Where is he now, working all the time? (*Begins drawing dots on paper.*)

Dr. Gilbert: (*Pauses.*) He's far away.

Jaime: "Far away"—silly, that don't answer my question. (*Raises her arms in the air and shakes her head as if my answer made no sense.*) Where does he live?

Dr. Gilbert: He's in heaven.

Jaime: (*Turns from her drawing to look at me.*) Do you want to be my friend? (*Begins drawing another picture of jellyfish and what she referred to as "pop-up fish."*)

Dr. Gilbert: I would be happy to be your friend.

Jaime: (*Returns to her other drawing and makes more dots on her paper.*) This is snow from the heavens, little circles. Your daddy sent them.

Dr. Gilbert: I like the snow and would like to see some here in Denver.

Jaime: What are you making? (*Looks over at my drawing.*)

Dr. Gilbert: I'm making an ice-skating princess.

Jaime: (*Frowns and points to my drawing.*) That is not an ice-skating princess. You're doing a awful job. She needs longer hair and a big dress, with a sparkly crown. Look at me draw my hand. (*Traces her hand with a marker on what looks like her third picture.*)

Dr. Gilbert: Can you write your name? (*Tries to enhance the ice princess.*)

Jaime: Yes, and because I like you, and your daddy in heaven, and because you're my new friend, I'm giving you my Christmas snow picture, this hand picture, and—let me see, that's two—and I'm going to make you a Broncos picture to take to your daddy.

Dr. Gilbert: This is fantastic. Thank you, Jaime! (*Claps and laughs.*)

Jaime: You're welcome. Do you and your daddy like the Denver Broncos? (*Draws a square on another picture.*)

Dr. Gilbert: I like the Broncos, but my dad was a Chicago Bears fan.

Jaime: Ooh no, this is a Broncos classroom and here is your Broncos stadium picture. (*Hands me a drawing with the square with her name she wrote on top.*)

Dr. Gilbert: You wrote your name so nice. Great work.

Jaime: I can write my alphabets too; I'll make some for you. (*Begins making letters.*) Did your daddy teach you your ABCs?

Dr. Gilbert: I believe my teacher taught me. (*Begins note-taking.*)

Jaime: (*Says in frustration.*) Well, because, I haven't seen my daddy in days and days.

(The child at the other end of the table leaves and Orin, another child, sits at our table and begins drawing.)

Dr. Gilbert: Well, I hope you get to see him soon. (*Turns to Orin.*) What are you drawing, Orin?

Orin: This is Mommy, Daddy, and my baby brother.

Jaime: (*Begins drawing people.*) This me, my daddy Richard, my sister Rochelle, who I also never get to see, and my nephew Q.

Orin: How do you know them if you never get to see them?

Jaime: (*Stops drawing and frowns at Orin. Sits back in her chair, looks at me, and slides her family picture to me.*)

Jaime: It's frustrating that Orin ask these questions about my family picture, that I don't know the answer. Take my family picture with you, too, to show your daddy in heaven.

Takeaways and Next Steps

Based on the information gained from Jaime's case, Ms. Kim and I believe that drawing and other art-based experiences can be used effectively across the curriculum as assessment-based activities. I also note that when conversing with the children, the more open ended the discussion, the more likely a child will want to converse. Over time, I am able to learn about Jaime's knowledge, skills, and abilities and observe her thinking processes and use of imaginative thinking. Further, supporting Jaime's individual purposes and passion for drawing through open-ended conversations will deepen her knowledge on drawing topics, a method that will also benefit other children.

Preschool children need to have a set of foundational social and emotional competencies (Vygotsky 1978). Essential social and emotional learning activities contribute to children's emotional competencies—the expression of feelings, building relationships, and supporting empathy and sympathy. Jaime's drawings are completed in response to her conversation about family and emotion; both her drawings and conversation indicate that she already knows a lot about her family dynamics.

Children's work can be revisited and discussed so children begin to learn that their work is important; it is not just something to hang on the wall or take home, never to be seen again. Revisiting work also provides children opportunities to evaluate their own growth and learning. For the example given, in a month or so Jaime can look at her pictures to see what she might add or change, and such revisions could reflect how her thoughts, emotions, or skills may have developed.

Case Discussion Questions

1. How does Dr. Gilbert relate to Jaime and maintain a meaningful dialogue with her? What is it about the nature of the questions he asks that encourages Jaime to express herself rather than lead to specific answers?
2. How do Jaime's drawings illustrate symbolic representation (using symbols to represent objects, ideas, and situations), including emergent writing skills such as name writing? How do the drawings, and the discussions about them, illustrate her emotions?
3. What is learned about Jaime's social and emotional development during the activity?
4. How can the observation described in this case fit into Ms. Kim's overall assessments?

General Discussion Questions

1. What early literacy skills predict young children's future academic learning and school success?
2. How is early literacy connected to social and emotional learning? How are each assessed?

Suggested Resource

Duke, N.K. "Resources." Literacy Research, Policy, and Practice. www.nellkduke.org/resources.

References

Gilbert, B.L. 2019. "Unarthodox: An Investigation of How Children Articulate Their Sense of Self Through Art." PhD diss., DePaul University. https://via.library.depaul.edu/soe_etd.

Vygotsky, L.S. 1978. *Mind in Society: The Development of Higher Psychological Processes*. Cambridge, MA: Harvard University Press.

3.5 The ABCs of Kindergarten Registration: Assessment, Background, and Collaboration Between Home and School

Bridget Amory

Connections to *Developmentally Appropriate Practice*

- Chapter 7: Engaging in Reciprocal Partnerships with Families and Fostering Community Connections
- Chapter 8: Observing, Documenting, and Assessing Children's Development and Learning

Case Overview

Manny is an emergent bilingual learner enrolling in kindergarten in a rural public school—the first in his family to go to kindergarten. As Manny slowly adjusts to school, his teacher, Mrs. Brooks, is unsure that she adequately understands Manny's learning and consults with the school's English Learner (EL) teacher. Later, she shares observations and evidence of Manny's progress with his family. This case features the use of typical assessment tools, beginning with Manny's kindergarten screening, as he begins his first formal school experience.

Learning Objectives

1. Interact with performance data for one kindergarten student and describe the effectiveness of assessment processes used.
2. Analyze links between data collection and instructional decision making.

Case Narrative

Mrs. Velazquez enrolls her 5-year-old son, Manny, in kindergarten. He has never been away from his father and mother, and she worries whether he is ready for a full day of school. Nonetheless, she makes a registration appointment. Mrs. Velazquez gathers the documents she has been told she needs to bring, such as birth certificate, shot records, and proof of residence, and tells Manny they are going to visit his new school.

Manny holds onto his mother's hand tightly when they arrive and stands wide-eyed beside her. Mrs. Velazquez introduces herself in English; however, when Manny pulls her arm for attention, she responds in Spanish, "Shhh. Ahora no Manny!" Manny willingly separates from his mom and enters the gymnasium. There, he and many other children rotate through a variety of stations with engaging materials, sometimes answering questions and sometimes completing tasks. Mrs. Velazquez completes paperwork and answers questions. When Manny's screening is completed, he excitedly whispers to his mother, "Me gusta tirar la pelota" (I liked throwing the ball). Mrs. Velazquez thanks the staff.

Data gathered during the registration process include the following:

- Spanish is the primary language at home. Mom uses English and Spanish; Dad speaks only Spanish. The family is trying to use English more to assist both Dad and Manny with vocabulary development.
- Manny has no formal child care experience.

- Manny qualifies for free and reduced lunch.

Mrs. Velazquez provided the following information as part of the screening:

- Manny was not born prior to the 37th week of pregnancy.
- Sometimes Manny has difficulty following directions at home and sometimes says no, but more often complies with the requests.
- Sometimes he has difficulty soothing himself when angry or upset.
- Sometimes he does not share well with others.
- Manny often does not handle change in routines and can become overstimulated.
- He always has difficulty settling himself after an exciting activity, getting overstimulated. He responds to the prompt "Take a deep breath."
- He often has difficulty using words to explain feelings and needs.
- Manny responds best to a direct approach.
- Manny has not experienced any recent traumas; however, he does have a new baby brother.

Manny's scores on the WIDA (World-Class Instructional Design and Assessment) Screener for Kindergarten, given to students to determine English language proficiency and eligibility for language support services, indicate that he performs at the lowest proficiency level. This establishes Manny's eligibility for English language services.

Transitioning into Manny's Kindergarten Year

The first day of school, Manny rides the bus and is greeted by a swarm of children and adults. He follows the other children and enters the building, but he cannot remember where to find the kindergarten classroom. An adult asks Manny his name; he responds with wide eyes and nothing more. When asked the question again in Spanish, Manny blinks in response. Another adult asks, "¿Cómo te llama tu mamá?" Manny lights up and responds, "Mi nombre es Manuel. Mi mamá me llama Manny." The adult takes Manny by the hand and walks with him to his classroom.

With teacher guidance and the lead of peers, Manny successfully navigates first days of school with only a few moments of seeming overwhelmed. During these first months of kindergarten, Manny finds school is sometimes confusing, but he likes the bumpy bus ride and the driver's singing with the children. At school he likes singing, too, although he does not always sing along. He enjoys swinging fast and high on the playground swings.

Instruction in Mrs. Brook's class is primarily in English, and Mrs. Brooks also uses the Spanish words she knows. When Manny feels overwhelmed, he puts his head down at his table. His teacher asks, "¿Estás bien?" (You okay?). Manny responds, nodding his head; Mrs. Brooks tells him, "Descansar" (Take a rest), and pats his shoulder. This behavior continues the first few months of school. Mrs. Brooks reflects on the screening interview notes and uses the WIDA skills information to plan for Manny; she also relies on other forms of assessment, like observing and recording brief notes, as Manny engages in daily routines and learning experiences. However, she is concerned about Manny's emergent literacy development.

While Manny is well behaved and appears to be engaging through listening and watching others, Mrs. Brooks is concerned that he does not talk or engage socially with peers. She connects with the EL teacher about Manny and explains, "I am not sure how to help him. He is well behaved, appears to be bright and capable, but he doesn't respond orally. He points or use body language. How do I help him to use words? I know when he is frustrated, as he shuts down." Mrs. Brooks's colleague explains that often, emergent bilingual learners *are* learning despite not yet verbalizing. She advises Mrs. Brooks to increase her use of visuals with Manny, such as pictures of common vocabulary words that she can point to and supply both the Spanish and English word for, such as roja and red. She can continue to praise his communication efforts as well. The EL teacher encourages Mrs. Brooks to find something Manny is particularly interested in to entice him to engage in activities. After the meeting, Mrs. Brooks feels energized.

One day Manny wears his favorite shirt, showing a shark. When Mrs. Brooks asks, "Manny, what would you like to learn today?" Manny points to the shark. Mrs. Brooks responds, "Oh, wow. I like tiburónes (sharks) too. Let's see what we can learn about sharks." Manny nods. The following morning, the discovery center has books about sharks and fish as well as plastic sharks and fish in a bucket of water. Manny eagerly explores these resources, and Mrs. Brooks begins to hear a few shark-related English words from him.

As the year progresses, Mrs. Brooks busily collects data. She uses a system of pizza boxes to store student work and anecdotal notes. While she maintains electronic records, she finds the pizza boxes are particularly helpful for work samples. Plus, students love decorating them.

During family–teacher conferences, Mrs. Brooks meets with Manny's mother and father. She notes that Manny appears to be adjusting well to full-day kindergarten and that he is a sweet boy who gets along nicely with everyone. She shares the following observations about Manny's progress and behavior:

- Often responds with nonverbal signals, such as wide eyes, a smile, and head nods during stories
- Always pleasant but often keeps to himself
- Enjoys swings at recess
- Copes with stress by putting his head down on the table
- Works well with other students
- Appears to enjoy learning about sharks
- Enjoys using whiteboards and dry-erase markers; often doodles
- Enjoys having a classroom job like turning off the lights or being line leader
- Responds favorably to verbal praise and rewards for participation

Mrs. Velazquez translates some of this for her husband and then turns to Mrs. Brooks.

Mrs. Velazquez: Oh, this is wonderful news. I worry about Manny. He comes home from school so tired each day and does not want to talk about his day.

Mrs. Brooks: That often happens at the start of kindergarten. There is a lot of information Manny is processing. When he gets home, it is best to give him the chance to rest or have some quiet playtime. I do notice that Manny often tires in the afternoon.

Mrs. Velazquez: He loves to sleep. I must wake him every morning for school.

Mrs. Brooks: Well, thank you for getting him up. He has a wonderful attendance record, which is very important in establishing learning routines.

Mrs. Velazquez: De nada. Oh, I mean, you are welcome. Sometimes I forget and use Spanish.

Mrs. Brooks: That's okay. I understand. I appreciate you using Spanish. I often hear Manny use Spanish when he interacts with others. He is quickly learning to use English. He seems proud to share Spanish with others. I initially worried about his English skills, but he is making progress. I work very closely with our English Learner teacher to support Manny.

Mrs. Velazquez: I really want Manny to learn English. His dad is trying to learn too.

Mrs. Brooks: Our school district offers evening EL classes for adults.

Mrs. Velazquez: (*Translates the opportunity to Mr. Velazquez, who nods his interest and smiles.*)

Mrs. Brooks shares the pizza box of Manny's work and the following specifics about his academic progress:

Academic Target in English	Progress Not Yet / Developing / Proficient
Produce three rhyming words	Developing
Produce three initial sounds	Proficient
Identify 30 upper/lowercase letters	Developing: Identifies three uppercase letters and two lowercase letters (*M*, *X*, *O*, *o*, and *x*)
Produce eight letter sounds	Developing: Produces one letter sound (*M*)
Identify three concepts of print	Developing: Distinguishes by pointing
Write name with and without a model	Developing: Traces name
Answers comprehension questions after reading and/or listening to a story	Developing: Often shrugs his shoulders when asked about the stories they read, although he actively attends and appears interested

At the end of the conference, Mr. and Mrs. Velazquez thank Mrs. Brooks for all she does to help Manny. Mrs. Brooks thanks them for sharing Manny with her.

Takeaways and Next Steps

During Mrs. Brooks's annual evaluation with her building administrator, she shares reflections on her practice. She had known Manny's readiness levels from WIDA; however, she'd had limited experience with emergent bilingual learners. "I learned more about the process of language learning from my conversations with the EL teacher. She suggested several techniques to help Manny, and I've seen growth in him. I also learned about the power of patience . . . I remember learning about wait time in college, but I hadn't thought about it in relation to the acquisition of language skills." She continues, "Also, I am reminded of the importance of collaborating with colleagues, especially when learning new ways to teach. I am incredibly grateful for the opportunity to engage with colleagues to discuss best practices and brainstorm ways to reach all of our students."

Case Discussion Questions

1. Review ways Mrs. Brooks collected evidence of students' learning and the assessment data sources included here. Do you believe the assessments effectively captured Manny's development and transition to kindergarten? Why or why not? What other assessment strategies and types of data would be helpful?
2. How does this case study illustrate developmentally appropriate observation and assessment?
3. Is it important to know whether the teacher conducted assessments in English or Spanish? Why or why not?
4. How could Mrs. Brooks document her observations of Manny to support discussion with the EL teacher?
5. Based on the family's comments and the details about Manny's progress Mrs. Brooks shared with them, suggest one or more specific strategies or next steps to follow up with the family.

General Discussion Question

1. Identify examples of how to support families in the school registration process.

Suggested Resources

Amory, B. 2021. *Shazam! So You Want to Become a Classroom Crusader?* Dubuque, IA: Kendall Hunt.

Amory, B., & S. Rowser. 2022. *Kapow! Becoming a Differentiation Crusader*. Dubuque, IA: Kendall Hunt.

¡Colorín! colorado: www.colorincolorado.org.

Strasser, J. n.d. "Transitioning to Kindergarten." www.naeyc.org/our-work/families/transitioning-to-kindergarten.

WIDA. 2020. *WIDA English Language Development Standards Framework, 2020 edition: Kindergarten–Grade 12*. Madison: University of Wisconsin School of Education, Wisconsin Center of Education Research.

3.6 Creating Opportunities for Individualized Assessment Activities for Biliteracy Development

Esther Garza

Connections to *Developmentally Appropriate Practice*

- Chapter 7: Engaging in Reciprocal Partnerships with Families and Fostering Community Connections
- Chapter 8: Observing, Documenting, and Assessing Children's Development and Learning

Case Overview

All of the children in Ms. Hernandez's first grade bilingual class are of Latinx heritage. The majority of the children speak Spanish as their primary language, and they are all learning both Spanish and English in the classroom. This case focuses on how Ms. Hernandez assesses the English proficiency of one of her emergent bilinguals (EBs) as part of his biliteracy learning using the *Performance Descriptors for Language Learners* (American Council on the Teaching of Foreign Languages [ACTFL] 2015) to inform instruction and communicate the child's progress to his family. Ms. Hernandez creates a language proficiency checklist based on the ACTFL descriptors, which provides a necessary assessment of English linguistic (oral), reading, and writing skills taught explicitly in the classroom. Jorge, a first grade EB, is the primary student in this case.

To further inform her instruction, Ms. Hernandez also records each of her students' family information relating to home languages spoken and read and considers this as part of the holistic assessment of student performance. Jorge's family is from Mexico and their heritage language is Spanish. His parents are both immigrants and first generation in the United States. Jorge's father primarily speaks Spanish and his mother is bilingual. During a family conference with Jorge's parents, Ms. Hernandez refers to the checklist and her own notes about the family's language practices to discuss his academic learning with the family.

Learning Objectives

1. Describe ways that individualized assessment activities assess language and content proficiency in EBs.
2. Identify how an EB's linguistic and cultural background factor into individualized assessment.
3. Identify ways that individualized assessment results can inform suggestions for language and literacy activities families can do at home.

Case Narrative

During English as a second language (ESL) time, Ms. Hernandez engages Jorge in an oral retell and a writing activity to assess his language and content proficiency. The writing activity prompts Jorge to recount a story in English using his own thoughts and words and is an assessment of his use of narrative story structure connected to his linguistic proficiency and cultural knowledge and background. An EB's bilingualism and biliteracy development is the result of having access to not only two linguistic but also two cultural systems that are observed in using a narrative story structure learned by the child in their first language and transferred to their second language.

The following dialogue ensues between Ms. Hernandez and Jorge when Ms. Hernandez asks him to tell her about the book *Stellaluna,* which he read from the first grade bilingual leveled classroom library.

Ms. Hernandez: Tell me the story.

Jorge: There is a mother. She has a baby. A little baby. She's flying with her baby. And . . .

Ms. Hernandez: You can keep going. That's okay.

Jorge: She is a bat.

Ms. Hernandez: Okay.

Jorge: She is a bat. (*Pauses.*) The the owl came, the bat let the new baby go. The bat pushed the mother.

Ms. Hernandez: Okay, go on.

Jorge: She land at the tree. She was cold. (*Pauses longer.*) There was a . . . a . . . the three babies. And the bat fall down at the baby nest. The bird, the mother bird, came and she give a grasshopper to the bat. The bat eat the bat—eat the grasshopper. And the bat he was sleeping upside down and the birds try it and the mother bird got . . . the bat got . . . wait, the mother bird said, you teaching the baby birds bad. They go up, they fly around and he land to a tree. I want to say he pushes the birds away.

After the retell, Ms. Hernandez asks Jorge to write about what he read in the story. In Jorge's writing, he presents his recount in a different way than in his oral retell. Jorge writes the following about his retell of the book:

> She is a Bat she can fly at night she like to fly. She land in the nest the Bird. The mom Bird carn Back to the nest. The Bat get in Big tuBuB The mom Bird tel the Bat dot do nuten to my baby. Now day stat to fly. He went to fast. The Bird stop. And the Bat of fo down. He likes to fly.

Ms. Hernandez's weekly practice is to collect samples of children's speech and writing to have a continuous evaluation of language proficiency. In the above example, she reviews Jorge's oral recorded retell and her observational notes to assess his linguistic proficiency, reading comprehension, and writing development using the language proficiency checklist and ACTFL Performance Descriptors. The ACTFL Performance Descriptors are organized into three ranges of performance (novice, intermediate, advanced) and are situated in three modes of communication (interpersonal, interpretive, presentational) according to certain language features, including content topics that the learner can understand and discuss. For this case study, some examples are focused on (1) the interpretive mode of communication, in which the receiver interprets what the author or speaker is communicating, and (2) cultural awareness, which describes the cultural products, practices, or perspectives needed to communicate successfully in a cultural setting (ACTFL 2015).

In the example above, Ms. Hernandez assesses Jorge for language proficiency (grammar usage, pronunciation, comprehension, fluency) while assessing his content learning (vocabulary, reading comprehension, writing story structure and elements). Ms. Hernandez identifies Jorge's specific linguistic (oral) skills and determines that Jorge is at an intermediate range of speaking English, expressed in his ability to retell by using vocabulary related to a familiar topic such as family and his sentence-level, straightforward language use. Based on Jorge's use of the descriptive, action, and reactive sequencing of writing narrative story structure, Ms. Hernandez identifies that he is at an intermediate high level in reading and writing. The evaluation of Jorge's oral proficiency and reading and writing skills supports the linguistic and content standards required for success in first grade. These assessments also provide a picture of Jorge's writing organization skills by using a discourse sequence structure, which demonstrates his development of vocabulary, grammar, and style (ACTFL 2015) by building and extending his cultural knowledge of the English narrative structure.

Following these assessments, Ms. Hernandez requests a family conference to speak with Jorge's parents about his linguistic development and his academic progress based on goals established earlier in the year and supported by state standards. During the conference, Ms. Hernandez presents her assessment of Jorge's proficiency levels in English and Spanish, along with examples of different class literacy activities. Based on additional assessments, Ms. Hernandez informs Jorge's parents that his Spanish proficiency levels are at the advanced level in speaking and writing while his English proficiency is at the intermediate level (as referenced above). As a collaborative partner, Ms. Hernandez also inquires about the family's goals for Jorge's biliteracy and how the family supports his language and literacy learning at home. Ms. Hernandez offers additional language and literacy activities for them to try at home, such as creating a story retell and written recount of a rich, authentic cultural family tale or experience in Spanish, English, or both. With the instruction Jorge is receiving in school, along with the support he is receiving for his biliteracy development in his bilingual household, Jorge is progressing academically in English literacy.

Takeaways and Next Steps

1. On a daily basis, Ms. Hernandez supports the educational standards, both linguistic and academic, created for her students' success. As a bilingual educator, she understands the critical role of students' linguistic and cultural backgrounds for learning and assessment. By assessing students' language proficiency, including their cultural knowledge, bilingual teachers can help students connect what they learn in one language to new learning experiences in another language—also known as creating bridges between both languages for cross-linguistic transfer (Beeman & Urow 2013).
2. Ms. Hernandez has created an assessment practice and process to understand how to effectively create bridges to accelerate learning for all EBs, who on a daily basis demonstrate that they are eager to learn and engage in their biliteracy development. For example, Ms. Hernandez applies her prior knowledge about the second language acquisition process and the importance of linking children's learning to their home languages and cultures. The use of the ACTFL Performance Descriptors also provides her with guidance to create an assessment as a proficiency checklist to understand Jorge's functional language ability and narrative structural development in writing. Ms. Hernandez can target her instruction to create cross-linguistic transfer opportunities to improve Jorge's reading comprehension and narrative writing in English and Spanish. In addition, Ms. Hernandez will take a step further to attend to Jorge's linguistic and academic needs by individually conferencing with Jorge, as she has with his family, about the assessment results. She will continue to discuss Jorge's learning with his family and exchange ideas on how to extend his learning both at home and at school.

Case Discussion Questions

1. Why is it important that an EB's oral language skills be assessed separately from their reading and writing skills?
2. How might Ms. Hernandez use the results of her assessments of Jorge's linguistic proficiency to plan learning experiences for him? In what ways could she expand her assessment practices to facilitate Jorge's learning?
3. How does Ms. Hernandez use her discussion with Jorge's family to enrich her assessment process? What more could she do to welcome the family as partners in his learning?

General Discussion Questions

1. Why is it critical for teachers to understand the language proficiency of EBs in both their home and second languages and the role it plays in successful learning? Which principle of the position statement on developmentally appropriate practice does this support?
2. A key to accurately assessing the language and content proficiency of EBs is understanding "that assessment results are impacted by [educators'] own perspectives and biases and the way the assessment process is carried out . . ." (Scott-Little, with Reschke 2022, 168). How can teachers identify their own biases and increase their knowledge of the lived experiences of the EBs they teach—who may be recent immigrants, refugees, first generation, undocumented—and the children's varying language and content proficiencies?

References

ACTFL. 2015. *Performance Descriptors for Language Learners.* Alexandria, VA: ACTFL. www.actfl.org/resources/actfl-performance-descriptors-language-learners.

Beeman, K., & C. Urow. 2013. *Teaching for Biliteracy: Strengthening Bridges Between Languages.* Philadelphia: Caslon.

Scott-Little, C. With K.L. Reschke. 2022. "Observing, Documenting, and Assessing Children's Development and Learning." In *Developmentally Appropriate Practice in Early Childhood Programs Serving Children from Birth Through Age 8,* 4th ed., NAEYC, 159–80. Washington, DC: NAEYC.

3.7 Observing Second-Graders' Vocabulary Development

Marie Ann Donovan

Connections to *Developmentally Appropriate Practice*

- Chapter 8: Observing, Documenting, and Assessing Children's Development and Learning
- Chapter 10: Planning and Implementing an Engaging Curriculum to Achieve Meaningful Goals

Case Overview

Observing to assess while teaching a lesson might seem impossible to juggle. Yet when educators have a focused purpose for what they plan to learn, it quickly becomes a natural part of their everyday process. Formative curriculum-based assessments inform curriculum planning and provide a structured way to witness how individual students make sense of what educators are teaching in the moment.

In this case, a new second grade teacher has realized that some of her students' middle-of-year standardized test scores indicate less growth in certain aspects of reading than she expected. She decides to meet with the school's curriculum specialist to explore possible causes for these results.

Learning Objectives

1. Identify the essential elements of observation-based assessments that inform curriculum planning, individualize instruction, and communicate learning to stakeholders.
2. Explain how to create observation-based assessment tools and methods that capture students' strengths and areas for growth in meeting planned learning outcomes.

Case Narrative

Six months into the school year, Alex is puzzled. Her large, urban district's February standardized tests indicate that five of her 27 students' vocabulary knowledge scores remain below benchmark since the fall. The district continues to experience an influx of students new to English, so academic vocabulary development is this year's districtwide curriculum emphasis. While Alex noticed a few children struggling to understand and remember certain content-area words, she's surprised by the number of children still not achieving. She's keen to figure out why, so she meets with the school's curriculum specialist, Sam.

Before the meeting, Alex turns to the position statement on developmentally appropriate practice. She considers the statement's key factors in developmentally appropriate planning, focusing on guideline 5D.3, "Educators plan curriculum experiences that follow logical sequences and that allow for depth, focus, and revisiting of concepts." She recognizes her need to conduct concentrated, ongoing observations of children as they refine their new knowledge. As she heads to Sam's office, she remembers the statement's guidance about ensuring that observational assessments and documentation methodology are purposeful, strategic, and reflective.

Alex: Thanks for meeting. I'm trying to understand why five of my students' vocabulary growth scores are stagnant. I teach vocabulary every day.

Sam: Let's look at your context first. You've a large class—27—and nine are learning English. It's hard to keep track of every learning dimension for each child—that's where these types of standardized measures help guide your noticing. Tell me what you know about these five students as readers.

Alex: They're all below benchmark in vocabulary, like they were in November. Two are close to reading at grade level. The other three just started reading at grade level. None is a dual language learner or has been identified for any intervention, though.

Sam: What do the score analyses say about their relative weaknesses in specific vocabulary-learning skills?

Alex: They all need to work on affixes, multiple-meaning words, and subject-matter words.

Sam: How tests like these assess vocabulary growth might be different from the specific words and word-building strategies you're teaching. How do you know which vocabulary skills your students use to understand new words? How are you selecting the core vocabulary to teach in your social studies and science units?

Vocabulary Terms

affix—a word part attached at its beginning (e.g., prefixes such as *un-* or *re-*) or its end (e.g., suffixes such as *-ing*, *-less*) that affects its overall meaning, part of speech, or grammatical usage.

morpheme—any word part that holds meaning or affects a word's usage. The word *disloyalty* has three morphemes—the prefix, *dis-*; the root, *loyal*; and the suffix, *-ty*.

Alex: I rely on the unit tests in our phonics and spelling series to tell me how students break words into morphemes to get at meaning. I directly teach the core vocabulary listed in the teacher's manual or in the district's curriculum plans for our common units. I require students to use the core vocabulary in their writing assignments for each unit. I check to see if they're using their new words correctly.

Sam: At this grade level, those series' tests help you see which specific morphemes children are learning. Students need more experience with morphemes than what they get through the series though. That's where subject-matter vocabulary instruction comes in. How do you connect your morpheme instruction with your social studies and science vocabulary instruction?

Alex: We post the "most important" unit words on the walls and review their definitions throughout each unit, especially before writing about what we're learning. I point out the morphemes in those words as they come up.

Sam: Making those incidental connections is good—but not enough. Can you be more intentional in connecting your subject-matter vocabulary and morpheme work?

Unit Title: How Do Rules and Laws Help Our Society? **Date:** 2 March
Student: Shiloh
Words Selected: rules, citizen, government
Rationales/Relevance to Unit Content: Lessons to date focused on ***rules*** and ***laws***, and how laws are enforced by the ***government*** to ensure every ***citizen's*** well-being
Morphemic Knowledge Evidenced: She connected *citizen* to *citizenship*; explained how the suffix *-ship* means "You're being a citizen." Could explain what a *citizen* is through use of age-appropriate language and examples from other countries. She connected *government* to *law* by saying, "The government makes the laws we have to follow to stay safe."
Confusions/Inaccuracies in Meaning-Making Observed: She doesn't differentiate between *rule* and *law*, sees them as having the same meaning /context.

Figure 1. Anecdotal note-taking organizer: Example from Alex's class

Alex: Hmm . . . I have so many students and a packed curriculum. I don't know when I'd do more.

Sam: I understand. What if instead of *doing* more instructionally, you focused on *learning* more about how your students think about new vocabulary? Here's an idea for your word wall work: Use word jars in your next social studies or science unit. At the start of the unit, give all students a jar to decorate plus three blank cards. After three or four days, ask them to write one "most important" unit word learned so far on each card—don't suggest any, you want to see how they think. Then ask them to explain on the back of each card why they believe it's important. Once they've finished their cards, pair students to share their words and rationales. Use this anecdotal note-taking form (see Figure 1) to organize your observations of these five students while working with their partners. Listen for words they select that relate to essential ideas in the unit and any morphemic knowledge they evidence. With the whole class, hold a vote on which jar words should be added to the *Most Important Words About* . . . wall. After each voting session, look for patterns in the types of words all students picked, such as similar morphemes, parts of speech, or specialized terms for the unit's content. Share what you notice with the class, connecting these words to any previous instruction, especially that in the phonics and spelling series. You also could lead students in categorizing the words on the wall according to their *use*—"words for directions" such as *north, south*—or words that *connect* the big ideas of the unit—"words about community types" such as *rural, urban.* If you can, note any categorizing ideas these five students volunteered during your class discussions. Try collecting two or three weeks of data on these five students in an upcoming unit. Let's examine your data together next month.

Alex: This seems doable and not a lot more work than I'm already doing with my word walls. I like how this approach involves students in talking about what they're learning.

Sam: Something else to learn about these five students is what they do when they can't figure out a word's meaning. I can help you find short grade-level texts connected to your social studies or science units to use during small group reading with these five. Once they've worked through the text in their group, find time to sit separately with each and ask them to read it aloud. Record notes on their word-solving skills (see Figure 2). See if they use *immediate* context clues such as rereading the sentence or *extended* ones such as rereading the paragraph or checking illustrations. If they don't struggle in reading it aloud, point to a few core unit concept words in the text and ask them to define each. Also ask them to explain how the text helps them understand what each word means. If they struggle to read the text either in the group or alone with you, that's okay. By rereading and discussing it with you, they'll become more proficient in tackling grade-level text.

Alex: I see what you mean. I'll use these tweaks and record what I learn about these students' vocabulary strategies. I'll bring my observation notes next month.

Sam: Great! Aim to try the read-aloud at least three times before we meet again, so we'll have some data to discuss. I'll share how your findings tie to the vocabulary instruction initiative underway in the district too.

Lesson:

Date:

Student:

Word 1:

- Sounds out: **with without** syllabicating
- Looks for **morphemes**
- Considers **immediate extended** context
- Looks at: **illustration table chart**

1. Defines meaning: **yes no with assistance**

Figure 2. Anecdotal note-taking organizer: Students' personal vocabulary-building strategies

Takeaways and Next Steps

Through following Sam's advice, Alex will see how anecdotal note-taking and observational checklists work best when they're used to target specific skills and concepts. Educators should try not to observe too much at once—less is more. Maintaining focus ensures they'll have time to observe and simultaneously document without impeding instruction and classroom management. Routinely using anecdotal note-taking approaches with students lessens any anxiety they might have about being observed. Being open about the purpose (e.g., "I need to remember all that you say as we talk") does too. Given that these five students are known to struggle, it's critical for Alex to take this more natural and personal approach in studying them so they won't feel scrutinized.

Alex will be using a sampling approach in collecting these assessment data. She's examining only certain aspects of her literacy curriculum that interact to develop children's vocabulary, the aspect the standardized test scores point to needing her attention. Alex is focusing solely on the children who are not yet meeting the benchmark. As you learned, Alex uses other assessments to document all students' growth in various ways too. Sampling these five students observationally will give her ample, usable data for planning next steps not only with these students but also all the other children in her class.

Case Discussion Questions

1. How might Alex compare data from Sam's observation tools with data she's already collecting or has access to?
2. How might Sam's observation practices help Alex become more intentional in vocabulary instruction?
3. How might the data Alex collects with Sam's tools inform her quarterly student progress reviews?
4. What else might Alex do to build these students' vocabularies? To formatively assess their growth?
5. Do you think Alex will need to keep using these tools after a few months? Why or why not?

General Discussion Questions

1. What are the strengths and limitations of the anecdotal observational tools Sam designed for Alex?
2. How might the observational data Alex is collecting be shared with grade-level teacher teams? Families? Students?
3. Overall, what should any teacher expect to learn through administering standardized tests? What's important to remember when reviewing standardized test scores and using their data?

Suggested Resources

Duke, N.K., & K.B. Cartwright. 2021. "The Science of Reading Progresses: Communicating Advances Beyond the Simple View of Reading." *Reading Research Quarterly* 56 (S1): S25–S44. https://doi.org/10.1002/rrq.411.

Foorman, B., N. Beyler, K. Borradaile, M. Coyne, C.A. Denton, J. Dimino, J. Furgeson, L. Hayes, J. Henke, L. Justice, B. Keating, W. Lewis, S. Sattar, A. Streke, R. Wagner, & S. Wissel. 2016. *Foundational Skills to Support Reading for Understanding in Kindergarten Through 3rd Grade* (NCEE 2016-4008). Washington, DC: National Center for Education Evaluation and Regional Assistance (NCEE), Institute of Education Sciences, US Department of Education. http://whatworks.ed.gov.

Hiebert, E.H. n.d. "Vocabulary Instruction." TextProject. https://textproject.org/teachers/vocabulary-instruction.

3.8 Writing Isn't the Only Way! Multiple Means of Expressing Learning

Lee Ann Jung

Connections to *Developmentally Appropriate Practice*

- Chapter 8: Observing, Documenting, and Assessing Children's Development and Learning

Case Overview

As Mr. Jacobs prepares reports on his third-graders' progress for families, he struggles with how to give a meaningful account of some of his students' work—Alicia, in particular. Alicia struggles with writing, but when she can speak about what she knows, she seems to really understand the concepts she is learning. Even though Mr. Jacobs has a sense of what Alicia knows, understands, and is able to do, he questions whether his assessments reflect this. He is sure that her family will be concerned about her poor writing skills; they have already shared their goal of a college education for Alicia. They perceive college as a ticket to a successful life for their daughter. As well, Mr. Jacobs knows that the third grade team is invested in meeting all district and state learning standards. In this case, Mr. Jacobs must weigh whether to lean on the most valid information he has about Alicia's and other students' learning or to base his reports only on written assessments that may not adequately capture that learning.

Learning Objectives

1. Discuss and evaluate the teacher's handling of the dilemma he faces in preparing a full picture of the child's skills and knowledge for the family–teacher conference.
2. Describe ways to modify assessment to capture each child's understanding and skills and also satisfy standards.

Case Narrative

As Mr. Jacobs settles in at his desk, just after the final bell rings and students scurry to their busses or families' cars, he begins sifting through his third-graders' assessment measures in science to prepare report cards and the accompanying narrative to send to families. Mr. Jacobs stops when he reaches Alicia's report card, struggling to know what to do. Normally, he bases the scores for reporting on how students performed on the written assessments and assignments he uses in class. The dilemma he faces is deciding how to reconcile Alicia's written assessment performance with what he knows about her conceptual understanding in science.

On the one hand, Alicia performs very poorly on the written assessments and assignments, and her science experiment notes only loosely hang together and lack evidence of deep understanding. However, in his informal conversations with Alicia and through student-led conferencing, Mr. Jacobs knows that her understanding is far deeper than is evident on the assignments. He reflects on one particular conversation with Alicia as she and a small group of other students explored whether gravity has different effects on different types of objects:

Walking around the room, Mr. Jacobs stopped at the group. All the students were just as engaged as he'd hoped. As Mr. Jacobs listened, Alicia chimed in with, "Yeah, I think the rock will fall faster too, because the gravity will pull harder on it because it is heavier." The others in the group nodded in agreement. She was fully participating, making predictions, and supporting her predictions with her logic, and she clearly understood what gravity meant.

Mr. Jacobs watched as everyone in the group recorded their predictions on the sheet he'd provided and noticed that Alicia's sheet was missing most of the information on her predictions. As the group tested each of the items, Alicia compared her predictions with what they discovered. As she dropped the pencil, she commented, "Wow, I thought the pencil would fall a whole bunch slower! It went fast!" She was clearly able to make the comparison and articulate how her prediction contrasted with what they found. Fully engaged in the activity, Alicia did not record her findings.

Mr. Jacobs knelt next to Alicia and quietly prompted her, "Hi, friend. I'm so glad you're so into this fun activity! I don't see anything recorded or your prediction or in your notes. If you don't do it during the experiment, you might forget." Alicia responded, "Oh, yeah. I forgot." She fumbled to pick up her pencil and paper. As she started to work on the recording sheet, she did so with very little accuracy, seeming to be a bit disappointed with herself.

Mr. Jacobs felt a little disappointed too, but he wasn't sure why. He definitely wanted to help Alicia complete the written part of the activity, but he couldn't help but feel he had disrupted her engagement and joy to prompt her to show what she knew in a way that wasn't a strength for her.

He could tell that she was completely hitting the mark on the intended objectives of the lesson—engagement, inquiry, making predictions, and comparing predictions with results. But the way he is required to score students for the report card is by using the record sheet of their performance on written assignments, which include the science experiment notes.

For the science section of the report card, Mr. Jacobs must give a score of 1–4 based on students' mastery, as shown on written assignments. For each of eight science concepts from the school's third grade science standards, a rubric of four levels is used:

1. Excels at the success criteria
2. Meets the expectations of all success criteria
3. Meets the expectations of some success criteria
4. Is not meeting the expectations of the success criteria

After much reflection, Mr. Jacobs completes the report shown in Figure 3. In the end, he decides that what is most important about students' learning in science is their understanding and skills within science practices. The way students best show their learning varies, and he feels that a student's needs in writing shouldn't be the only factor in determining understanding of other subjects. Mr. Jacobs understands the importance of recognizing multiple ways for children to show accomplishment for the knowledge, skills, and dispositions of science from multiple dimensions. He attended a recent in-service program on Understanding by Design (UbD) (CAST, n.d.; McTighe & Wiggins 2012;) and realized that this approach to curricula would be in the best interest of all young children. UbD starts with the educator's consideration of standards and objectives, and then the educator creates curricular activities to help all children meet standards through differentiated approaches. Mr. Jacobs begins thinking about how in the future he can give all his students, not only Alicia but also others, options to help them best show their learning. As he brainstorms, he jots down the many ways these skills and understandings in science could be evident, such as building models, making audio recordings, and drawing charts and schematics. In writing, there is only one way, but Mr. Jacobs knows there are many ways for students to demonstrate their understanding of content.

My Learning Report

Student: Alicia

Grade: 3

Homeroom teacher: Mr. Jacobs

Science	Grade	Comment
Asking questions	1	During small group activity
Developing and using models	2	Does not document models in written work
Planning and carrying out investigations	2	Can accomplish the task with small group, but does not write up work
Analyzing and interpreting data	2	Can explain data, but does not write up
Using computational thinking	2	Does not write up lab work
Constructing explanations	2	Does not write up work, but can explain orally
Supporting with evidence	2	Can provide oral examples
Communicating information	1	Only in oral work

Grading Scale

1	2	3	4
The student excels at the success criteria.	The student meets the expectations of all success criteria.	The student meets the expectations of some success criteria.	The student is not yet meeting the expectations of success criteria.

Figure 3. Alicia's learning report

Takeaways and Next Steps

We all have preferences and conditions under which we perform best, and students are no different. For any given skill or understanding, there are countless ways to measure children's learning. When educators do not provide children with options for showing what they know, understand, and are able to do, they introduce significant barriers for many children. Barriers to learning for individuals occur when, for example, teachers say that all children must complete the following:

- Write a science experiment to show the effects of gravity.
- Memorize and dramatize a poem related to science.
- Draw to scale a model of a polygon.

The answer for assessment is never one size fits all. But all too often, there is a single, often teacher-designed assessment.

This case provides an understanding of how children's skills and understandings are not always best reflected in planned assessments. Once educators have identified the most important skills and understandings for children to learn within a content area—and thus the areas to assess—the next task is to ensure that assessments are measuring these and that nothing else is getting in the way.

As Mr. Jacobs has discovered, sometimes the most valid assessment is informal observation and conversation with a child. When it is time to report children's learning, teachers should use the most valid information they have rather than base their reports only on planned or written assessments (Jung 2020; Tomlinson 2017).

It is important that teachers individualize instruction to support children's development of long-term educational goals. For Alicia, this means including instructional supports in writing while appreciating the ways she verbally demonstrates knowledge, skills, and abilities. While individualizing and supporting individual children to expand their skills, teachers cannot expect the same work products from everyone for high-stakes assessment. Expecting standard products can frustrate and inhibit progress in learning.

Case Discussion Questions

1. Which principles outlined in the position statement on developmentally appropriate practice do Mr. Jacob's decision support?
2. Explain how this case provides examples of core consideration 1 (commonality) and core consideration 2 (individuality).
3. How does Mr. Jacobs employ child development principle 3 of the position statement?
4. In what ways does Mr. Jacobs arrive at a resolution in a way that recognizes individual variation in learners and allows children to demonstrate their competencies in different ways?
5. What other ways could Mr. Jacobs have students show what they know in the future? How would this benefit both teacher and students?
6. Mr. Jacobs recognizes that his interactions with Alicia during the activity seemed to detract from her engagement and enjoyment in the activity. What could he do differently to better support students' engagement and learning and still determine their understanding of the material?
7. Mr. Jacobs understands that Alicia's family may worry about her written language competence, particularly as they intend for her to go to college someday. How might Mr. Jacobs address this concern?

Suggested Resources

Graves, D.H. "All Children Can Write." LDOnline. www.ldonline.org.

LEAD Inclusion: www.leadinclusion.org/home.

Seravallo, J. 2017. *The Writing Strategies Book.* Portsmouth, NH: Heinemann.

thinkSRSD: www.thinksrsd.com.

References

CAST. n.d. "The UDL Guidelines." Accessed July 11, 2022. https://udlguidelines.cast.org.

Jung, L.A. 2020. "Does This Count?" *Educational Leadership* 78 (1): 34–39.

McTighe, J., & G. Wiggins. 2012. *Understanding by Design*. Alexandria, VA: ASCD.

Tomlinson, C.A. 2017. *How to Differentiate Instruction in Academically Diverse Classrooms.* 3rd ed. Alexandria, VA: ASCD.

PART 4

Teaching to Enhance Each Child's Development and Learning

Emily Brown Hoffman

In every early childhood context, effective educators build authentic relationships with children and engage in teaching that is inclusive, community and culturally sustaining, appropriately challenging, and equitable. Educators continually seek to develop the complex, extensive range of teaching strategies necessary to support children's development and stimulate critical thinking. They scaffold young children's learning through instruction that is play based and differentiated to respond to each child's interests, skills, and knowledge. To support specific learning experiences and meaningful goals, educators strategically use different learning contexts and carefully tend to all aspects of the learning environment—emotional, social, physical, cognitive, and linguistic.

The cases in Part 4 showcase how early childhood educators can implement meaningful, accessible, and responsive instruction with infants, toddlers, preschoolers, kindergartners, and primary-age children to support genuine learning that affirms children and all their identities. The teaching and learning described in these cases are rooted in social justice and student and family empowerment and directly align with developmentally appropriate practice. The authors have taken the utmost care to provide examples of how early childhood educators can enact high-quality instruction through offering children culturally affirming experiences. Their cases illustrate examples of rigorous and developmentally appropriate instruction through authentic and contextualized descriptions of anti-bias education.

The cases address the following topics:

- Incorporating family values and priorities in teaching decisions to strengthen infants' security and sense of identity within their family and cultural contexts
- Considering how children's individuality influences their decision making and adapting instruction to best support each child's learning
- Exploring identity and community through creative movement and art making
- Developing culturally and linguistically relevant materials to teach phonological awareness and letter recognition more effectively
- Using a humanizing and restorative approach to support development of self-regulation and responsibility
- Highlighting the skills and strategies a mother uses to create a joyful, developmentally appropriate learning experience that supports her daughter's literacy and problem-solving skills and emerging racial identity

The authors of these cases represent diverse perspectives and concentrations within early childhood education. They are specialists in child development, curriculum and instruction, special education, educational psychology, and community education and represent different ages, gender identities, races, ethnicities, abilities and disabilities, and geographic locations. All authors have extensive experience and expertise in the teaching of young children, some within the context of classroom or early learning program experience and others within higher education. Through these cases, the authors characterize the interdisciplinary knowledge and practice that effective early childhood teachers must embody.

4.1 Engaging with Families to Individualize Teaching

Marie L. Masterson

Connections to *Developmentally Appropriate Practice*

- Chapter 3: Context Matters: Reframing Teaching in Early Childhood Education
- Chapter 7: Engaging in Reciprocal Partnerships with Families and Fostering Community Connections
- Chapter 9: Teaching to Enhance Each Child's Development and Learning

Case Overview

This case study illustrates "developmentally appropriate teaching practices that include a wide range of skills and strategies that are adapted to children's ages, development, and individual characteristics and to the family, social, cultural, and linguistic contexts of each child" (Masterson 2022, 181). This goal requires educators to "communicate frequently with families to incorporate preferences in feeding, napping, and care routines and families' knowledge of children's interests and needs" (193).

In the case study, the teachers encounter unfamiliar practices a family uses with their infant daughter. At first, the teachers are unsure what steps to take and don't know if the requests are allowable with licensing standards. They recognize their need to learn more about the family language, culture, and beliefs, as these are different from their own. The teacher and director work with a cultural broker to understand differences and to align the program's practices with those the family requests. They learn that even when a family communicates through orientation meetings and demonstration visits, participation in the classroom can bring to light cultural priorities and differences that affect decisions. The family requests challenge the teachers' assumptions and require them to adjust their perspectives and practices.

Learning Objectives

1. Explain the importance of building on family values and priorities in teaching decisions to strengthen infants' security and sense of identity within their family and cultural contexts.
2. Identify examples of hidden beliefs, practices, and priorities that influence communication and decision making.
3. Describe ways to incorporate family knowledge and insights and adjust teaching decisions to support the development and learning of each child.

Case Narrative

On the day 8-month-old Adella joins the classroom for the first time, Ms. Livy removes the infant's outer knit suit. Adella is wearing a beaded necklace and a bracelet. The bracelet, which has small beads woven through the red and black laces and a larger bead in the middle, leaves a red mark on Adella's arm. Adella has sucked on the bracelet, and it is damp from her saliva. Ms. Livy is concerned about cleanliness. She wonders if the beads present a choking hazard, but she doesn't say anything, not wanting to upset Ms. De Costa, Adella's mother.

Before leaving, Ms. De Costa places a small metal pot of homemade ointment into Ms. Livy's hands. She wants Ms. Livy to use it for diaper changes. Ms. Livy is unsure what to do, because the program has a written policy that all medications and ointments must be clearly labeled with the name of the child and a list of ingredients. She smiles and places the pot into the diaper bag. She plans to find out if this is allowable.

Ms. Livy wants to help Adella feel comfortable adjusting to the program. She also wants to honor the family's request and help Adella take pride in her family and culture. Ms. Livy and her director contact a cultural broker, a social worker from the community center, who understands the language and culture of the family and can share some ideas for incorporating the requests.

The cultural broker explains that in many cultures around the world, including Native American, Asian, and Latin American traditions, charms, beads, necklaces, bracelets, and anklets may be worn by infants for protection against disease or evil. In some religious traditions, jewelry is believed to provide protection from a guardian angel or saint and ward away evil spirits. Each bracelet or jewelry type may have a specific meaning to the family. Families believe this protection is essential for the safety of the child.

Ms. Livy and the director understand the importance of the jewelry to the family. In addition, they realize that making natural balms to aid in healing is part of Ms. De Costa's way of showing care for Adella. Ms. Livy talks with a licensing representative who works with programs to incorporate family requests. The representative says that the jewelry is okay since it is securely fastened. She also has a suggestion about how to incorporate the family's request to use the ointment. As a result, Ms. Livy asks Ms. De Costa for the list of ingredients. Ms. Livy records these on a card, adds Adella's name and the date, and places the card with the balm in a plastic bag.

The licensing representative shares some other family requests she is familiar with, such as touching infants while talking about them to avoid passing on negative energy, the use of gripe water (a liquid herbal supplement thought to soothe various infant ailments), and the preference for strict adult-determined sleep and feeding practices. She notes that many of these can be incorporated. However, she points out that when family practices are determined to be unsafe for children, additional consultation with the family will be necessary. For example, teachers must always place infants on their backs to sleep, and the crib may not contain clothing, restraints, or blankets that pose a strangulation risk. Non-negotiable guidelines should be placed in the family handbook and discussed with families before children are enrolled. When licensing does not allow a practice, the director and teacher need to show sensitivity during conversations with the family.

The teachers come to know the De Costa family well and find caring ways to incorporate home practices into procedures and routines. While Ms. Livy and Ms. Sara, her coteacher, are not native Spanish speakers, they use the internet to find and learn frequently used words like *diaper, bottle, nap,* and *drink* in Spanish. They use the familiar names for the children's family members and use labels and captions to help them communicate. Over time, they continue to incorporate strategies to encourage Adella's development and learning.

One day Ms. Livy holds Adella on her lap. They sit on the soft carpet next to Ms. Sara, who is stacking cups with Gabe and Eva. The teachers have made personal photo books for each of the children. For the two infants from Spanish-speaking families, including Adella, the laminated books include captions in English with simple translations in Spanish.

Ms. Livy points to the colorful cover of Adella's book and says, "Where is Mamá? There's Mamá!" Adella smiles. "Is Mamá reading a book? You and Mamá like to read books together," says Ms. Livy as she turns the page. "Is this your dog? Es este tu perro?" Ms. Livy asks. She turns the page, covers up the photo of Adella with her hand, and asks, "Where is Adella?" She pulls her hand away and says, "There's Adella!" Adella laughs and claps her hands.

While changing Adella's diaper, Ms. Livy uses a picture guide above the changing table that shows a baby with each part of the body labeled in English and Spanish. Ms. Livy holds Adella's feet gently and says, "These are your feet. Esta son tus pies. And here are your toes. Dedos de los pies." Then she tickles Adella's fingers and says, "Tus dedos—your fingers." Ms. Livy uses ointment and slips on a clean diaper before replacing Adella's clothing. "All done, Adella! You are warm and dry," she says.

Ms. Livy spends time with Ms. De Costa to learn how Adella is rocked and fed. At first, Ms. Livy forgets, and she holds Adella facing toward her to take the bottle. She turns Adella around to rock against her shoulder, but Adella fusses and pushes away. Ms. Livy remembers that Ms. De Costa faced Adella outward, where she could watch Ms. Sara and the others. Ms. Livy adjusts Adella outward and tries to read *Tengo diez deditos* (*Ten Little Fingers*), but Adella doesn't seem interested.

Ms. Livy asks Ms. Sara to play a recording of "Duérmete Mi Niño" ("Fall Asleep My Child"). It was recorded by Ms. De Costa. Within a few minutes, Adella is asleep. Once she is placed in the crib, Ms. Livy plays soft music from *Canciones de cuna: Spanish Lullabies*. These are songs that are soothing and familiar to Adella. The other children are going sleep and enjoy the melodies too.

As the teachers learn more about the families, they build trust as they honor the priorities that are valued. They continue to ask the families to demonstrate ways of playing and supporting the children. They gain deeper understanding about the families' practices and the children's unique ways of developing to help them make effective teaching decisions.

Takeaways and Next Steps

The teachers find that discovering and responding to hidden expectations and norms requires patience and sensitivity. They explore the internet, hold many conversations with the family, and talk with a cultural broker to gain new insights and adjust their perspectives and practices. When unsure of appropriate actions, they reach out to a licensing representative to explore the options. Their goal is to individualize teaching for Adella, so that the family's ideas are incorporated. They also realize that it is important to explore the larger context of the family's language, culture, and context, rather than focus narrowly on the details of a specific request. They learn to use questions and conversations to build a strong relationship with the family and to expand their range of teaching approaches.

This case study illustrates the complex issues that require teachers to seek out family perspectives and to explore ways to incorporate family requests into infant teaching. It shows that trusting relationships develop with reciprocal communication over time and require sincere willingness to understand and support families whose practices may be different from a teacher's own.

Case Discussion Questions

1. How do the teachers' responses reflect genuine desire to learn about the families and support their choices?
2. Even after initial meetings between families and teachers, why can expectations and norms related to care routines and teaching remain hidden?
3. How did the teachers honor the child's individual characteristics and incorporate the social, cultural, and linguistic contexts of the family?
4. What additional strategies can the teachers use to build trust and engage the families in ongoing communication about teaching and caregiving routines?

General Discussion Questions

1. Identify a situation where you experienced or observed cultural differences in care routines with infants. How were these practices the same or different from your own cultural approaches?
2. Why is it important to identify and reflect on your own beliefs and values related to teaching practices with infants and to discuss these with colleagues?
3. What practical considerations need to be evaluated when a family's requests do not fit with the program's accepted practices or with licensing standards? How can educators honor families' identity and childrearing norms when they feel they must ask the family to adjust or conform with program expectations? How can educators create a sense of belonging and trust while they talk with families about differences?

Reference

Masterson, M. 2022. "Teaching to Enhance Each Child's Development and Learning." In *Developmentally Appropriate Practice in Early Childhood Programs Serving Children from Birth Through Age 8,* 4th ed., NAEYC, 181–214. Washington, DC: NAEYC.

4.2 Tumbling Towers with Toddlers: Intention and Decision Making Over Blocks

Ron Grady

Connections to *Developmentally Appropriate Practice*

- Chapter 1: Intentional Teaching: Complex Decision Making and the Core Considerations
- Chapter 6: Creating a Caring, Equitable Community of Learners
- Chapter 9: Teaching to Enhance Each Child's Development and Learning

Case Overview

This case study takes place in a classroom of 2-year-olds in a Reggio-inspired preschool. Children range in age from 2 years, 1 month to 2 years, 10 months. At this stage of development, children present a wide array of skills, interests, and dispositions that make learning both a joyful and complex process. A challenge of working at this center is that while the program is grounded in child-centered, play-based pedagogies, educators are responsible for providing ample evidence of children's learning according to a specific framework informed by the curriculum of the larger K–12 school of which this early childhood center is part.

Blocks are often seen as both tools for constructive play and as a material that provides insight into children's mathematical development. However, blocks also provide opportunities for complex decision making and social interaction that, properly scaffolded, build confidence, deepen relationships, and promote logical–mathematical intelligence. In this case, you will observe children of varying ages building with blocks and Magna-Tiles. Case vignettes are followed by brief reflections on the teaching strategies involved.

Learning Objectives

1. Identify effective teaching strategies (Masterson 2022, 183–84) used in the case study.
2. Analyze the benefits of using a small group format for open-ended play experiences with specific materials.
3. Identify methods to extend children's inquiries through multiple modes.
4. Elaborate on ways to meaningfully engage with children of diverse interests and varying levels of skill and development.

Case Narrative

Sunlight fills the room with a cool autumnal light. Mere minutes have passed since 15 two-year-olds have dispersed throughout the classroom, seeking their own pursuits. Some head directly for the sensory table, which is sloshing with blue-hued water. Others visit the atelier, eager to get their fingers to work with wire and clay. Most popular, however, is the block table.

As the final children leave the meeting rug, I pull a chair up to the block table. The children are enthralled by the smooth, bright, wooden blocks, as am I. Some transition swiftly into building, stacking blocks up high. Others, however, I invite to begin with a simple prompt: "I wonder how you will use these blocks today?"

A minute or so into our building, I encourage Alana (2 years, 3 months—henceforth 2y, 3m) to begin building by handing her a wooden block. She takes the block, examines it, and then places it on the table. As she does this, I place another block on top of it, demonstrating one way to use the material (Masterson 2022, 183). We share a brief look, and Alana retrieves another block and stacks it. We continue stacking blocks for the next couple of minutes, taking moments in between each additional block to admire the evolving creation. Will (2y, 10m) approaches us at the table.

"What are you making?" Will asks.

"You might ask Alana," I offer.

"What are you making, Alana?" Will asks.

Alana remains silent, and so I narrate her process so far.

"She seems to be stacking up blocks, one by one, on top of one another."

"Oh, like this? I like to stack blocks," Will says, and begins stacking some himself. "One, two, three . . ." Each additional level is carefully added, and eventually the blocks tumble.

As they fall, I observe Will, not intervening, noticing the way he repositions the blocks on top of one another, sure to balance them. I remain silent and sit with the children at the table, observing. All continues in this way until Will grabs a box of Magna-Tiles from the nearby shelf and starts to build with them. He makes a square and then begins to put blocks on top of the Magna-Tiles.

Narrating, both for Alana and for Will, Alana's thinking about her own intentions is an example of scaffolding metacognition. This narration also connected two children to one another by revealing, in a sense, the mind of a silent peer to a child who was more wont to share their thoughts through words. Through "narrat[ing] the children's actions and strategies," I was able to "engage [the children's] thinking and to draw attention to [the] effective strategies and interesting ideas" (Masterson 2022, 196) that Alana had. These ideas, in turn, inspired Will down his own path of inquiry and improvisation. Given that expressive language skills develop along highly differential trajectories, this translation between children's minds, ideas, actions, and educators' words may not only be helpful but sometimes vital.

Notably, despite the challenges I observe Will experiencing, I do not intervene. A patient observation can be as powerful and as intentional as direct scaffolding of social and metacognitive processes. I felt comfortable allowing Will, the oldest in our class with a wealth of experience with school-like contexts and materials, the cognitive and technical challenge of figuring out how to balance his creation. Will was a unique individual, which meant that despite my knowledge of his personality and interests and my ideas about where his ideas may be leading, I had to acknowledge that his intentions might be changing as our interaction evolved. Therefore, refraining from action was ideal. (See core consideration 2, individuality, in Bredekamp & Willer 2022, 13.)

This distance and my own intentional silence also provided an opportunity for Will to strengthen already strong skills in executive function. He would likely have had less success "filter[ing] distractions and maintain[ing] the focus necessary to manage [this] activit[y]" had I begun intervening (see Masterson 2022, 186).

As Will builds with a new combination of Magna-Tiles and blocks, a child at the other end of the table attempts to do similarly, but with less success. A cry of frustration erupts across the table, and I move myself closer to James (2y, 5m).

"You seem upset! I notice your tower is falling down." I lay a hand on James' shoulder.

"I can't do it!" James says, sadness evident his voice.

"You're trying to stack all the Magna-Tiles on top of one another, it looks like," I say.

James confirms that this is true. I turn to Will, still building and balancing.

"Will, I wonder how you did it. James is trying to do the same thing that you did."

Will approaches us and turns his head to one side. "It's just going like this," he says, taking the block and arranging it with care.

I interpret: "It seems that when it's like this, the blocks aren't too heavy. They balance."

"Yeah, balance," Will says.

James and I make two structures using the technique explained by Will. "Will really helped us out. Thanks, Will!"

As a 2-year-old with less experience, James needed a more direct intervention. Masterson (2022, 197) writes that a key component of effective teaching with toddlers is to "provide gentle assistance when children need help coping or handling frustration or disappointment" (197). In response to this need, I both consoled James *and* invited Will to teach him how to work with the materials. This encouraged the sort of "direct interactions" (193) that, despite my facilitation, constituted an important initial step toward solidifying a community of learners where it is simultaneously alright to not know *and* to consult one's peers for help.

Within fifteen minutes, the children have transitioned to other pursuits; the atelier with its paints, the sensory table with its water and scoopers, and the dramatic play area with its comforting ritual of family life have all beckoned them away. Nonetheless, the next time that these three are ready to approach the building table, it will be there, waiting, and ready to offer new challenges, new wonderings, and new opportunities to learn, connect, and grow together.

Takeaways and Next Steps

Toddlers are always in awe, constantly curious, and endlessly emotional. Effectively teaching and engaging with them, therefore, requires both flexibility and intention. This case illustrates that the intentional provision of materials can lead both to new insights and to frustration. Had, for example, our classroom included only traditional wooden, non-magnet blocks, Will would not have devised a new scheme of building, and James would not have had an opportunity to manage disappointment and be supported by a peer. Had building been a one-on-one endeavor, perhaps Alana and Will would not have ever connected over their mutual interest in constructive play. The list could go on and on, and yet at its core rests the tenet that every choice matters.

There are a variety of possibilities for potential directions in which to take this learning as well as a few important takeaways that guided the interactions detailed here.

For instance, first and foremost, there is the maintenance of open-endedness: Rather than directing children, for example, to build a particular structure or even asking them something like "What do you *plan* to build?" inviting them into a dialogue with a question like "How do you plan to use this material?" leaves room for possibility. It is an implicit invitation, permission even, for a child to explore their own interests and give them "active agency in decision making and ownership of [their] learning" (Masterson 2022, 189).

A potential next step might be to document the unfolding learning. Documenting children's work through photographs and video is both a chance to explore process and to allow children to take their efforts on one day and bring these efforts and experiences forward to another. For example, on a subsequent day I might bring in a photograph of Will offering his assistance to James to remind them of their previous work together. I might also use a video of the two building in order to show, in motion, the process of their building. Such documentation can then be used for other purposes, such as assessment, to share with families and even for larger group discussions with the children.

Extending and integrating children's learning across multiple domains (for example, large and small motor engagement, play, literacy, math) is a critical piece of early childhood pedagogy and enables children to engage with an idea or ideas in ways that are most accessible to them. Although the above case focuses primarily on building, there are myriad ways that children's learning could be enriched and extended. For example, how might books about structures (both successful and failed) link children's interests in building with their development of literacy skills? How might we facilitate other opportunities (for instance, for dramatic play or math) that integrate children's affinity for building?

Case Discussion Questions

1. How does the teacher model intentional scaffolding of children's learning? What else could he have done? What might you have done differently?
2. Where do you see the children being invited into the metacognitive processes of considering their own intentions, goals, and actions?
3. How might this case have looked different if the teacher had stepped back from the activity and participated merely as an observer? What avenues might the children have explored?
4. What could have been done to increase challenge for each child?
5. What are some ways you might connect some of your own learning goals and professional objectives to the situation described in the case?
6. How might provisioning the block table with a clipboard, a few sheets of paper, and a writing implement have influenced and/or extended children's work there?
7. What might have happened if, later that week, the teacher had printed photographs of the children working together and put them up near the building table for the children to reference?

General Discussion Questions

1. What particular supports might a community of toddlers need to effectively engage with open-ended materials such as blocks?

2. What could have been done in the environment to support children diagnosed with disabilities who are learning to use materials such as blocks? How might the teacher have used tools such as photos, pictures, or sequences to support a child who is just learning to build with blocks?

References

Bredekamp, S., & B. Willer. 2022. "Intentional Teaching: Complex Decision Making and the Core Considerations." In *Developmentally Appropriate Practice in Early Childhood Programs Serving Children from Birth Through Age 8,* 4th ed., NAEYC, 5–23. Washington, DC: NAEYC.

Masterson, M. 2022. "Teaching to Enhance Each Child's Development and Learning." In *Developmentally Appropriate Practice in Early Childhood Programs Serving Children from Birth Through Age 8,* 4th ed., NAEYC, 181–214. Washington, DC: NAEYC.

4.3 What My Heart Holds: Exploring Identity with Preschool Learners

Cierra Kaler-Jones

Connections to *Developmentally Appropriate Practice*

- Chapter 6: Creating a Caring, Equitable Community of Learners
- Chapter 9: Teaching to Enhance Each Child's Development and Learning

Case Overview

This case explores teaching strategies used by a preschool teacher to "foster positive self-identity and help children develop appreciation for their own and others' diverse cultures, languages, and social experiences" and to "facilitate anti-bias conversations with children" (Masterson 2022, 190). In this case, the teacher uses guideline 4 of the position statement on developmentally appropriate practice to plan and implement a lesson in which a diverse class of preschool children use art making to learn about identity. Ms. Cierra and the children draw and discuss the things they love about themselves, issues they care about, and people they love who can help make a change. This experience and the strategies used by Ms. Cierra also support the goals of anti-bias education, particularly the first goal, "Children will demonstrate self-awareness, confidence, family pride, and positive social identities" (Derman-Sparks & Edwards with Goins 2019, 2).

Learning Objectives

1. Identify ways to bring each child's home culture(s) and language(s) into the shared culture of the learning community.
2. Identify ways to encourage children to tell personal stories using drawing, dictating, and movement.
3. Explain the use of specific, positive feedback to acknowledge learners' efforts and observations.

Case Narrative

The children and Ms. Cierra huddle into their daily opening circle where she introduces the activity for the day. The learners in the class love to wiggle and move their bodies, so Ms. Cierra incorporates movement-based routines into the class's daily routines. "For circle time today, you'll share your name and a pose that represents you. I'll share mine. My name is Ms. Cierra and this is my pose," she says. Ms. Cierra stands with her chest puffed out and hands on her hips. The class giggles.

Jalen: My name is Jalen. (*Crouches down to the ground and puts his hands in front of him, like Spiderman.*)

Alexis: My name is Alexis. (*Twirls in a circle.*)

Bria: My name is Bria. (*Points her right finger in the air and has her left hand on her hip.*)

Josh: I'm Josh. (*Uses his walker to steady himself as he nods his head up and down.*)

After each child has a turn to share their name and pose, Ms. Cierra asks them to place their hand on their heart. "What do you feel?" Ms. Cierra inquires.

Lily: I feel my heart hitting my hand.

Sabina: My heart is like a butterfly!

Ms. Cierra: Those are great observations, Lily and Sabina. We started our time together by introducing ourselves, saying our names, and choosing a pose to represent us. Today, we're going to explore something called *identity*. Our identities are important parts of ourselves. They are the things that make us different, but there are also things we have in common. For example, we all chose different poses. After we posed and felt our hearts, all of our hearts beat. This is something we have in common.

Ms. Cierra asks the children to head to their art tables where they will work in small groups to draw, play, and reflect.

Ms. Cierra: Today we're going to explore the things that our hearts hold. What do we know about our hearts?

Jamal: We felt them in circle time.

Ms. Cierra: Amazing, Jamal! That is a great connection you made to our circle time activity. We have a few options. On the paper, we can practice drawing things that we love about ourselves. We can talk with a partner. We can also act it out.

As an example, Ms. Cierra shows her paper, draws a book, and says, "I love that I am a learner and share information with others." After a few minutes of children scribbling their artistic creations and talking at their tables in groups of three to four, Ms. Cierra walks around the room to check in with each of them individually.

Ms. Cierra: What do you love about yourself, Alexis?

Alexis: I love my shirt!

Ms. Cierra: I love that your outfit expresses who you are and it's something that makes you feel good. Let's think together. What are some other things you love about yourself?

Alexis: I am nice to animals. I help take care of our dog.

Ms. Cierra: That is wonderful. I love hearing you talk about how kind you are. Let's also try writing out the word *dog* together. D-o-g.

Ms. Cierra checks in with Bria and Josh.

Ms. Cierra: What do you love about yourself, Bria?

Bria: I love my hair!

Ms. Cierra: That's beautiful. What do you love about it?

Bria: My hair is big. It is like a crown, my dad says. (*Pats Ms. Cierra's curly hair as Ms. Cierra crouches next to her.*) Your hair is like mine.

Ms. Cierra: Your hair *is* like a crown. I appreciate how you named something we have in common. What else do you love about yourself?

Bria: I like to be a helper.

After individual check-ins with a few more children, the class seems ready to move on to the next prompt. Ms. Cierra says, "I would like for you to draw or talk about the loved ones in your life that support you. This could be your family, your community, or someone you love." Ms. Cierra holds up her picture that represents one of the other teachers. "This is Mr. Jaylon," she says. "Whenever I need help, I know that they will support me."

Ms. Cierra: Who is that you drew, Lily?

Lily: That's my abuela!

Ms. Cierra: Wow, that's a great drawing of your abuela. Can we spell *abuela* together? A-b-u-e-l-a. (*Writes the letters on Lily's paper.*)

Dawan: What is an abuela? That sounds like a silly word. (*Practices trying to say the word and laughs.*)

Ms. Cierra: I'm glad you asked us what abuela means, Dawan. It's actually a word in Spanish. Isn't that cool? Lily, do you know what abuela means?

Lily: (*Looks uncertain.*) I don't know.

Ms. Cierra: That's okay. Abuela means *grandma* in Spanish. It's so beautiful that in our classroom community, we speak different languages.

Ms. Cierra stops at each child's station to ask them who they drew or talked about. Jalen drew his mom, Alexis talked about her tía, Sabina drew her tita, Josh drew his grandma, Bria told the table about her dad, and Dawan drew his cousin. Ms. Cierra asks them to share whom they drew or talked about in small groups with the class so they could talk about appreciating the diversity of whom they represented and the languages they use in our families. The class practices saying words like *tía* (*aunt* in Spanish) and *tita* (*aunt* in Tagalog) to note the different words that they called the aunts in their families. Sensing that the class was ready to be active, Ms. Cierra puts on their favorite class song and they have a short dance party. Afterward, Ms. Cierra starts the last part of the activity:

Ms. Cierra: What can we do to help our community? Draw, talk with each other, or act out how you can help. (*Walks around.*) What are you drawing, Jalen?

Jalen: A garden.

Ms. Cierra: I can see the different plants you drew with all different colors. How does your garden help people?

Jalen: It helps people . . . not be hungry.

Ms. Cierra: That is very thoughtful. It reminds me of how you said one of the things you love about yourself is that you like going outside. What are you drawing, Josh?

Josh: Me and my grandma. We make cards for people who are sick to make them feel better.

Ms. Cierra: I love that you are drawing someone you love that is helping you make a difference.

Ms. Cierra hears her name being called and sees Sabina waving at her. "Ms. Cierra, I need help," Sabina says. "How do you spell *love*?" "That's a great question, Sabina. I'm so glad you asked me for help," says Ms. Cierra. "Let's spell it together. L-o-v-e."

Ms. Cierra listens in on some of the other children's conversations.

Sabina: This is me making a sign. I like to draw. (*Acts out making a sign by finding a sign in the classroom and pretending to draw on it.*)

Lily: This is me picking up trash. (*Picks up some of the class blocks up from the ground, pretending it is trash.*)

Sabina: Oh, I see the trash. Picking it up keeps things clean.

Lily: What does that say? (*Taps Sabina's pretend sign.*)

Sabina: Love.

Takeaways and Next Steps

This case illustrates Ms. Cierra's use of supportive teaching strategies within the context of an anti-bias activity in which children reflect on their identities, highlight their families, and consider ways they can help others. Ms. Cierra also engages in movement activities, drawing, and discussion to build on children's motor skills and literacy. Aligned with guideline 4 of the position statement on developmentally appropriate practice, Ms. Cierra helps preschoolers explore others' cultures and experiences by inviting conversation about family, languages, interests, and self-expression (Masterson 2022, 190). The activity is designed to support children with varying abilities to participate and work in community with their peers. During early childhood, children build their self-concept and begin to think about the values, attitudes, beliefs, and interests that define them. Engaging children in identity-based activities in preschool can help to build a positive sense of self.

Preschoolers notice differences and begin to ask questions about those differences. When Ms. Cierra hears some of the children sharing their languages, she needs to quickly pivot to create space for the children to share and hear from the rest of the class. She also recognizes that she has to intervene when one child laughs about a word. She tries to offer a teaching moment that emphasizes the beauty of different languages by communicating positive messages. When faced with these questions and situations, it is crucial for teachers to encourage children to ask questions and then honestly answer those questions, holding conversations that facilitate understanding and respect for others.

Case Discussion Questions

1. How did Ms. Cierra intentionally use multiple teaching strategies to support children in making connections and telling stories? Which principle in the developmentally appropriate practice position statement does this reinforce? What challenges or modifications might you add to the lesson to meet the needs of each child?
2. How did Ms. Cierra use specific, positive feedback to acknowledge learners' efforts and observations? How was this helpful to children?
3. How was Ms. Cierra's response to Dawan helpful for him, Lily, and the other children? What else could Ms. Cierra have said or done?
4. What challenges might arise when doing this activity? What might you do in those situations?

General Discussion Questions

1. What are some ways to make the importance of identity clear for preschool children in developmentally appropriate and anti-biased ways?
2. What are some experiences that could encourage children to explore other aspects of identity, such as ability?

References

Derman-Sparks, L., & J.O. Edwards. 2019. "Understanding Anti-Bias Education: Bringing the Four Core Goals to Every Facet of Your Curriculum." *Young Children* 74 (5): 6–12. www.naeyc.org/resources/pubs/yc/nov2019/understanding-anti-bias.

Masterson, M. 2022. "Teaching to Enhance Each Child's Development and Learning." In *Developmentally Appropriate Practice in Early Childhood Programs Serving Chidlren from Birth Through Age 8,* 4th ed., NAEYC, 181–214. Washington, DC: NAEYC.

4.4 "I See a Really Big Gecko!" When Background Knowledge and Teaching Materials Don't Match

Germaine Kaleilehua Tauati and Colleen E. Whittingham

Connections to *Developmentally Appropriate Practice*

- Chapter 1: Intentional Teaching: Complex Decision Making and the Core Considerations
- Chapter 9: Teaching to Enhance Each Child's Development and Learning
- Chapter 10: Planning and Implementing an Engaging Curriculum to Achieve Meaningful Goals

Case Overview

This case demonstrates the way educators in a native Hawaiian organization respond to the lack of culturally and linguistically relevant materials for teaching phonological awareness and letter recognition to preschool children. The preschool classroom in this case uses a research-based early literacy curriculum to help children develop phonological awareness, alphabet knowledge, and oral language skills. The materials provided by the commercial publisher include an alphabet flip chart containing an illustrated scene and an accompanying rhyme for each letter of the alphabet. The *kumu* (teacher) and *keiki* (children) engage in the activities using traditional materials; later, the kumu derives a culturally rich solution to using these antiquated materials: creating an alphabet flip chart composed of local photographs that reflect local items, places, and people of interest while incorporating ʻōlelo Hawaiʻi, or Hawaiian vocabulary, where possible. This example of creating and then using materials that center the local lived experiences of keiki and their *ʻohana* (family) to teach phonological awareness and alphabet knowledge is designed to generate ideas for consideration when creating similar resources in any cultural context.

Learning Objectives

1. Identify the core goals of culturally and developmentally appropriate language-rich interactions, specifically in a preschool space (Masterson 2022).
2. Identify connections between guideline 4D of the position statement on developmentally appropriate practice and the case described here, specifically on how it relates to providing equitable opportunities for all children to learn.

Case Narrative

On the first day of instruction using the curriculum, Kumu Akina facilitates a conversation with keiki about the illustrated scene on the Western alphabet flip chart. The scene depicts cartoon-like images of mismatched animals and objects that begin with the letter A, for example, an alligator with an apple and an armadillo flying an airplane. (On subsequent days, the kumu will label the images that keiki name to reinforce the focus letter and the multiple sounds the letter can represent.)

Kumu: Aloha kakahiaka (Good morning).

Class: Aloha, Kumu.

Kumu: I have some fun things planned for us today. Let's begin with our alphabet flip chart.

Leilani: Ooh, what letter are we going to do today?

Kumu: Today we are going to do the letter *a*. (*Flips the chart to the letter* a.) Let's focus our attention on the pictures in the middle of the page. Tell me what you see.

Alika: I see mangoes.

Kimo: My kupuna uses li hing powder to make the mango yummy!

Kumu: They do look like mangoes, but they are a little different. Can someone else tell me what this fruit is?

Kalei: Apples.

Kumu: Yes, Kalei, those are /a/pples. Apples begin with the letter *a*. What else do you see?

Ka U'i: What is an apple?

Kumu: An apple is a fruit that grows on trees like a mango, but it grows in a cooler climate. You can use it to make apple juice, and many people bake yummy desserts with them!

Pua: I see a monkey.

Kumu: Oh, it looks kind of like a monkey, but we call that an *ape*. (*Emphasizes the initial sounds in* monkey *and* ape.)

Kimo: I have never seen an ape in Hawai'i. I only seen the monkey at the zoo.

Pua: One time I saw a monkey eat a banana.

Kumu: That's right, we have monkeys at the zoo. What else do you see in the picture?

Leilani: I see the airplane.

Kumu: Yes, an airplane flying in the sky.

Alika: I see a really big gecko!

Kumu: Alika, this is an alligator.

Alika: I never saw an alligator here.

Kalei: I think I saw that on TV.

Kumu: Yes, you might have. What else do you see in the picture that starts with the /a/ or /ā/ sound?

Pua: I see the ant. We have fire ants outside.

Kumu: Yes, a fire ant bite can hurt.

Kimo: Kumu, what is that big brown bug on the grass?

Kumu: Kimo, that is an armadillo. An armadillo is a mammal that eats bugs.

Leilani: Yuk, that's gross!

Kumu: Has anyone seen an armadillo before?

Alika: Nope.

Kumu: Okay, well, it looks like we have a lot of new things to talk about in this picture! During choice time I will look through our classroom library to find a few books that might help us learn about these new plants and animals.

Concerned about the lesson with the alphabet flip chart, Kumu Akina is deep in thought while passing out snack later that morning. Why is the letter *a* lesson such a miss? She realizes that while the poster activities are intended to spur conversation between keiki about the items in the picture, it is nearly impossible for her preschoolers to engage in an authentic back-and-forth without prior experiences with these items to draw on. A lesson intended to create authentic talk has quickly turned into her correcting the children's interpretations of the illustrations in order to match the vocabulary it was meant to reflect.

Kumu Akina thinks keiki can have a rich conversation about the mangoes that grow on the side of the road as they walk along to get to school, discussing the different colors that tell if and when the fruit is ripe enough to be picked, or talk at length about the different geckos they have seen in their yard—everyone has a story about being surprised by those tricky little lizards! She hopes keiki will have an opportunity to share these stories when working with the letters *m* and *g* but thinks it unlikely that these familiar items will be included in the posters provided.

She decides to approach the objective from a different angle. Instead of showing keiki pictures intended to represent the letter *a*, why not have them curate their *own* pictures reflecting objects that start with the letter *a*? This would allow all keiki to contribute their lived experiences and would produce a classroom artifact for each letter of the alphabet.

The next day, Kumu Akina tells the keiki they will be going on an adventure. "*Adventure* begins with the letter *a*! We talked about some things that start with the letter *a* yesterday, and now it is our turn to find words that start with *a*," says Kumu Akina. "Let's start by remembering two of the sounds that the letter *a* can represent. We can hear /a/ like in *after*. We wash our hands *after* we paint. Or we can hear /ā/ like in *angry*. *Angry* is one of the words on our feelings chart."

Takeaways and Next Steps

Teachers have the *kuleana* (responsibility) to provide children with materials that are culturally appropriate, developmentally appropriate, and accessible (NAEYC 2020). And, they have the power to choose materials that make sense for the children and the families they serve.

In this case, the kumu prioritized providing keiki with opportunities to think and talk about things that are familiar to them, capture their interest, and are readily present in their environment. She created a list of nouns familiar to the children's environment that began with each letter of the alphabet, including ʻōlelo Hawaiʻi where appropriate (not all letters in English are a part of the Pīʻāpā, or Hawaiian alphabet). The kumu then gathered as many of the items as possible for each letter of the alphabet into a single scene; took a picture; and wrote a poem to accompany each photo. She created one image and matching poem for the letter A, for the letter B, and so on.

When teaching skills such as phonological awareness and alphabet knowledge, the kumu made the intentional choice to eliminate the need for keiki to also have to build background knowledge about snow or aardvarks or yaks. Eventually the kumu wants children to know what all of those things are, but when teaching something as new and fabulous as letters and sounds, she will focus on things like mud, cinder, and taro, which are relevant to keiki every day.

Case Discussion Questions

1. How does the lesson created by the kumu reflect guidelines 1 and 4 of the position statement on developmentally appropriate practice?
2. Which principles outlined in the position statement on developmentally appropriate practice does this case support?
3. What are some possible challenges the kumu may encounter as she and her keiki begin to seek evidence of letter sounds in the environment rather than relying on the commercial materials provided?
4. Think about how the kumu responds to Alika and Kalei as they discuss the alligator. How else could she have engaged the keiki during that exchange?
5. Based on the discussion that the kumu had with her keiki, describe any additional strategies, materials, or activities she could use when planning future lessons using the alphabet flip chart.

General Discussion Questions

1. Does the use of commercial alphabet charts, posters, or other such materials pose any challenges or concerns for teachers? If so, what are they? How can educators overcome these challenges and address the concerns?
2. In what other ways can teachers revise, modify, or supplement the curriculum to ensure that children's interests, experiences, and culture are not only reflected but celebrated?

References

Masterson, M. 2022. "Teaching to Enhance Each Child's Development and Learning." In *Developmentally Appropriate Practice in Early Childhood Programs Serving Children from Birth Through Age 8*, 4th ed., NAEYC, 181–214. Washington, DC: NAEYC.

NAEYC. 2020. "Developmentally Appropriate Practice." Position statement. Washington, DC: NAEYC. www.naeyc.org/resources/position-statements/dap.

4.5 Using a Humanizing and Restorative Approach for Young Children to Develop Responsibility and Self-Regulation

Saili S. Kulkarni, Sunyoung Kim, and Nicola Holdman

Connections to *Developmentally Appropriate Practice*

- Chapter 3: Context Matters: Reframing Teaching in Early Childhood Education
- Chapter 6: Creating a Caring, Equitable Community of Learners
- Chapter 9: Teaching to Enhance Each Child's Development and Learning

Case Overview

Restorative justice in education includes the following six key areas: (1) defining misbehavior and a harm done to others, (2) expressing feelings in a dialogue for problem solving, (3) seeking restoration of relationships, (4) recognizing wrongdoing and misbehavior as an opportunity for learning, (5) giving all those affected voices in the restorative process, and (6) accepting responsibility (see Kulkarni & Chong 2021). This case provides an example of using a humanizing and restorative approach for young children to learn individual/classroom level responsibility and self-regulatory behavior during a kindergarten story hour. It illustrates a series of developmentally appropriate teaching strategies that draw from principles of restorative justice, using examples that can be modified and adapted for *all* young learners, including children with identified disabilities and children from culturally, racially, and linguistically diverse backgrounds.

Learning Objectives

1. Identify developmentally appropriate teaching strategies for helping children develop responsibility and self-regulation, drawing from approaches that humanize children's unique experiences and embrace restorative justice.
2. Explain ways to individualize approaches and strategies to help children recognize individual and classroom responsibility and self-regulate their behavior.
3. Contrast collaborative and cooperative approaches to behavior in the classroom that encourage a classroom community response with deficit-oriented approaches that problematize the individual child.

Case Narrative

Mr. Williams's kindergarten class includes students of diverse ability profiles, language backgrounds, and racial and cultural backgrounds. Jamal is a 5-year-old with a developmental disability in Mr. Williams's class who identifies as a Black boy and lives with his mother, grandmother, and baby sister. Jamal enjoys listening to stories and speaking up in class. His disability, however, sometimes also manifests in difficulty following instructions and communicating clearly with his peers. Mr. Williams identifies as a Black male without any disabilities.

Mr. Williams calls students to the rug to read *Whistle for Willie* by Ezra Jack Keats. A discussion will follow about the main character, Peter, who tries to whistle to his dog. Before starting to read, Mr. Williams starts by walking through expectations with the class.

"Before we start this story, let's talk about what we might expect during this reading time," says Mr. Williams. Esperanza, a dual language learner without identified disabilities, sits up on her knees and says, "Well, maybe we could raise the hand for question?" Mr. Williams gives Esperanza a high five and draws a picture of a student's hand being raised on chart paper at the front of the rug. He turns to the group, with an added hand-in-the-air gesture, "Yes, let's raise hands when we have a question or need to talk during the story."

Julio, a student with complex support needs, raises his hand next. Julio uses his iPad to communicate. Mr. Williams gives some extra time for Julio to compose a response: "I . . . like . . . the . . . sounds . . . but . . . they . . . can . . . be . . . loud. I like the sounds but they can be loud." Mr. Williams thanks Julio and agrees, "Yes, sound effects in the story can be fun, but sometimes they can also be too loud or startle us. How can we make sure that the sounds are fun for all of us?" Jamal's hand shoots up and, without waiting to be called on, he says excitedly, "Ohh, but what about the whistle in this story . . . like I can whistle!" Jamal lets out a small, screechy whistle. Some of the students, including Julio, put their hands on their ears. Mr. Williams smiles calmly at Jamal and says, "Wow, that's great, Jamal, but the whistle might be too loud for some of our friends if we don't wait until it's time. What can we do if we want to whistle during the story? Could we all try together when it's time?" Jamal squirms on the carpet and exclaims, "Yes!" Mr. Williams suggests, "Jamal, do you want to remind us when it is time?" He points to his watch as he asks this question. He also uses the chart paper to draw a clock. Jamal nods, and Mr. Williams asks students to get comfortable for the reading.

When the time comes to whistle, Jamal's hand shoots up and he runs to point at the clock. As he comes up to the chart paper, his leg kicks Esperanza's knee. She cries out, "Ouch, Jamal!" Jamal looks back and says, "It was on accident!" Mr. Williams counts to three silently and then responds, "Okay, Jamal, what might you say to Esperanza to tell her that you didn't mean to kick her when you came up to the front?" Jamal looks at Mr. Williams, then Esperanza, and says, "I'm sorry I kicked you on accident." Esperanza looks up and says, "It's okay." Mr. Williams thanks them both. "Thanks for solving this conflict so quickly. What's something we can all do to make sure we don't accidentally bump into each other on the rug?" Julio raises his hand and replies, "We . . . can . . . walk. We can walk." Mr. Williams repeats Julio's suggestion, "Yes, we can walk instead of run. Jamal, do you want to try again so we can all try out the whistle together?" Jamal slowly walks up to the chart paper and then pokes the clock picture. Mr. Williams asks Jamal to lead the next transition. "Excellent walking, Jamal. Can you tell us what it's time for?" Jamal faces the class and says, "It's time to whistle!" Mr. Williams leads the class together. "How about we try whistling together, everyone? Let me show you how we might do this." Mr. Williams does a countdown, showing his fingers and writing the numbers on the dry-erase board: "3, 2, 1." He then lets out a small whistle. "Whoa, you can do that?" say some students. Mr. Williams then gives the students an opportunity to practice whistling. He asks Jamal to lead the countdown this time.

Mr. Williams resumes reading the story. When Peter, the main character, learns to whistle, Mr. Williams pauses and asks, "Does anyone else feel like they want to whistle with Peter?" A couple of students squirm in their seats and say, "Yeah!" Mr. Williams counts them down using his fingers. "Okay, three, two, one . . ."

Later that afternoon, in his Class Dojo, an online communication tool to families, Mr. Williams shares that families might expect a few practice whistles at home. He also includes a video of the students when they whistle, with Jamal leading the countdown.

Takeaways and Next Steps

Mr. Williams uses several techniques to enact restorative or humanizing practices while simultaneously recognizing and celebrating a classroom filled with students of color, students with disabilities, and dual language learners.

First, Mr. Williams makes use of literature that centers diverse main characters and their experiences. His choice of literature allows his kindergarten students to make tangible connections to their own experiences. Second, Mr. Williams is able to turn a situation that could be perceived as challenging into a positive learning experience for the entire class.

Third, Mr. Williams's use of "three, two, one" serves a purpose both for himself in reacting to Jamal (taking three deep breaths) and to prepare students with expectations for participation in the story and whistling. He understands the importance of wait time for supporting children's various learning needs.

Mr. Williams also makes family connections by sharing what students learned in class and to expect that the students might try out their whistle at home.

Case Discussion Questions

1. Mr. Williams used several effective teaching strategies (Masterson 2022) in this situation. Describe how he used the following strategies:
    - Acknowledgment
    - Encouragement
    - Modeling
    - Offering specific feedback
    - Scaffolding
2. Which instructional strategies applied to Jamal do you think were most helpful or relevant in this learning context, and why?
3. Discuss Mr. Williams's approach to using a whole class discussion versus individually pulling Jamal aside and talking to him. What are some benefits and drawbacks of each approach?
4. What other approaches might Mr. Williams have used to address Jamal's behavior? What would have been the outcome of these approaches, and how might Jamal and the other students have been affected differently?

General Discussion Questions

1. Explore one or more of the suggested resources below. How can educators support humanizing behavioral goals with the whole class while also individualizing strategies to help students (1) understand how their behaviors affect others and (2) learn alternative ways to communicate specific needs within classroom spaces?
2. How can educators help students understand what their behaviors communicate in a safe, supportive learning environment?

Suggested Resources

Harris, M. 2021. "3 Restorative Practices for Classroom Conflict." Teaching Channel. www.teachingchannel.com/blog/restorative-conflict.

WeAreTeachers Staff. 2021. "What Teachers Need to Know About Restorative Justice." We Are Teachers. www.weareteachers.com/restorative-justice.

References

Kulkarni, S.S., & M.M. Chong. 2021. "Teachers of Color Implementing Restorative Justice Practices in Elementary Classrooms: A DisCrit Analysis." *Equity & Excellence in Education* 54 (4): 378–92. https://doi.org/10.1080/10665684.2021.2000519.

Masterson, M. 2022. "Teaching to Enhance Each Child's Development and Learning." In *Developmentally Appropriate Practice in Early Childhood Programs Serving Children from Birth Through Age 8*, 4th ed., NAEYC, 181–214. Washington, DC: NAEYC.

4.6 Joyful, Developmentally Appropriate Learning Environments for African American Youth

Lauren C. Mims, Addison Duane, LaKenya Johnson, and Erika Bocknek

Connections to *Developmentally Appropriate Practice*

- Chapter 3: Context Matters: Reframing Teaching in Early Childhood Education
- Chapter 7: Engaging in Reciprocal Partnerships with Families and Fostering Community Connections
- Chapter 9: Teaching to Enhance Each Child's Development and Learning

Case Overview

Wallace "Wally" Amos Jr. made his first homemade cookies with his Aunt Della when he was a child. Later, he would go on to create and sell Famous Amos chocolate chip cookies across the world (MacIntyre 2021, 2–3). To inspire African American children to dream big, learn important foundational skills, and cultivate relationships with their first and most important teachers—their caregivers at home—a team of child development researchers and educators asked families with young children living in the Midwest to work together to dream up a family cookie recipe using a box of materials sent directly to their homes. A researcher virtually observed and recorded the families working together. Through this activity, the researchers hoped to learn more about how learning, specifically cognitive development and domain-specific learning, occurs at home.

In this case, an African American mother works with her 6-year-old daughter to create the family cookie recipe. She uses developmentally appropriate practices as she builds her child's cultural knowledge by talking about her own experiences and perspectives.

Learning Objectives

1. Apply knowledge of high-quality learning experiences and intentional teaching strategies to an interaction between an African American mother and child.
2. Describe developmentally appropriate teaching practices occurring within an African American child's home learning environment.
3. Describe ways to connect home and classroom learning to craft meaningful, developmentally appropriate classroom experiences for African American youth.

Case Narrative

After opening their box of materials, which includes chefs' hats, aprons, cookie cutters, and recipe cards, one family begins to dream up a new cookie recipe and write it down.

Mom: No. Okay. So let's start first. Let's do the ingredients. I'll pick first. I want oatmeal in my cookie.

Child: Okay.

Mom: So is that the, yeah, ingredients? Oatmeal. O.

Child: How do you s-

Mom: Oatmeal.

Child: O-A-T-

Mom: Meal.

Child: M-E?

Mom: Mm-hmm (affirmative).

Child: L? A-L.

Mom: Mm-hmm (affirmative).

Mom: So sprinkles. Can you help me? I don't think I might know how to spell it.

Child: S.

Mom: Okay.

Child: P-I-

Mom: What-

Child: R?

Mom: Mm-hmm (affirmative).

Child: I-N-K-L-E.

Mom: Is that one sprinkle or two sprinkles?

Child: No, two sprinkles.

Mom: Is that singular or plural?

Child: Plural.

Mom: Good job. Okay. So oatmeal, milk, sprinkles. What else do we need? (*Reads what her daughter is writing.*) Wait, wait, wait. Does that make sense, "Put the ingredients the"? Put the ingredients. So what are we going to do? We going to—

Child: In.

Mom: Okay.

Child: In.

Mom: What I learned when I was . . . actually, I didn't learn until college, that you have to read things out loud to see if it makes sense. So when you're writing, you have to really read. Because if you was just writing it, you thought it was right. But when you read it out loud, "Put the ingredients the," you could see how it don't make sense. So always read it out loud, okay?

Child: Okay. So—

Mom: You're doing excellent.

Child: Thank you. So did my grandma teach you when you was little in school? Did she teach you how to read it out loud? Or no?

Mom: I learned that my freshman year in college. I just used to always just write. And then just figure out mistakes. But it's so much easier when you read it out loud.

Child: Well, do your teacher used to know you did that?

Mom: She is the one that told me. It's a professor in college.

Child: (*Reads the full sentence she wrote to find any mistakes.*) Oh. I—that's a "I" right there.

Mom: Okay.

Takeaways and Next Steps

This case example displays developmentally appropriate skills in a nonschool setting and highlights a family's existing strengths and cultural knowledge. Through play and developmentally appropriate interactions, the mother promotes listening, speaking, reading, writing, and vocabulary skills while also fostering her daughter's confidence. The case example demonstrates authentic, intentional teaching practices. Educators who build strong partnerships with families recognize that families' funds of knowledge, or existing strengths and capacities (Moll et al. 1992), increase children's educational achievement and emerging self-concept.

Case Discussion Questions

1. In this example, how does this rich parent–child interaction serve the learning, the purpose for learning, and the individual skills and strengths of the child?
2. Using the list of teaching strategies on pages 183–84 of *Developmentally Appropriate Practice* (Masterson 2022), identify the strategies this mom used to support her daughter's learning.
3. How and in what ways does this interaction draw on the cultural, social, linguistic, and community contexts that this child knows and experiences?
4. Does this case mirror learning strategies typically seen in the school setting? If so, in what ways? What is different about the learning seen in this case?
5. Did this case study challenge any biases you hold about learning contexts? How?
6. How might an educator build on and translate the practices illustrated in this case to the classroom setting?

General Discussion Questions

1. What does it mean for educators to learn from children's first teachers—their caregivers? How can that knowledge be translated to positive family–school relationships?
2. What other activities could build children's foundational skills and cultivate relationships, which enhances children's development and learning?
3. In Chapter 9 of *Developmentally Appropriate Practice*, the author writes in a vignette, "Ms. Encinas helps the children connect what she is reading to their own life experiences, knowing that doing so encourages deeper engagement and pleasure and enhances the children's learning" (Masterson 2022, 182). If connections to children's lives can increase engagement at school, how do you view the role that learning at home plays in children's overall trajectories? For example, do you view these experiences as similar, in that home-based connections in any context increase engagement with concepts, or do you

view unique processes taking shape through this vignette? Consider the role that learning at home plays in children's identity development as well as academic self-concept, and also consider how learning at home may build on itself through repeated experiences.

4. How can you apply, or continue to apply, a funds of knowledge approach to working with African American families and other families of color?

References

MacIntyre, J. 2021. *Cookie King, Wally "Famous" Amos: Mini-Biography of Famous Amos Cookies Founder*. Content Media Group.

Masterson, M. 2022. "Teaching to Enhance Each Child's Development and Learning." In *Developmentally Appropriate Practice in Early Childhood Programs Serving Children from Birth Through Age 8*, 4th ed., NAEYC, 181–214. Washington, DC: NAEYC.

Moll, L.C., C. Amanti, D. Neff, & N. Gonzalez. 1992. "Funds of Knowledge for Teaching: Using a Qualitative Approach to Connect Homes and Classrooms." *Theory into Practice* 31 (2): 132–41.

PART 5

Planning and Implementing an Engaging Curriculum to Achieve Meaningful Goals

Daniel R. Meier

At its foundation, developmentally appropriate curriculum requires careful and thoughtful planning of meaningful, engaging, and play-based activities, materials, and environments that stimulate children's holistic growth and learning. A well-designed curriculum for all young children also integrates critical features of child-responsive and culturally and linguistically responsive pedagogy. Meaningful learning outcomes are identified for children in all domains of development and content areas, as well as site- and program-specific learning goals for educators at the local, state, and national levels. Whatever curriculum a program or school follows, educators use their knowledge of the children and their teaching expertise to make adjustments to the curriculum that address children's individual needs in all areas of growth and development, maximizing learning for each child. An effective curriculum is never static; it is continually changing as educators seek to make meaningful connections in children's learning experiences, with the overall goal of creating a foundation for lifelong learning, play, and discovery.

The case studies in Part 5 cover a range of developmental areas related to curriculum planning, implementation, and reflection: social and emotional learning, language and literacy development, physical and motor growth, and cognitive and subject-matter learning. In these cases, children's play, curiosity, imagination, and interests are at the center of curricular conceptualization, planning, implementation, and reflection.

The case studies also focus on a range of specific issues and challenges that early childhood educators face in connecting theory and knowledge of curriculum to effective practice. These successful connections include

- An infant and toddler teacher "prioritizing social and emotional learning by supporting children's needs, telling social stories, and reading books about emotions" and using "co-regulation to scaffold emotional competence" (Masterson 2022, 226)
- A preschool teacher "infusing into the curriculum ways to help children recognize, label, and manage emotions" into the curriculum (232)
- A preschool teacher "selecting appropriate technology tools that integrate with the curriculum to extend and deepen learning" (236) through the use of early coding activities that foster student agency and problem solving
- A preschool teacher implementing emergent inquiry-based curriculum that emphasizes how children's "investigations have practical application and meaning in their lives" (221)
- A preschool teacher adapting outdoor spaces and scaffolding physical skills and socialization for a child with a disability through "ongoing adjustments that are responsive and individualized" (215–16)
- A preschool teacher describing the power of children's dual language learning in nature activities to illustrate key ideas for "supporting children in exploring interdisciplinary content more deeply and developing skills for collaborative learning and problem solving" (219)
- A kindergarten teacher describing and illustrating key strategies for choosing read-aloud texts with "rich and descriptive vocabulary" and the use of books "that reflect many diversities, help children identify with characters and themes, and discover new information, ideas, and experiences" (234)

A talented group of dedicated and committed early childhood educators, the authors of these cases all live and work in the San Francisco Bay area and represent the wonderfully rich tapestry of languages, history, cultures, and world views found in this region. Three of the authors grew up internationally, and all but one are multilingual speakers, readers, and writers. They include teachers and administrators working across infant and toddler programs, preschool programs, and kindergarten. The authors also represent a range of public and private/independent sites, English-medium and dual language programs, and programs supporting children with disabilities. All of the authors hold advanced degrees in early childhood curriculum, teaching, and/or leadership and advocacy, and their teaching experience ranges from 5 to 25 years. Two of the authors have published in the field of early childhood education previously, and the remaining authors are eager to contribute their first published work to advance early childhood educators' understanding of the place of curriculum in developmentally appropriate practice.

Reference

Masterson, M. 2022. "Planning and Implementing an Engaging Curriculum to Achieve Meaningful Goals." In *Developmentally Appropriate Practice in Early Childhood Programs Serving Children from Birth through Age 8*, 4th ed., NAEYC, 215–51. Washington, DC: NAEYC.

5.1 Using the Environment and Materials as Curriculum for Promoting Infants' and Toddlers' Exploration of Basic Cause-and-Effect Principles

Guadalupe Rivas

Connections to *Developmentally Appropriate Practice*

- Chapter 9: Teaching to Enhance Each Child's Development and Learning
- Chapter 10: Planning and Implementing an Engaging Curriculum to Achieve Meaningful Goals

Case Overview

This case study reflects the integration of developmentally appropriate materials and opportunities for infant exploration and how a curriculum is influenced by planning and in-the-moment decision making. Ms. Lupe works at a campus-based center that provides children with an emergent, child-centered, play-based curriculum to support their natural curiosity and exploration within a safe, supportive, and nurturing environment. Ms. Lupe and her colleagues carefully and thoughtfully plan play spaces and experiences that support curricular goals based on infants' and toddlers' play interests and talents "through both pre-planned, teacher-directed, intentional activities, and child-initiated, emerging play activities" (Shin & Partyka, 2017, 127).

From observations of Andy, who is almost 1 year old, Ms. Lupe notices Andy's increasing curiosity about the effect of his actions on objects and materials. She provides Andy with different opportunities and materials to scaffold his understanding of cause and effect. In this case narrative, Ms. Lupe introduces Andy to a long, clear tube, mounted to the wall and elevated at one end, which he explores by observing its physical properties and placing cars inside. Reading Andy's social and visual cues, and offering guidance only as he needs it, Ms. Lupe uses oral and nonverbal language to scaffold Andy's exploration of the tube and how objects move through it.

Learning Objectives

1. Describe ways to support infants and toddlers in routines and interactions to develop trust and confidence.
2. Explain how providing materials, time, and scaffolding for an infant's or a toddler's environment promotes exploration of how actions have an impact on (cause) what happens (effect).

Case Narrative

At almost 1 year of age, Andy stands on his own but is not walking yet. Ms. Lupe notices that he is starting to throw toys and other objects and watches as they land on the floor. Andy will throw objects from the top of the infant loft and roll them down the loft ramp. When he is standing, he will pick up an object and raise his arm to throw it, and sometimes the object will land on a peer. Ms. Lupe wants to provide Andy with additional, safer ways to explore cause-and-effect relationships.

The dramatic play/block area in the infant classroom has a long see-through plastic tube fastened to the wall so that it is elevated at one end to make an incline (see the photo on page 105). The teachers put the tube in this fixed position so that children can put materials inside it and see what happens: Which ones fit in the tube? Which ones don't fit? In which end of the tube should you try to put an object if you want it to move through the tube? Which objects move through the tube? Which objects don't? Some objects slide, some objects roll. Some objects need a push, some objects don't.

Ms. Lupe wants to encourage Andy to roll wooden cars inside and down the tube to support his understanding of cause and effect and to give Andy an opportunity to continue to build his trust in her by interacting with him one-on-one. Ms. Lupe places a car inside the tube, and Andy watches as it slides down and exits the other end. "Bye-bye, car," Ms. Lupe says as the car rolls down. Andy crawls to the end of the tube and picks up the car. He places it on the bottom of the tube, but it rolls back down almost immediately since it has only a short distance to roll. Ms. Lupe says, "Andy, look!" and rolls another car from the top of the tube. Andy picks it up and puts the car in the space between the tube and the wall. He laughs and looks at Ms. Lupe. She claps, smiles, and says, "Yay!"

A few days later, Ms. Lupe notices Andy standing in front of the clear tube and holding a car. It is the first time he appears interested in the tube without her prompting. He holds the car in his left hand (his nondominant hand) and places it in the tube, but he seems to have a hard time opening his hand in the tube so he can let the car go. He pulls out his hand and tries again. Andy furrows his brow and babbles. "Andy, are you frustrated because the car isn't going in the tube?" Ms. Lupe asks. He looks at her and babbles some more. Wondering if it might be easier for Andy to let go of the car if he uses his dominant hand, Ms. Lupe says, "Try again. Try your other hand." Andy looks up at Ms. Lupe as she speaks but does not respond to this suggestion. After a few more tries, Andy is able to put the car in the tube and let go of it, but it gets stuck because the car is on its side. Andy puts his whole hand through to push the car, and the car goes halfway down. "Yay! Andy, you did it! You pushed the car through!" Ms. Lupe says enthusiastically. Even though the car did not roll all the way down, Ms. Lupe still wants to celebrate Andy's efforts to explore cause and effect by manipulating the car so it would fit into the tube.

The following week, Ms. Lupe notices that her group of children are becoming more interested in balls. She decides to focus the curriculum on balls and also ties that focus to Andy's interest in the tube. At the time, Ms. Lupe has only soft balls and bouncy balls the size of a volleyball. She orders some smaller plastic balls that fit inside the tube. Ms. Lupe thinks Andy will have an easier time rolling the balls than the cars, though he will still have the choice of both materials. Ms. Lupe hopes that Andy will feel successful if he can place the ball inside and watch it roll all the way down. This might keep up his motivation to try the cars again and to make a further connection to cause and effect.

The following week, Ms. Lupe invites Andy back to the tube to see if he prefers the ball or car to roll down the tube. She wonders if he has made the developmental connection that rolling the ball is not as challenging as setting the car on its wheels in the tube to roll down. She also wonders if he knows that rolling the ball in the tube always has the same results. Ms. Lupe offers Andy the car first, and he tries to place the car inside the tube. When he can't, he tries it with his other hand. Although Ms. Lupe thinks that Andy might be able to open his hand on the first try and let the material go if he uses his dominant hand, this does not seem to be the case. He is also still working on understanding that the car needs to be on its wheels when he lets go to make the car roll down the tube. Eventually, Andy throws the car on the ground, and Ms. Lupe offers the car and ball to him. He takes the car but then drops it to pick up the ball. He places the ball into the elevated end of the tube and watches it roll down the tube. About three weeks has elapsed since Ms. Lupe first introduced Andy to the tube. After this, when given the option between the ball and the car, Andy almost always chooses the ball.

Takeaways and Next Steps

This case narrative reflects how play, when initiated by young children, can also be "educationally focused, directed by the teacher or parent to reach specific educational goals" (Zigler & Bishop-Josef 2006, 22) as part of an emergent curriculum for infants and toddlers. During the initial tube interaction, Andy doesn't seem to understand that placing materials at the top of the tunnel makes them slide down to the other end. When Andy shows signs of frustration, Ms. Lupe provides responsive caregiving—an example of "reflecting and validating a child's feelings and behaviors" to help "very young children make sense of their world" (Darling-Kuria & Bohlander 2014, 94). While Ms. Lupe continues to invite Andy to experiment with objects in the tube, eventually Andy explores it on his own. Ms. Lupe uses Andy's interest in things that move and cause and effect to strengthen his cognitive, physical, self-regulation, and relationship skills.

Ms. Lupe can also extend this activity by reading books about objects that roll and move, singing and moving to songs about emotions, and writing a social story and Learning Story on Andy's tube exploration for Andy's family. Ms. Lupe can also provide Andy and his peers with different-sized materials to help the children differentiate between objects that fit or don't fit into the tube and build on each other's actions, essentially extending the curricular play and exploration toward the beginning stages of classification.

As often happens in emergent curriculum planning for infants and toddlers, Ms. Lupe does not expect to create a month's curriculum on cause and effect for her whole group of children initially based on Andy's interest in the tube. Throughout the month, the children roll balls down an open ramp and through a tunnel ramp; participate in water sensory activities and hit water with their palms, causing water to splash; create music by shaking rattles or hitting notes on a xylophone, and use a sticky wall to stick and pull materials off it.

Case Discussion Questions

1. In her actions and language over the three weeks, how does Ms. Lupe help integrate self-regulation, language, cognitive, and social competencies for Andy?
2. How is principle 8 of the position statement on developmentally appropriate practice reflected in this narrative?
3. How did Andy's exploration of basic cause-and-effect principles inform Ms. Lupe's thinking in planning curriculum to achieve a meaningful goal?

General Discussion Questions

1. What is the value for infants and toddlers of exploring cause and effect through objects in the environment?
2. What is the value of teachers closely interacting with infants and toddlers to inform their curriculum planning and implementation?

Suggested Resource

Escamilla, I.M, L.R. Kroll, D.R. Meier, & A. White. 2021. *Learning Stories and Teaching Inquiry Groups: Reimagining Teaching and Assessment in Early Childhood Education*. Washington, DC: NAEYC.

References

Darling-Kuria, N., & A.H. Bohlander. 2014. "Promoting Social-Emotional Development: Helping Infants Learn About Feelings." *Young Children* 69 (3): 94–96.

Shin, M., & T. Partyka. 2017. "Empowering Infants Through Responsive and Intentional Play Activities." *International Journal of Early Years Education* 25 (2): 127–42. https://doi.org/10.1080/09669760.2017.1291331.

Zigler, E.F., & S.J. Bishop-Josef. 2006. "The Cognitive Child Versus the Whole Child: Lessons from 40 Years of Head Start." In *Play = Learning: How Play Motivates and Enhances Children's Cognitive and Social-Emotional Growth,* eds. D.G Singer, R.M. Golinkoff, & K. Hirsh-Pasek, 15–35. New York: Oxford University Press.

5.2 Social Play Connections Among a Small Group of Preschoolers

Leah Catching

Connections to *Developmentally Appropriate Practice*

- Chapter 10: Planning and Implementing an Engaging Curriculum to Achieve Meaningful Goals

Case Overview

Three children have been together for three years in a toddler program with the same teacher, and they are all now together in the preschool program. The children often choose to play together and are learning to navigate each other's emotional expressions and occasional biting and hitting behaviors. The teacher (and author of this case study) responds to their emotional and social needs by incorporating self-regulation activities and environmental changes. These changes support this small group with prosocial peer interactions and emotional regulation as the children learn to recognize their peers' emotional signals.

Learning Objectives

1. Describe ways to support peer dynamics for children experiencing big emotions.
2. Explain ways to plan for and adapt small environmental changes that support social, emotional, and linguistic skill development in peer relationships.

Case Narrative

Cassie, Simone, and Elena, all age 3, are in a small group together. They transition from routines and activities together, sit at the same table for meals, and often choose to play together during self-directed play.

The lead teacher, Teacher Leah, observes that Cassie has begun to bite and hit her peers when she becomes overwhelmed or upset. As a result, Simone and Elena start choosing activities without Cassie and often walk away when Cassie expresses her emotions by screaming, biting, or hitting. During these times, Cassie wants to engage with her peers even more, creating a more challenging situation for all three children. Teacher Leah and her coteachers note that this behavior occurs throughout the day. They begin addressing the situation by helping Cassie label her emotions and offering a variety of words for Cassie to use, such as *angry, mad, frustrated,* and *upset*. In addition, the teachers observe that Simone is starting to have big emotional reactions when her peers want to engage in activities different from what she wants, and Simone often runs away from them screaming and crying. If a teacher approaches to help, Simone often says, "Go away," and runs to a new spot.

In reflecting with her teaching team, Teacher Leah notes that many children in the class have been enjoying the yoga stretches and breathing at the beginning of large group time. The teachers also share observations about the physical space and note that many of the classroom spaces that see conflict are limited to two peers at a time. Using these observations, Teacher Leah and her coteachers decide to address the small group of girls' needs by implementing two practices: yoga with deep breathing and altering the classroom environment to better suit the needs of the group.

First, Teacher Leah tries yoga and deep breathing exercises with the whole class and separately with the small group of three girls. The small group especially loves practicing the deep breathing technique that the teachers and children call "lion's breath," where the children take a big breath in and breathe out a roar with their mouths open wide. The children practice both loud and quiet roars together. The teachers help children practice their lion's breath when they begin to feel overwhelmed, guiding them through breathing in and out by modeling it for the children and practicing with them. After a few weeks, the children remind each other to use lion's breath when they are upset, echoing the same language and modeling practices the teachers use. Cassie and Elena remind Simone by saying, "Simone, breathe. Like a lion." Simone practices the deep breathing regularly. Simone even begins to do the breaths on her own, saying to herself "lion breath" each time she becomes upset instead of running away. Then, Simone and Elena prompt Cassie to try it when they notice her feeling overwhelmed, often saying, "Cassie, it's okay—breathe, like this" as they breathe in and out. It does not work as consistently with Cassie, but because Cassie's peers are supporting her in moments of stress and big emotions, Cassie turns less frequently to screaming, biting, or hitting when she becomes upset.

Teacher Leah and her coteachers reflect on the classroom physical environment and what changes they can make to better support social interactions for the small group and the whole class. They adapt the classroom so that each child can expect more one-on-one time with their preferred peer and set up spaces to be available to more children at a time. During group time, Teacher Leah and the children talk about the changes that will be made in the classroom and she shows them the new labels for each area that are changed to "For 3 Children" instead of "For 2 Children." Teacher Leah rearranges the meal tables so Cassie and Simone each sit on one side of Elena, their preferred peer. Teacher Leah sits at the table with them during lunch and asks how they feel about their new spots. Cassie, Simone, and Elena tell Teacher Leah that they like their new spots. Over time, Teacher Leah and her coteachers notice that all three children engage in more conversations with each other during mealtimes.

Teacher Leah also adds a third set of materials in their most-visited spaces, like the dramatic play kitchen and the loft, to support the extension of the play between the children to include all three girls. While Cassie, Simone, and Elena notice some of these changes, at first Teacher Leah supports their play by showing them the new materials available and the spaces where all three children can play together. She remains close by as the three girls begin to navigate three-person dramatic play scenarios. Teacher Leah provides guidance and language for the children to use and often points out that it is possible for all three children to engage with the same materials together.

As Cassie, Simone, and Elena realize that there are enough materials and space for them all, their play happily expands beyond a two-person interaction, especially during their dramatic play. Their role-playing as a parent and a baby becomes either two parents and a baby or a parent and two siblings, usually with one child directing the other two. They also extend their play to include animals, and one child will often be the pet owner while the other two choose which pet they want to be.

Takeaways and Next Steps

This narrative connects to the social and emotional development of young preschool-age children, as mentioned in Chapter 10 in *Developmentally Appropriate Practice*: "Educators create spaces and provide materials . . . that help children develop their social and emotional skills" (Masterson 2022, 232). In this narrative, the teacher also demonstrates her ability to "infuse into the curriculum ways to help children recognize, label, and manage emotions" (232).

This case example reflects the teacher's focus on supporting the social and emotional development of a small group of preschool children. This group has been with the same teacher and with each other for three years. Teacher Leah, who has primarily worked with infants and toddlers, has to reflect on her teaching practices and how to adapt these to fit the needs of this group of children as they grow and develop. As new expressions of emotions emerge, the dynamic of the group begins to change, creating more challenging situations for the three children. Teacher Leah and her coteachers also give the children developmentally appropriate tools to regulate their emotions and model the language and behaviors; with repetition and support, the children begin to support each other with reminders. The environmental changes eventually enable the trio of children to engage in more complex play together with more collaboration and joy.

Case Discussion Questions

1. What is the value of the teachers in this case brainstorming new opportunities and strategies to supplement and extend their curriculum around social and emotional learning, play, and language?
2. In terms of the teachers' curricular planning and adaptations, how is this case an example of integrating children's developmental capabilities for friendship, social interaction, and problem solving?
3. In what ways did Teacher Leah and her teaching team "create spaces and provide materials . . . that help children develop their social and emotional skills" (Masterson 2022, 232)?
4. What additional forms of verbal and nonverbal language can Teacher Leah and the other teachers provide to help children develop their own ways of supporting their peers during emotional moments?
5. What information could these teachers have gathered about the children's problem-solving and conflict resolution skills? How might they have incorporated this information into the program's overall social emotional and language curriculum?

General Discussion Questions

1. How does the careful shaping of indoor and outdoor environments support child-responsive, developmentally appropriate curriculum to promote children's social, emotional, and linguistic development?
2. What tools and materials in the early learning environment can support children's self-regulation? How can these tools empower children to support each other in a time of need?
3. What is the role of teacher collaboration and dialogue to problem solve new possibilities for enhancing the curriculum to further support children's prosocial learning and friendships?

Reference

Masterson, M. 2022. "Planning and Implementing an Engaging Curriculum to Achieve Meaningful Goals." In *Developmentally Appropriate Practice in Early Childhood Programs Serving Children from Birth Through Age 8*, 4th ed., NAEYC, 215–51. Washington, DC: NAEYC.

5.3 Can Preschoolers Code? A Sneak Peek into a Developmentally Appropriate Coding Lesson

Olabisi Adesuyi-Fasuyi

Connections to *Developmentally Appropriate Practice*

- Chapter 10: Planning and Implementing an Engaging Curriculum to Achieve Meaningful Goals

Case Overview

Ms. Stephanie's class of 4-year-olds is learning about life cycles. Ms. Stephanie follows her students' interests by planning a study on the life cycle of chickens that will make rich connections across multiple domains and subject areas. The children explore the topic through photographs, videos, manipulatives depicting the different stages of a chicken's life, and a visit from a local farmer who brings in chickens and several other animals. The class even partners with a farm to hatch baby chicks in a small incubator at the school.

Throughout the year, Ms. Stephanie incorporates coding activities as part of her classroom's curriculum to provide students with more opportunities to practice and master new concepts. This case study focuses on one of the coding lessons with a small group of children who review the life cycle of a chicken, using the classroom robot named Dash. The students have engaged in multiple step-by-step playful coding lessons without a robot before Ms. Stephanie introduced Dash. In addition, prior to this lesson, the students have used Dash during self-directed play and as part of other weekly activities.

Learning Objectives

1. Explain strategies to introduce early coding skills that offer children experiences that integrate communication, thinking, and problem solving.
2. Articulate a plan for effective ways to support student learning through the creation and editing of a sequence of instruction.
3. Describe a learning environment that uses STEM (science, technology, engineering, mathematics) integration to foster collaboration and problem solving through the use of multiple tools.

Case Narrative

Ms. Stephanie's classroom rug is set up with white rectangular lapboards placed together, a robot, an iPad, and diagrams showing the life cycle of a chicken. As the children come into the classroom from outdoor recess, they squeal, "Dash!" as they see the setup on the rug.

Ms. Stephanie says, "Okay, if you want to play with Dash, wash your hands and join me at the rug." Soon Bruce, Angela, and Cynthia come over while others play at different play centers in the classroom. The three students at the rug hold the iPad, each trying to get the first turn. Ms. Stephanie claps five times, and the students all quiet down and clap five times.

Ms. Stephanie: (*Turns to the three students at the rug.*) Okay, I know you are all excited to play with Dash today, but what do you think we will do with Dash today?

Children: (*Hands go up in the air.*)

Ms. Stephanie: Bruce?

Bruce: We are going to teach Dash the life cycle of a chicken. Look, look, he has to go to the egg first. (*Points to the robot.*) And then the robot will go all the way to the chicken. (*Gets to his feet, excitedly pointing out the path the robot will take to the chicken.*)

Ms. Stephanie: Thank you, Bruce; you may sit down now. Who would like to use the iPad to show Dash where to go?

Children: (*Hands go up in the air.*)

Ms. Stephanie: Angela, come on over. Now we all need to help by teaching Dash what happens at each stage of the life cycle of a chicken.

Angela: (*Sits by the teacher, picks up the iPad, and places the robot by the picture of eggs in a nest.*) Dash will start here.

Ms. Stephanie: Can you tell us why?

Angela: Because the life cycle of a chicken starts from an egg—the hen lays an egg and then after 21 days a baby chick comes out. (*Moves a rectangle block to the bottom of the iPad screen with her finger.*)

Ms. Stephanie: Angela, can you tell us what you are doing?

Angela: I am trying to tell Dash how to get to the egg, but I have to think about it first. (*Pauses.*) He goes forward, I think, then he will go two steps, and then turn this way one time. (*Motions right.*)

Ms. Stephanie: How do you tell Dash what to do using the iPad?

Cynthia: Ms. Stephanie, you have to connect Dash to the iPad using Bluetooth and then you have to put the start block down to the bottom of the screen so that when you press enter, Dash knows it's time to start.

Ms. Stephanie: Great, look, Angela has the start block at the bottom. Can we hit that start button now?

Two other children, Sophie and Cindy, join the other three children on the carpet.

Angela: I have to tell Dash what to do before I hit the start button. See . . . (*Stands up and points at Dash.*) Dash has to take . . . (*Pauses.*) Hmm, two steps forward, make one . . . hmm, if he turns this way, is it right or left?

Cindy and Cynthia: That's right.

Cynthia: Just one right turn or Dash will go in circles. (*Spins her head around as she speaks.*)

Angela uses her finger, pulls the "move forward" block, and stacks it on the start block. She repeats this action and now has two steps of "move forward" blocks.

Cindy: Now Dash has to turn right once. (*Puts one finger up.*)

Angela pulls the "turn right" block and adds it to the stack of "start, move forward, move forward" blocks.

Ms. Stephanie: What if we try those instructions first and see where it takes Dash?

Angela: Okay. (*Hits the go button and Dash moves a few steps forward, makes a right turn, and then turns off the lapboards.*)

Children: Oh, no!

Ms. Stephanie: Great try, Angela. It's okay if you don't get it right the first time; you just have to keep on . . .

Children: Trying and never give up!

Ms. Stephanie: I love how you were thinking, Angela; you tried to estimate how many steps Dash needs to take to get to the right spot for a right turn. Estimation is a great way to make an educated guess, and if you don't get it right the first time, you just try again. Who would like a turn?

Children: (*Raise hands.*)

Ms. Stephanie: We're going to start again. Come on over, Sophie. Now remember, we all have to work together to help Sophie and Dash.

Cindy: (*Whispers.*) Let's make Dash take only one step forward.

Sophie: Wait, I have to think and estimate it for Dash. (*Stands and uses her hand to measure the space between Dash and the picture of eggs in a nest.*) Yes, just one step forward.

Sophie picks up the iPad and moves the "start block" to the bottom of the screen. She pulls down the "move forward" block and stacks it on the start block.

Ms. Stephanie: Okay, what do we do next?

Angela: Pull the right turn down. Just one time, okay?

Sophie: (*Pulls down the "right turn" block and stacks it on the "start" and "move forward" blocks.*) Can I press the start button now?

Ms. Stephanie: Sure.

Sophie hits start. Dash moves forward, takes a right turn, and stops right in front of the picture of the nest of eggs.

Children: (*Cheer excitedly.*)

Ms. Stephanie: (*Smiles.*) You all did great working together to help Dash. Now before we help Dash move to the next picture, let's talk about what happens to the chicken eggs. Do all eggs hatch into chicks?

Children: No.

Ms. Stephanie: So what happens to the egg? We will start with Sophie.

Sophie: First the hen has to lay an egg that fertile.

Ms. Stephanie: It's called *fertilized.* That means an egg that has everything it needs to hatch into a chick, right? Okay, Cynthia, what happens next?

Cynthia: Then the hen has to sit on it for 21 long days.

Ms. Stephanie: Why does the hen have to sit on the eggs for so long?

Bruce: So she can keep it warm, like the incubator is keeping our chicken eggs warm.

Ms. Stephanie: So why do the eggs need to stay warm?

Angela: So the chick can start to grow inside the egg. First it has a red spot, and then every day it just changes and grows its head, wings, legs, everything, and when it's 21 days a baby chick comes out—it's all done.

Ms. Stephanie: Awesome, okay, do you think I should increase the temperature in the incubator so the chicks hatch faster?

Children: No!

Cindy: It can't be too hot, no, just the right temperature or it will become boiled egg.

Children: (*Giggle.*)

Angela: We have to be patient, Ms. Stephanie, and not make it too hot.

Ms. Stephanie: Okay, we will be patient. We will wait for the eggs to stay in the incubator for 21 days at the right temperature. I think it's time we help Dash move to the next picture.

Takeaways and Next Steps

Ms. Stephanie has learned that connecting the intentional use of coding with children's daily lives helps them recognize and understand how to identify a problem, gather information, and make decisions to solve it. As children learn to code, they communicate and build on their vocabulary (Lee & Junoh 2019). In this case, Ms. Stephanie uses problem solving, group work, visuals, discussion, and technology tools to extend her students' learning of scientific concepts and processes. She knows, for instance, that using a robot will engage the students in active problem solving in a group setting and deepen their involvement with the scientific process of making multiple attempts to observe and understand physical and scientific phenomena. In addition to the initial curricular planning of this project, Ms. Stephanie uses observation and reflection to ensure that all students have the opportunity to engage in the lesson and experiment with the technological tools. Her observations allow her to uncover some of the more problematic aspects of using technology; for example, with only one iPad, students have to wait for a turn, and some of them do not get a chance to use the iPad to code.

Using new forms of technology for developmentally appropriate learning in the early years goes beyond simply pushing buttons and finger slides. Early coding activities offer children experiences in integrating communication, thinking, and problem solving. While Ms. Stephanie is thrilled to see how much her students have learned, she also identifies opportunities to be more intentional with her questioning techniques to support students' use of directional language.

Case Discussion Questions

1. How might Ms. Stephanie have advanced the learning objectives included in the case? For example, what might Ms. Stephanie say when Bruce answers that they are going to teach Dash the life cycle of the chicken or Dash will go first to the egg?
2. What else could Ms. Stephanie say to Angela after her unsuccessful attempt to move the robot the way she intended to help her revise her thinking and try another plan?
3. What else could Ms. Stephanie say to the students after Sophie's successful attempt?
4. How did Ms. Stephanie integrate children's learning within and across emotional, social, linguistic, and cognitive developmental domains?
5. What else could Ms. Stephanie have done to facilitate the children's higher-level thinking skills?
6. How does this narrative highlight the role of discussion and playful learning within a classroom community to support children's learning as part of a STEM curriculum?

General Discussion Questions

1. How might precoding be integrated in other curricular areas such as art, math, science, and physical movement?
2. What are the implications of this case study for your use of plugged and unplugged technology in your teaching practice, whether current or future?
3. How can the developmentally appropriate use of technology and coding support children's social and emotional development and cooperative learning?
4. What guidelines and principles can educators keep in mind to ensure equitable gender access to technology in preschool?

Reference

Lee, J., & J. Junoh. 2019. "Implementing Unplugged Coding Activities in Early Childhood Classrooms." *Early Childhood Education Journal* 47 (6): 709–16. https://doi.org/10.1007/s10643-019-00967-z.

5.4 **Everyday Gifts: Children Show Us the Path—We Observe and Scaffold**

Martha Melgoza

Connections to *Developmentally Appropriate Practice*

- Chapter 6: Creating a Caring, Equitable Community of Learners
- Chapter 10: Planning and Implementing an Engaging Curriculum to Achieve Meaningful Goals

Case Overview

This case study is written by a preschool director of a parent cooperative school who is also a teacher there. It illustrates key ideas for a curriculum that "includes interdisciplinary connections" (Masterson 2022, 220). The school follows an emergent inquiry-based curriculum that emphasizes how children's "investigations have practical application and meaning in their lives" (221). The narrative explores how children's engagement with the outdoors can be integrated in a school's emergent curriculum when teachers provide children the space to think, move, talk, and interact on their own. The outdoor space, then, allows for movement of mind and body through playful interaction with the environment and peers.

Learning Objectives

1. Describe how to support connections between curriculum content and children's explorations of the world around them.
2. Describe ways to use observation, analysis, and reflection to apply principle 3 of the position statement on developmentally appropriate practice.
3. Explain ways to support play and its key components (choice, wonder, and delight) that arise from children's everyday conversations.

Case Narrative

This case study describes and analyzes how Teacher Martha, a veteran early childhood teacher/director of a parent cooperative school, supports children's thinking and problem solving, respecting their ideas and using intentionality to organize and support developmentally appropriate learning environments for the children's play, interaction, and self-discovery. Teacher Martha also has a great deal of experience using the processes of observation, inquiry, documentation, and reflection to refine curricular goals and strategies to support children's emergent interests. In this narrative, Teacher Martha describes the children's play and discoveries and reflects on her reasons for observing and interacting with the children and the overall meaning and value of these actions for supporting play and the environment as the foundation for developmentally appropriate emergent curriculum.

The case specifically describes the children's learning in an outdoor play area. The school site is surrounded by a nature area that includes a hillside, a view of the bay, and a dirt and wood chip area for the children to run and play. During the COVID-19 pandemic, the school's classrooms were outdoors. The teachers and families utilize the outdoor spaces as a nurturing and inviting environment for play and social interaction, where child-initiated discoveries and problem solving are supported. The teachers and families view every environment as a third teacher (Edwards, Gandini, & Forman 2011) and revel in the immediate access to varying "curriculum" (e.g., the offerings nature provides that differ from indoor learning) and the feeling of freedom outdoors.

Teacher observation is critical for understanding how to plan certain elements of the curriculum and for supporting children's interests as they arise within the emergent curriculum framework. During the long pandemic, for instance, the teachers and families noticed that being outside calmed everyone; this environment provided a powerful new learning space for social and emotional growth, physical development, and discoveries about nature education and science. The change of seasons alone made for a joyful and natural engagement for children with their surroundings and the larger world around them. Through careful observation, the teachers and families learned to adjust the curriculum to children's interests and use thoughtful questions and other small, specific scaffolding strategies to support and extend children's interests and discoveries.

There are two enormous piles of wood chips left over from 10 trees cut down in the outdoor space, which the children love to climb. One day, the teachers, families, and children visit the wood chip piles and bring chalk for the children to use on the nearby pavement. The children immediately gravitate to interesting explorations: some draw with the chalk; one categorizes the chalk by size, shape, and color; others run to the wood chip pile; and still others go exploring. Teacher Martha notices the children discussing their activity and play choices and notes Oliver's discovery of a hole in the asphalt to investigate. As this child's discovery motivates others to join in, Teacher Martha continues to observe the children's interactions in play, noting the depth of the children's engagement as they explore the hole with their fingers and considering possible prompts and strategies to use to validate and extend the children's language, interactions, and nature interests.

Oliver: (*Gestures toward the hole.*) There could be worms!

Cort: Or monsters.

Oliver: Or monsters, but I think worms . . . or bugs . . .

Alden: How do we get them?

Oliver: We need tools. Teacher Martha, can we go back inside to get some shovels?

Teacher Martha: Not right now . . . we need to wait for Annie to come back with the other kids.

Oliver: But we cannot wait.

Teacher Martha: I am sorry to hear that. I wonder what you could use to help you explore your hole.

The teacher's comment here validates the children's immediate interests and motivation to explore. It also extends the children's potential actions and tool use to support their collaborative exploration of the hole.

Oliver: Well, it's really a tunnel.

Teacher Martha: Okay. My mistake. What could you use to explore your tunnel?

The teacher again uses an open-ended question to prompt children's thinking and problem solving around possible tools to find or adapt to extend their collaborative play and discovery making.

Alden: A stick.

Cort: Yeah. A stick . . . but it could break.

Oliver: We won't break it. Go find sticks, everybody.

Alden, Cort, Mia, and Irene search for sticks while Oliver stays behind to watch over the tunnel. Soon, Irene and Mia give up on the stick search and decide to go back to their chalk drawing. Cort get sidetracked with sorting the chalk by color and shape. Alden is left to find a stick. He finds two and brings them to Oliver.

As they dig and poke around in the tunnel, Oliver and Alden talk of bugs, worms, and monsters. The monster conversation leads to a conversation about nightmares they have had and how those are not good. Their conversation flows from one topic to the next with no interruption in the digging or exploring of the tunnel. As she observes, Teacher Martha realizes that there is a certain level of harmony in the children's play and social interaction and that her direct scaffolding is not needed at the moment. She continues her close observation and physical proximity to the children.

Cort brings his chalk over near Teacher Martha and asks to sit on her lap. Together they sit and listen to Oliver and Alden as they chat. Picking up on the conversation about nightmares, Cort comments to Teacher Martha that he sometimes has nightmares too. Irene says nightmares are scary and then you can't get to sleep unless you go to your parents' bed. Cort agrees. Will they have nightmares about the monster in the tunnel, they all wonder? Oliver, still looking for worms but unable to find any, chimes in.

Oliver: No, because there is no real monster in the tunnel. Worms are not going to get into your nightmares. They are not scary. They only make soil healthy. We have to get the worm out of here and over to the soil so it can get healthy.

Collectively, the children recall that the last time they were out here with a parent, they found worms. Then there is a sudden flurry of memories from the children.

Child: And another time we played hide-and-seek.

Child: And remember, we climbed the hill and almost got stuck.

Child: And we jumped in the mud puddles.

Child: Remember, Teacher Martha, we also made those designs with rocks and flowers and sticks.

Child: Then one day Liyan helped me climb up the rock wall, but he could not get Kaila up there, so she practiced climbing the fence to get roses.

Mia: Remember when we rode our bikes out here in the rain! That was fun.

Child: Remember the trees!

Child: And then they cut them!

Child: That is bad!

Oliver: And good. Teacher Martha said they were sick and dead and the church needed to cut them down.

Child: Remember the tree that fell on the church?

Child: And the wood chipping.

The children's conversations keep evolving and returning to memories of learning and discoveries in the outdoor nature area. An important aspect of emergent curriculum, their shared reminiscences support and solidify nature-based content learning as well as their sense of community. Teacher Martha realizes that these kinds of important connections usually come about when children feel connected to each other and to the environment and are in close physical proximity with teachers for comfort, trust, and problem solving and scaffolding as needed.

Oliver and Alden never do find a worm on this day . . . or a monster. They do, however, have a great deal of fun and want to come back another day to look for the worm. The children and adults take a group walk around the property as the children play a variety of chase and imagination games. They climb the wood chip pile and sit atop it as they wonder if it will rain tonight and provide jumping puddles for tomorrow . . . "Like last time, remember?" someone chimes in.

Takeaways and Next Steps

As a veteran educator, Teacher Martha has many years of experience intentionally organizing learning spaces, using observation, taking notes, and judging when to insert herself into a play sequence and when to step back, all with the goal of respecting children's play interests while mindfully supporting collaborative problem solving and content learning. Trust and openness within the collective group form the backbone for emergent curriculum for this age group, and it is important for teachers to provide certain kinds of open-ended supports for children's play, interaction, and talk. For example, Teacher Martha uses an "I wonder" statement ("I wonder what you could use to help you explore your hole") (Sisk-Hilton 2020) to help the children build their understanding of the world around them and their connections to it (principle 5 of the position statement on developmentally appropriate practice). Given that learning does not divide itself by academic domains (principle 7), thoughtfully conceptualized and implemented emergent curriculum plays an important role in connecting children's interests with play-based discoveries and collaborative problem solving.

Case Discussion Questions

1. How does this experience reflect guideline 5, especially 5D, of the position statement on developmentally appropriate practice? How does the children's revisiting of past outdoor experiences help further their understanding of the natural and physical phenomena they are observing? What else could Teacher Martha do to facilitate this?
2. What learning goals might Teacher Martha have had for this day's experiences? How can she build on what the children discovered, talked about, and learned?
3. How do the children themselves build into their community of learners, and what does the teacher do in terms of observation and direct support of their collaborative play and discoveries?
4. How is this narrative an example of a developmentally appropriate learning environment that motivates and enables children to make discoveries individually, with other children, and with adults?
5. In terms of principle 3, what is the value of Teacher Martha's use of observation, close physical proximity, and open-ended questions for promoting joyful learning, self-regulation, and content knowledge?

References

Edwards, C., L. Gandini, & G. Forman, eds. 2011. *The Hundred Languages of Children: The Reggio Emilia Experience in Transformation*. 3rd ed. Westport, CT: Praeger.

Masterson, M. 2022. "Planning and Implementing an Engaging Curriculum to Achieve Meaningful Goals." In *Developmentally Appropriate Practice in Early Childhood Programs Serving Children from Birth Through Age 8,* 4th ed., NAEYC, 215–51. Washington, DC: NAEYC.

Sisk-Hilton, S. 2020. "Science, Nature, and Inquiry-Based Learning in Early Childhood." In *Nature Education with Young Children: Integrating Inquiry and Practice*, 2nd ed., eds. D.R. Meier & S. Sisk-Hilton, 11–30. New York: Routledge.

5.5 Learning to Conquer the Slide Through Persistence and Engaging in Social Interaction

Sueli Nunes

Connections to *Developmentally Appropriate Practice*

- Chapter 6: Creating a Caring, Equitable Community of Learners
- Chapter 9: Teaching to Enhance Each Child's Development and Learning
- Chapter 10: Planning and Implementing an Engaging Curriculum to Achieve Meaningful Goals

Case Overview

The early learning program described in this case study uses a play-based approach to support children's social competence, positive approaches to learning, and the preacademic skills children need to succeed as learners. This case study looks at the efforts of a group of teachers who individualize the outdoor curriculum to nurture engagement, agency, and joyful learning for 3-year-old Daisy, a dual language learner with mobility challenges. The author and narrator of the case, who is the coeducation director, served as a participant observer collecting data and documenting the child's actions outdoors.

This case study describes and illustrates key strategies that "create spaces and provide materials. . . that help children develop their social and emotional skills" (Masterson 2022, 232). The case specifically emphasizes the value of supporting Daisy's physical exploration in outdoor play areas, illustrating that "educators actively seek to ensure that all children, including those with disabilities, are included in social relationships, play, and learning experiences; they model and provide support where needed" (Wright 2022, 132). The overall goal is to provide scaffolded opportunities for Daisy to develop important physical skills, such as grasping and climbing, and socialization with peers through the teachers' "ongoing adjustments that are responsive and individualized" (Masterson 2022, 215–16).

Learning Objectives

1. Describe ways to individualize curriculum planning around outdoor activities for a child with mobility challenges.
2. Identify interactions that help build children's confidence through participation in physical activity outdoors.

Case Narrative

Daisy was born with a tailbone disorder that caused a delay in walking. She started as an infant at the Family Developmental Center, part of a nonprofit social services provider, and has received early intervention services since then. As a toddler, Daisy used a walker to support and facilitate her walking. However, before moving to a preschool classroom at age 3, she started showing progress in balancing her body and walking independently by pulling her legs and moving slowly.

During the transition to the preschool area, her mom and the new teachers are concerned that the outdoor yard, which has a large play structure and spacious areas, might intimidate Daisy and restrict her exploration and learning. To support Daisy, her mother, the teachers, and the early interventionist team spend two weeks bringing Daisy to the preschool yard during the afternoons when it is calm and only a few children are present. In her first month as a preschooler, Daisy prefers to crawl on the yard's rubber surface. As she gets used to the yard, she starts walking independently and exploring the environment confidently. Her favorite area is the sandbox, and she would crawl out of it to observe other children climbing the play structure or riding bikes.

One day, I go into the preschool yard to observe how Daisy is exploring the environment and engaging in social play as well as her interactions with the teachers. Before I observe how Daisy explores the outdoor environment, I speak with her teacher, Ms. Maya, who is supervising one area of the yard near where Daisy is playing. She mentions that Daisy is doing well and playing more and more with her peers. Ms. Maya mentions that Daisy is playing with Amelia, who is carrying a small exercise mat.

As I approach Daisy, Amelia points to a blue slide, looks back at Daisy, and walks toward it. Amelia approaches the slide from the chute end and quickly climbs up the top. Daisy slowly follows her and starts to climb up the chute, but she slips back and makes a frustrated sound. I approach her and ask if she needs help. Daisy says "Sí," and I start guiding her.

I put my hands on the side of the slides while I talk to her. "Hold both hands on the side of the slide."

Daisy follows my guidance and starts climbing. Then, she slips back down again and makes the same frustrated sound. I stand next to the slide and say to her, "I am next to you; you can try again." Daisy goes up again. As she climbs and her legs spread apart, she loses her balance. I keep encouraging her and show her where to hold on the slide. "I am next to you," I say. "Hold your hands to the side and keep your legs together." Daisy adjusts her legs and brings them close together. I reassure her by saying "Yes, like that" and give her a thumbs-up.

This time Daisy starts climbing the slide slowly. She pauses, looks at me, and keeps climbing up the slide. Daisy rests when she reaches the top and looks at Amelia, who quietly waits for her. I say to Daisy, "You made it all the way up by yourself!"

Amelia places the small exercise mat she brought up with her in front of Daisy and points to the picture on the mat. On the mat, it says "Toe Touch" and shows an illustration of a child demonstrating the toe touch. Daisy looks at it, stretches her legs, and touches her toes.

After that, Amelia sits on the edge of the slide and says to Daisy, "Vamos" (Let's go). Daisy sits next to her, and they slide down next to each other. Amelia walks toward the spiral steps leading to a climber from which the slide can be accessed, and Daisy follows her. Amelia quickly climbs the steps. Daisy approaches the spiral steps and starts climbing them. She becomes frustrated and says to Ms. Maya, "Ayuda" (help). Ms. Maya approaches and supports Daisy to climb the steps by keeping her right hand close to Daisy's body while she goes up. Ms. Maya encourages Daisy by saying, "Puedes hacerlo" (you can do it).

When Daisy gets to the top of the play structure, she sees Amelia next to the big red slide. Daisy does not follow Amelia and instead walks toward the small blue slide and goes down alone. While sitting at the bottom of the slide, Daisy spots a bubble station and walks toward it. She approaches the table and says, "Quiero bubble" (I want bubble).

Ms. Linda, who supports this activity, points to the wands on the table and says, "Please choose a wand." Daisy chooses a green wand, dips it slightly into the tray of bubble solution, and swings it. No bubbles appear, and Daisy says, "No bubbles." Ms. Linda says, "You need to dip the wand in the liquid." She demonstrates for Daisy. Daisy keeps trying, but few bubbles appear. Daisy approaches the table again and watches Ms. Linda demonstrate to other children how to dip the wand in the liquid. Daisy looks very attentive, observing the motions.

Daisy tries again, firmly dipping the wand deeper into the bubble solution while holding on to the table to keep her balance. She moves away from the table and swings the wand. Her eyes brighten as she sees the bubbles flying around. As she keeps dipping the wand deeper into the bubble solution, her bubbles become larger and larger. She pops some with her other hand while saying, "Bubbles."

As I stand next to her, I say, "You are making huge bubbles, Daisy; you are a pro." Daisy continues to make and pop bubbles with the other children.

Takeaways and Next Steps

Research shows that children need to be active in developing healthy habits and supporting their cognitive, social, and emotional development (Kinsner 2019). This case study highlights the benefits for children of playing outside and exploring materials and activities that enhance their curiosity, social engagement, and physical development. It also emphasizes the role of both adults and children's nonverbal and verbal communication and interactions to facilitate physical, social, and emotional growth for young children with disabilities.

The case further illustrates how close observation and timely support from educators can help children with disabilities rely on their agency, strengths, and interests. In terms of the next steps, it's important to continue supporting Daisy's physical exploration and social inclusion and using suitable forms of documentation that teachers can share with Daisy and her family. Further, since Amelia positively influenced Daisy's engagement in outdoor play, the teachers might pay close attention to how Amelia or other children encourage and support Daisy so they can plan for including them more intentionally in activities with Daisy.

Case Discussion Questions

1. How does the environment support Daisy to develop her gross and fine motor skills?
2. In what ways did the teachers individualize the outdoor curriculum for Daisy?
3. What role do other children, such as Amelia, play in Daisy's physical exploration and social interaction?
4. What else could the adults have done to support Daisy's communication and physical skills?
5. How could the teachers use documentation of Daisy's efforts to further support her physical exploration and social inclusion?

General Discussion Questions

1. How would you respond in developmentally appropriate ways to a child who is struggling while engaging in challenging tasks?
2. In planning outdoor curriculum for young children with physical disabilities and delays, what is a developmentally appropriate balance of risk and safety?

References

Kinsner, K. 2019. "Rocking and Rolling. Fresh Air, Fun, and Exploration: Why Outdoor Play Is Essential for Healthy Development." *Young Children* 74 (2): 90–93. Washington, DC: NAEYC. www.naeyc.org/resources/pubs/yc/may2019/outdoor-play-is-essential.

Masterson, M. 2022. "Planning and Implementing an Engaging Curriculum to Achieve Meaningful Goals." In *Developmentally Appropriate Practice in Early Childhood Programs: Serving Children from Birth Through Age 8*, 4th ed., NAEYC, 215–51. Washington, DC: NAEYC.

Wright, B.L. 2022. "Creating a Caring, Equitable Community of Learners." In *Developmentally Appropriate Practice in Early Childhood Programs: Serving Children from Birth Through Age 8*. 4th ed., NAEYC, 111–44. Washington, DC: NAEYC.

5.6 "Sabes que todos los caracoles pueden tener bebés? Do You Know that All Snails Can Have Babies?" Supporting Children's Emerging Interests in a Dual Language Preschool Classroom

Isauro M. Escamilla

Connections to *Developmentally Appropriate Practice*

- Chapter 4: Teaching Content in Early Childhood Education
- Chapter 8: Observing, Documenting, and Assessing Children's Development and Learning
- Chapter 10: Planning and Implementing an Engaging Curriculum to Achieve Meaningful Goals

Case Overview

This case study describes and illustrates how children in a dual language public preschool program, fourth grade students, and teachers embark on an emergent project on snails that reflects developmentally appropriate practices for responding to children's interests. An emergent curriculum approach emphasizes using multiple media and a variety of forms of representation within long-term investigations. This case also highlights how teachers and children can collaborate on inquiry-based learning that is centered on children's individual and group interests and questions (Masterson 2021).

The focus of this case study originates from a half dozen snails provided to the preschool class by a fourth grade teacher, Ms. Kristen, who teaches at an elementary school adjacent to the preschool. The preschool children's eager curiosity serves as a catalyst for teachers in preschool and fourth grade to support their inquiry, exploration, and learning of specific living organisms. Working alongside the preschool children, the fourth-graders take on the role of topic experts to explain the significance of snails in a healthy garden environment. The fourth-graders also create dual language visuals that further support the preschoolers' interests and learning in a joyful manner. This case study affirms that when learning is meaningful and relevant, children are more engaged and eager to learn: "With self-agency, they make active choices and take responsibility for their effort and progress" (Wright, Counsell, & Tate 2015 in Masterson 2022, 219).

Learning Objectives

1. Describe ways to individualize curriculum planning and provide effective support for dual language learners (DLLs) to foster active engagement, self-agency, and joyful learning.
2. Explain how early childhood educators can support content learning in developmentally appropriate ways for young children.

Case Narrative

The preschool children are eagerly anticipating this moment—the snails' arrival in the classroom in a small see-through container. Ms. Kristen, the fourth grade teacher who has kindly offered the small creatures as pets to the preschool teachers and children, has plenty of advice. Ms. Kristen comes in with three of her students, Melany, Daniel, and Aaron, who were in this very same preschool classroom almost five years earlier. The preschool children gather around the small table to take a closer look at the "familia de caracoles" (snail family), as 4-year-old Keyben describes them. The children excitedly offer their first impressions, and Keyben asks numerous questions.

Keyben: ¡Están bien bonitos! Qué comen los caracoles? ¿Porqué unos caminan y otros no? ¿Dónde están los pies? No se los puedo ver. ¿Muerden? ¡Mira, ese va dejando baba por donde pasa! ¿De dónde le sale la baba, de la boca o de la cola? ¿Cómo se llama lo de arriba? Yo creo que unos caracoles quieren dormir. ¿Y dónde están los ojos? ¿Son niños o son niñas?

(They are very nice! What do snails eat? Why do some walk, and others don't? Where are their feet? I can't see them. Do they bite? Look, that one is leaving drool where it goes! Where does the drool come from, from the mouth or from the tail? What is the name of the thing on the top? I think some snails want to sleep. And where are their eyes? Are they boys or girls?)

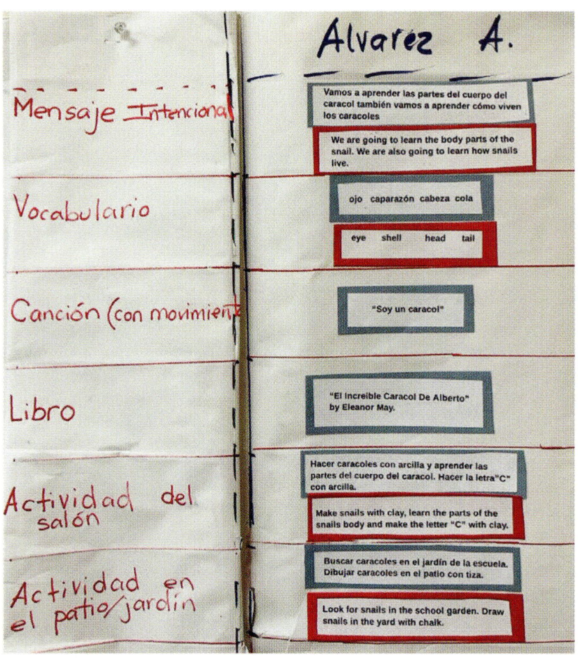

In just a few minutes, Keyben's questions and comments provide the teachers with many ideas that will guide their curriculum planning for the next several weeks. These questions launch the teachers and children on an exploration of a real-life event and concrete topic that children can explore in their immediate environment. So begins an emergent nature and art curriculum that also uses Personalized Oral Language Learning (POLL) strategies (Oliva-Olson et al. 2019). Following this process, teachers select a book, focus on certain vocabulary, and use other key POLL elements (see the poster shown at left). This particular POLL plan is created by preschool teacher Ms. Alicia with support from her two coteachers, Ms. Sahara and me. Ms. Sahara and I also design our own POLL plans based on the interests and learning dispositions of the small group of children (between five and eight children) we are each working with. A nonfiction book will help children familiarize themselves with specific words such as *tentacles, slime,* and *shell* (*tentáculos, baba,* y *caparazón*) while a song or chant will help children internalize the meaning of the words with movement/gestures associated with the new words.

During the snail investigation, a dance and movement teacher works with the children 30 minutes a week. I ask her to help the children understand how snails move and to speak with them about the body parts of a snail. I make this request because the children will be making sketches of the snails, and I think it will be beneficial for them to have a clearer understanding of the characteristics of snails. In this playful context, the children learn about how snails extend and retract their neck, how they use their one foot to drag themselves forward, and how the slime they produce facilitates their mobility.

During the investigation, which integrates a study of nature, science concepts, POLL elements, and dual language use, the children make and revise several observational drawings and paintings on paper and canvas and create mini-sculptures with modeling clay that represent their fascination with the snails.

To help the children represent their emerging understandings and the knowledge they are coconstructing, we ask them to create acrylic paintings on canvas, a process that takes several days.

At the end of the investigation, the preschoolers explain in a video for their classmates what they have learned about the snails and how they represent that knowledge in their paintings. What follows is their commentary while showing their paintings. Some children speak in Spanish; others express their ideas in both Spanish and English.

Keyben: Los caracoles ponen huevos, las hembras y los machos. Es el huevo de un caracol en una hoja. Los caracoles ponen huevos y cuando sean más grandes van a poner más huevos. (Snails lay eggs, the females and males. This is the egg of a snail on a leaf. Snails lay eggs and when they are bigger they will lay more eggs.)

Daniel: Yo me llamo Daniel y yo hice un caracol y este es su pie y la cabeza y estas son las antenas. (My name is Daniel and I made a snail and this is its foot and head and these are the antennae.)

Keyri: Hola. Yo me llamo Keyri. Hice un dibujo de los caracoles que viven en el agua y en la tierra. Y este es el cuello y estos son los tentaculos. Me gusta tanto mi caracol por qué eres tan hermoso. Y esta es su concha. (Hello. My name is Keyri. I drew a picture of the snails that live in water and on land. And this is the neck and these are the tentacles. I like my snail a lot because it is so beautiful. And this is her shell.)

Alice: Hola, yo me llamo Alice, este es mi caracol. Yo hice un caracol y los caracoles producen una baba para arrastrarse y para moverse. (Hello, my name is Alice and this is my snail. Snails produce slime for crawling and walking.) (*Says later, in English.*) Hello. My name is Alice. This is my snail. The snail is . . . um . . . slime. For walk. (*Makes a trail with her hand.*)

Sara: Hola, me llamo Sara y estoy pintando el caracol. Y saben que come el caracol? Come lechuga y toma agua. Y vive con su familia. (Hi, my name is Sara and I'm painting the snail. And know what the snail eats? He eats lettuce and drinks water. And lives with his family. (*Says in English.*) Hi, my name is Sara and I'm painting the grass and the snail. But you know how, what the snails, they eat? They eat grass, lettuce, and they drink water.

Ms. Kristen, the fourth grade teacher, has told the children that the snails' preferred meal is fresh tomato leaves, but 9-year-old Melany shares that her pet snails at home really like lettuce but not cucumbers or tomato leaves. We decide to listen to Melany and see what our snails prefer. We skip the tomato leaves and discover that our snails like cucumbers but love spinach and lettuce much more.

The fourth-graders happily share their knowledge of snail behavior with the younger children. For example, 9-year-old Daniel explains that snails are hermaphrodites.

Keyben: Y que quiere decir eso? (And what does that mean?)

Daniel: Quiere decir que los caracoles—ya sean boys or girls, o mejor dicho machos o hembras—pueden poner huevecillos and tener babies. (It means that both boy and girl snails—or better said, male and female snails—can lay eggs and have babies.)

Keyben: ¡Que bonito! (How cool!) (*Continues to observe the snail on the table and wonder aloud what other details she can add to her drawing of the snail.*)

Later in the project, the fourth-graders create a bilingual book to share with the preschool children their expertise on snails. The preschool children continue learning more about the snail life cycle in hopes that, very soon, they will see tiny snail eggs in the terrarium they have built to host the familia de caracoles.

During the project, the children realize that the small plastic container isn't big enough for all the snails. After some brainstorming, we decide to use a discarded fish tank to make a terrarium. They help pour in a pound of gravel for drainage, four pounds of rich soil, and 10 bean seeds (Melany has explained that snails also like to eat bean sprouts), which they carefully sprinkle with water to keep them moist.

Takeaways and Next Steps

"Curriculum planning focuses on (1) selecting *what* to teach (the content) and (2) designing *how* to teach (pedagogy) . . . to motivate engagement and to ensure all children gain the desired understandings, knowledge, and skills associated with the curricular goals" (Masterson 2022, 217). Designing and implementing curricular activities derive in large part from the ways in which teachers are fully present and interact with children and the explicit and intrinsic perceptions they have of them as learners. Early childhood educators who are aware of the potential significance of small moments are keenly cognizant of the world around them from the child's point of view; become partners with children in the teaching and learning process; and emphasize documenting, analyzing, and reflecting on data through multiple media and forms of representation.

Being present requires teachers to pay attention to the dynamics of the classroom, the ways in which teachers and children relate to one another, and how teachers observe and support children in their explorations and discoveries. This is especially important in dual language classrooms, where teachers must be aware of how children use their linguistic talents in everyday conversations. The teachers in this study notice and document how children put into practice the exploration and integration of their dual language and creative capabilities. Further, the teachers organize the data they collected (photos, children's comments, teachers' insights, video clips) and create a narrative of the learning that took place. This narrative study is an example of making sense of the data, including analysis and reflection.

Case Discussion Questions

1. How did the teachers integrate a developmentally appropriate emergent curriculum with artistic and visual representation?
2. How did the preschool children benefit from collaborating with the fourth grade children? How did the older children benefit?
3. How did the focus on nature include other subject areas and developmental domains?
4. How did the teachers integrate support for DLLs into the curriculum in an organic way?

General Discussion Questions

1. How can teachers required to follow a particular curriculum integrate children's interests into their lesson plans, providing choice and agency?
2. What is the role of observation and documentation in curricular planning and implementation in emergent curriculum?

References

Masterson, M. 2021. *Transforming Teaching: Creating Lesson Plans for Child-Centered Learning in Preschool.* Washington, DC: NAEYC.

Masterson, M. 2022. "Planning and Implementing an Engaging Curriculum to Achieve Meaningful Goals." In *Developmentally Appropriate Practice in Early Childhood Programs Serving Children from Birth through Age 8*, 4th ed., NAEYC, 215–51. Washington, DC: NAEYC.

Oliva-Olson, C., L.M. Espinosa, W. Hayslip, & E.S. Magruder. 2019. "Many Languages, One Classroom: Supporting Children in Superdiverse Settings." *Teaching Young Children* 12 (2): 4–7.

5.7 "Can We Read this One?" A Conversation About Book Selection in Kindergarten

Larissa Hsia-Wong

Connections to *Developmentally Appropriate Practice*

- Chapter 6: Creating a Caring, Equitable Community of Learners
- Chapter 9: Teaching to Enhance Each Child's Development and Learning
- Chapter 10: Planning and Implementing an Engaging Curriculum to Achieve Meaningful Goals

Case Overview

In this case I explore critical literacy's assertion (Freire & Macedo 1987) that children can and should be equipped with the tools and strategies to critique, challenge, and disrupt dominant and racist narratives, discourses, and ideologies, and how this relates to several of the early literacy principles of developmentally appropriate practice. In this example, I integrate the developmentally appropriate practice of creating a culturally responsive literacy curriculum through read-aloud book selection with two kindergarten children. Critical literacy is "an evolving repertoire of practices of analysis and interrogation which move between the micro features of texts and the macro conditions of institutions, focusing upon how relations of power work through these practices" (Comber 2013, 589). (See "Critical Literacy" on page 128.) The case narrative specifically focuses on the parts of the position statement on developmentally appropriate practice that highlight choosing curricular materials and resources that serve as windows and mirrors to build on each child's funds of knowledge. Books that serve as windows encourage children to see into the lives of those who live and identify differently from them; books that serve as mirrors reflect a child's own life, identity, and experiences.

Prior to the conversation captured below, our class had done extensive work on understanding and unpacking identity around gender, race, and ability. Creating a classroom grounded in anti-bias pedagogy begins on the first day of school and consists of embracing critical discussions; creating a learning environment that honors children's questions and stories; and committing and modeling continuous personal critical self-reflection to identify my own biases, blind spots, and understandings I need to unlearn. At this point in the year, the children and I have already engaged in many conversations about how books can serve as windows and mirrors. Part of these lessons and discussions include teaching and modeling possible sentence stems, or starters, for children to use as they share their thinking about books, such as "I identify as . . . The character identifies as . . ." and "I notice that the author/character . . . It makes me wonder . . ."

Learning Objectives

1. Identify ways to plan authentic curriculum experiences that build on children's funds of knowledge.
2. Describe ways to incorporate the components of play (choice, wonder, and delight) during academic conversations with children.

Case Narrative

After helping Otto and Casey, this week's Library Liaisons, tidy up the classroom library, Ms. Larissa invites them to choose the class's read-aloud books for later in the week. In the following exchange with the two children, Ms. Larissa refers to the classroom's READ-O board. (The READ-O board is inspired by BING-O reading sheets that encourage children to read a wider variety of books. It contains descriptors that intentionally focus on author and character identity and encourages children to choose and read a diverse range of picture books during read-aloud times.) Whenever the class reads a book that meets a READ-O square, they add a sticky note to the board with the book's title. The critical reader poster referred to below is an anchor chart on critical reading that highlights six minilessons that guide children when thinking and talking about books (see the photo at left).

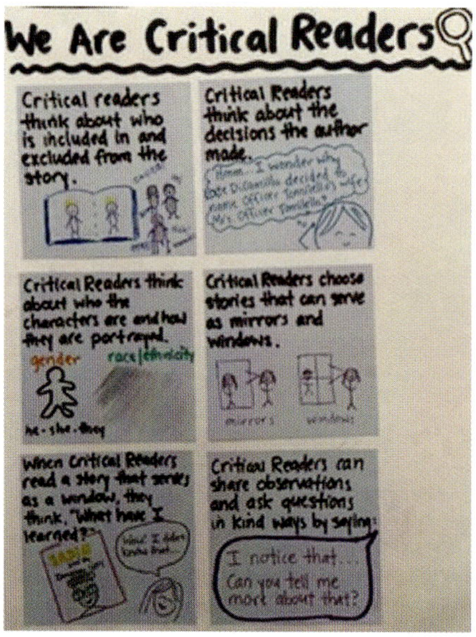

"Let's look at our critical reader poster and our READ-O board," Ms. Larissa says while gesturing to the two resources. "What books do you think we should read next as a class?"

After taking some time to browse through the book bins, Otto and Casey share their suggestions.

"Oooh, I think we should read this one," Otto says enthusiastically, holding up a copy of *Change Sings* by Amanda Gorman.

"What draws you to that book, Otto?" Ms. Larissa asks.

"I noticed the main character seems to identify as Black and on READ-O, it looks like it's time for us to read a book with a character who identifies as Black so we can learn more. Well, at least for me I could learn more because this book will be a window for me," Otto says, using several previously taught sentence frames.

"Great idea! It will be a window for me too! What are you thinking about, Casey?"

"Can we read this one?" Casey asks, holding up a copy of *Goldy Luck and the Three Pandas* by Natasha Yim.

"What interests you in that book, Casey?" Ms. Larissa asks.

"It looks really funny and, also, I think it is about Chinese New Year. See this page? There's a *hongbao* (red envelope), and my family is getting ready to celebrate it soon. And maybe after we read it, I can share some things I know too?" he asked, looking at Ms. Larissa expectantly.

"I love that!" Ms. Larissa says.

"Don't you celebrate Chinese New Year too? Maybe you can share too!" Casey says to Ms. Larissa.

"I do celebrate it, but now I'm too old to get hongbao, heh! And you know what, Casey? I've learned to call it 'Lunar New Year' because the festival is celebrated by many people and not all of them identify as Chinese," Ms. Larissa explains.

"You mean, it's kind of like how we can't just think everyone celebrates Christmas and just say 'Merry Christmas?'" Otto asks.

"Oh yeah, I remember! We can't do assumptions!" Casey chimes in.

"Exactly, we want to make sure we don't *make* assumptions about anyone's identity and that the words we use make everyone feel included," Ms. Larissa explains. "Casey, I love your idea about how we can invite people to share afterward!"

"Yeah! That would be so cool!" Otto says to Casey. "Part of my family celebrates it too, the part that comes from Malaysia."

"Malaysia? I didn't know they celebrated it too. Wow!" exclaims Casey.

"I can't wait to learn how your family in Malaysia celebrates the Lunar New Year. I can tell we are all going to get a chance to learn a lot from each other. These are great book suggestions, friends. Thank you for your help! I can't wait for our class to read them together!"

Takeaways and Next Steps

As a teacher of young children, I often feel the need to have everything planned, to direct all of our classroom and learning interactions (especially those with more serious and complex topics, such as identity and racism), and to have all of the right answers. However, my experience with Otto and Casey reminds me of the profound and authentic learning and growth opportunities that stepping back can provide. Giving Otto and Casey the opportunity and agency to choose our next read-aloud books allows me to connect with them in a way I might have missed. Giving them the space to build on their relationship with each other that centers their identities and their experiences enables them to connect in a more personal yet unforced way. The experience encourages me to think of how else I can follow children's leads and build in more opportunities for them to share authentically about themselves and learn from others. When joyful curiosity is expressed and nurtured, the bonds and connections between children and teachers become stronger, and the classroom becomes a true community grounded in authentic relationships that supports the growth of each individual.

Contrary to popular belief that they are too young and thus are incapable of engaging in complex and meaningful discussions, research shows that young children can comprehend complex issues such as race and racism (Fontanella-Nothom 2019; Piper 2019). Young children notice differences early on and pick up and internalize stereotypes and dominant narratives if these are not intentionally pointed out and discussed. Teachers who discuss these critical issues in an intentional way and honor children's knowledge and meaning making can help all children create a caring culture in which all selves and identities are embraced. Additionally, engaging young children in critical discussions on race provides them with cognitive, linguistic, and social models to identify, dismantle, and challenge biased and unjust ideas and information. Creating opportunities in which children can express and articulate their identities, learn about how others may identify, ask questions, and engage in dialogue at a younger age to develop their critical literacies is advantageous. As Vasquez, Janks, and Comber (2019) remind us, there is no one right way to engage in critical literacy; rather, it is most important for individual teachers to create our own way with our own voices.

Case Discussion Questions

1. Why is it important to help children develop critical literacy? Draw on specifics from the case narrative.
2. In what ways does Ms. Larissa employ principle 6 of the position statement on developmentally appropriate practice?
3. In what ways does Ms. Larissa plan a curriculum experience that builds on the funds of knowledge of Otto and Casey to offer culturally and linguistically sustaining literacy experiences?
4. Based on the discussion that Ms. Larissa has with Otto and Casey, what are some specific strategies, materials, or activities she could use to follow up on this conversation with the rest of the class?
5. Although this conversation does not take place during a play-based scenario, in what ways are the components of play (choice, wonder, and delight) integrated into the conversation?
6. Was Ms. Larissa's explanation of the term *Lunar New Year* necessary? How else could she have responded to the children to further develop their critical literacies in ways that are both child responsive and culturally responsive?

General Discussion Questions

1. What are some other ways teachers can incorporate meaningful and authentic conversations around complex curricular concepts such as identity, bias, and racism?
2. How can the framework of viewing books as windows and mirrors support identity-based conversations in a classroom? What might be some challenges or limitations to this approach?

References

Comber, B. 2013. "Critical Literacy in the Early Years: Emergence and Sustenance in an Age of Accountability." In *The SAGE Handbook of Early Childhood Literacy*, 2nd ed., eds. J. Larson & J. Marsh, 587–601. Thousand Oaks, CA: SAGE.

Fontanella-Nothom, F. 2019. "'Why Do We Have Different Skins Anyway?' Exploring Race in Literature with Preschool Children." *Multicultural Perspectives* 21 (1): 11–18. https://doi.org/10.1080/15210960.2019.1572485.

Freire, P., & D. Macedo. 1987. *Literacy: Reading the Word and the World*. Westport, CT: Bergin & Garvey.

Luke, A., & P. Freebody. 1999. "The Four Resources Model for Literacy." *Practically Primary* 4 (2): 5–8.

Piper, R.E. 2019. "Navigating Black Identity Development: The Power of Interactive Multicultural Read Alouds With Elementary-Aged Children." *Education Sciences* 9 (2): 1–12. https://doi.org/10.3390/educsci9020141.

Street, B. 2001. "The New Literacy Studies." In *Literacy: A Critical Sourcebook*, eds. E. Cushman, M. Rose, B. Kroll, & E. Kintgen, 430–42. New York: Bedford/St. Martin's Press.

Vasquez, V.M., H. Janks, & B. Comber. 2019. "Critical Literacy as a Way of Being and Doing. *Language Arts* 96 (5): 300–11.

Critical Literacy

Critical literacy maintains that all texts, as products of social, political, and cultural contexts, inherently deal with power and can serve as potential sites for transformation and liberation (Freire & Macedo 1987; Luke & Freebody 1999). Therefore, a critical literacy approach in a classroom creates opportunities for students to acquire the tools and strategies to critically examine texts, identify and problematize dominant narratives and discourses, and consider how the language of the texts perpetuates hegemonic ideologies (Street 2001). Proponents of critical literacy maintain that literacy education cannot be simply limited to teaching functional literacy skills; it must also include the skills and strategies to dismantle inequitable and oppressive systems of power.

PART 6

Demonstrating Professionalism as an Early Childhood Educator

Christyn Dundorf

Working with children and families in early childhood settings is among the most difficult and yet most rewarding service commitments. To bring to one's early childhood work an intentional awareness of and engagement with the complexity and entirety of developmentally appropriate practice elevates that practice to both an art and an exercise verging on impossibility. How, then, might an educator ever expect to realize the potential of developmentally appropriate practice?

In Part 6, the case writers suggest that the elements of professionalism make this possible. Professional early childhood educators are lifelong learners, seeking opportunities to engage with others to explore ideas and work through challenges. Professional educators also sustain their engagement and learning in the field through reflective and intentional planning and work with children and families. The first case in Part 6 shares ways in which a positive, supportive coaching relationship can build a teacher's confidence with new approaches and can expand perspectives on practice. The second case weaves together the interests, experiences, and needs of the children in the author's classroom with both the instructional expectations of her district and her commitment to nurturing the engagement of families in their children's education. The third case underscores the importance of ensuring that the voices of educators—those who know the realities of the everyday work—help inform early childhood policy decisions. The elements of professionalism portrayed in these case studies—lifelong learning, reflective and intentional practice, and professional advocacy—as well as the support provided to the early childhood professional by the NAEYC Code of Ethical Conduct and the thoughtful, intentional use of technology as a tool for communication and learning can help early childhood educators realize the potential of developmentally appropriate practices in their work settings and beyond. All of the cases describe experiences and opportunities that involve taking an extra step, a step away from the easy or predictable—to participate in a coaching relationship, to extend curriculum in child- and community-focused ways, or to advocate on behalf of the early childhood field. In each case, this professional risk taking, though challenging, is rewarded with confident classroom practice, with vibrant engagement of children and families, and with authentic consideration of provider needs.

These authors bring diverse backgrounds and experiences to their case studies. Throughout their careers, they have held roles as teachers, special educators, coaches, program directors, professional development providers, policy associates, presenters, and advocates for children and families, educators, and the early childhood profession. The authors hail from different areas of the United States and represent different sectors of the field (preschool, elementary education, and professional development/early childhood product support). Their diverse histories illustrate some of the multiple professional pathways traveled by those who seek to support the care and education of young children.

6.1 Take a Chance on Coaching: It's Worth It!

Lauren Bond

Connections to *Developmentally Appropriate Practice*

- Chapter 1: Intentional Teaching: Complex Decision Making and the Core Considerations
- Chapter 11: Demonstrating Professionalism as an Early Childhood Educator

Case Overview

This case explores how coaching relationships, a component of a commitment to lifelong learning for educators, support teachers' growing reflective and intentional practices for their classroom communities. These practices are vital for adapting standardized curricula to fit children's individual characteristics and experiences and to fit the social and cultural contexts of children, families, educators, and programs. In this case, the coach reflects on the elements of a coaching relationship that supported one teacher in implementing a statewide early childhood curriculum.

Learning Objectives

1. Identify the risks and rewards of participating in a coaching relationship to support professional practices.
2. Examine personal responses to observations of one's professional practice as well as reactions to constructive feedback.
3. Identify sources of potential mentoring and coaching support to grow one's reflective and intentional professional practice.

Case Narrative

Setting the Scene

In 2019, Maryland introduced an early childhood curriculum, Children Study Their World (CSW). CSW, developed at the University of Maryland, emphasizes project-based learning and playful exploration. The curriculum "consists of eight interdisciplinary, content-rich projects that build upon children's knowledge and increase in complexity. Each project supports children's common understanding of a topic and nurtures their innate sense of curiosity and discovery about their world" (University of Maryland 2018). The curriculum aligns with NAEYC's nine principles of child development and learning. Maryland also offers the Early Learning Assessment (ELA), and CSW includes a collection of activities and experiences aligned with this assessment tool.

During the curriculum pilot, programs were eligible for a year of coaching support; I was assigned to three preschool teachers at a multiage center in suburban Maryland. As a coach, one of my goals is to help teachers fit the curriculum and assessment to their community of learners. If children aren't responding as a teacher thinks they should, the teacher takes ownership to make a change or shift, using their professional knowledge of how children develop and learn, knowledge of individual children, and understanding of context.

I want teachers to experience personal growth through coaching. When teachers get a window into their practice through the coaching visits and observations and can reflect openly, they identify ways to productively change their practice. Coaching creates vital time and space for collaborative processing and reflection.

Charlie Ann Wright, one of the teachers at Wee Lad and Lassie, has three years' experience in the pre-K and 3-year-old rooms. I met with Charlie biweekly to monthly for one to two hours. Generally, I would observe a component of the day, such as a read-aloud. Then Charlie and I would debrief while the children had choice time. I would type up my observations and notes of our discussions, including what we shared and Charlie's reflections. These notes served several purposes: they helped me track our progress and reflect on possible next steps, ensured that the director was aware of our discussions, and reminded Charlie of our next meeting and planned areas of focus.

In the Beginning

Initially, Charlie was hesitant about coaching.

Charlie: When I heard the word *coach*, I was scared you were going to say, "You did this wrong, you should have done this." I did hear you were super nice and kind, so I thought, okay, I'm going to do my best and see what happens. Then . . . I loved the notes . . . you were so positive. You made me feel good that I was doing a lot of the things right.

I worked gently, asking Charlie questions intended to build her understanding of the curriculum and engage her in reflective thinking. I often asked, "How did that work?," "What would you do differently next time?," and "Why do you think that happened?" I didn't want her to feel as though she was doing things wrong. I wanted her to be confident in the knowledge she brought to the curriculum and the coaching relationship. I wanted her to be open to trying new things. My goal was to make our relationship a safe place for mistakes and tackling problems collaboratively.

The curriculum offered Charlie new ways of approaching read-alouds with children. It provided a rich and diverse selection of books representing a variety of children, families, cultures, and abilities and emphasized children's active engagement in the reading—moving like characters, making similar sounds, answering questions, talking about words from the text, and collectively retelling the story.

Charlie: When I first started reading to children, I wasn't the best at it. I would read and get it done in five minutes. But now, between talking to you and seeing the CSW video, I have the kids clapping. I have the kids jumping up—whatever is in the book. They love it. A book takes 20 minutes because they're moving so much.

Each time we met, Charlie would decide where to focus my attention. It could be something she was working on or something great that we could celebrate. Sometimes, I would ask permission to see a particular experience or component of the curriculum that I hadn't seen in a while. Though children were not used to the routines of the pilot curriculum, Charlie persisted.

Charlie: The kids say, "We read this already." And I say, "But are you learning the book? Do you understand the book? Can you help me read the book?" They say, "Yeah!" and they get excited about it. I help them understand why we're reading the book again. You were there to help me grow on that.

Charlie tended to use the curriculum guides as a script. Initially, the script helped build new adult routines, such as talking with children about the meaning of words and asking open-ended questions. I helped her see that to be authentic, she had to resist the urge to read the curriculum verbatim. For instance, as Charlie became comfortable with the curriculum and its guidance for read-alouds, she began to independently recognize words that might need discussion. Those could be any words in the book, not just those highlighted in the curriculum guide.

Charlie: I remember when you shared your "Wow Words," and I love that! You asked why I skipped over *pizzazz* in the story. After we talked about it, you mentioned the Wow Words. Like *pizzazz*. You said I could talk more about that. That will stick in my brain forever.

As Charlie began to ask more open-ended questions and involve the children, the children became more engaged, expressing their curiosity and wonder. It was exciting to see them adapt to the new read-aloud routine by sharing their thoughts about the book. As Charlie became more proficient with her read-alouds, she was able to creatively meet the needs of individual children. For example, when reading the book *Skeleton Hiccups* by Margery Cuyler, Charlie expanded the book text and joyfully joined with children in finding bones in their jaws and arms, feeling them move. These encouragements and explorations engaged the children in the book-reading experience.

Charlie: When I saw the video clip, it just made me excited to try it [an interactive read-aloud]. And then once I saw how children reacted to the read-aloud, I was like, this is exciting. They're into it now. They're not just sitting there saying, "This is boring."

Charlie was already good at her craft, so her progression with the curriculum was quick. I think this was reflective of her level of investment and commitment to the process. She would ask questions and ask for my professional opinion. This helped me to know that she saw me as a resource. She shared that families were reporting that their children were bringing home the stories and their reading experiences. I think the response from the children and families helped build her confidence and find joy in her work with children.

As the year progressed, it was evident that Charlie was also grasping the other aspects of the project approach articulated in the curriculum. For example, she was finding ways to connect the focus project into the various structures of their day, such as small group and whole group investigations, as well as into choice time. She was leaning into investigations that extended over several weeks and planning culminating events to celebrate the children's learning. Over time, she became more independently reflective and began to initiate reflective feedback without me having to ask the questions.

Now, two years later, Charlie is noticing the difference between her practice supported by coaching and the practices of the teachers around her.

Charlie: Now, I don't want to get a book done in five minutes. I want the children to understand everything. Some of the other teachers say, "Why do you do so much?" Because they just read the story. Other teachers here at the school weren't part of the curriculum pilot and didn't have a coach to teach them. But I am starting to see other teachers exploring it on their own.

Takeaways and Next Steps

In the beginning, Charlie was anxious about being in a coaching relationship with me. As our relationship evolved, Charlie made significant practice changes—such as transforming her read-alouds and increasing children's engagement and enthusiasm.

As a coach, I want everyone to grow using reflective processing and teaching strategies with intention and purpose. Not every coach will be the right fit. Coaches are growing too, seeking to best connect with and support teachers. Even a difficult coaching relationship will help an educator know what to look for next time. I encourage educators to take the risk of asking someone to coach them on something they are working on or to be a mentor. They will reap the wonderful rewards of expanding their understanding and improving their practice.

Case Discussion Questions

1. The danger of a standardized curriculum is that, if used as a script, it might not be developmentally appropriate for a particular community of children. What strategies and reflective thinking routines (for example, What did I plan? What happened? What would I do differently next time?) would you use to increase attention to individualization and context, aligning the curriculum with your community of learners (Bredekamp & Willer 2022)? Which additional chapters in *Developmentally Appropriate Practice* would support your efforts to increase the cultural and individual responsiveness of a required curriculum?

2. Sometimes standardized curricula will make recommendations such as "Children should be read to for 20 minutes a day." How might you use your knowledge of children's development at various ages (for example, 3-year-olds, 4-year-olds, mixed-age groups) to individualize this curriculum guidance?
3. Charlie shared that she would never forget the Wow Words to which the coach introduced her. What tricks of the trade have you picked up from your instructors, mentors, or colleagues? How have you internalized those practices and made them your own?

General Discussion Questions

1. How do you prefer to receive feedback? What would help you see feedback as having positive intent and being a growth opportunity?
2. Coaching is not always an available resource for programs. How might educators find coaches and mentors among their own communities of colleagues? How might they encourage themselves to take a professional growth risk?

References

Bredekamp, S., & B. Willer. 2022. "Intentional Teaching: Complex Decision Making and the Core Considerations." In *Developmentally Appropriate Practice in Early Childhood Programs Serving Children from Birth Through Age 8*, 4th ed., NAEYC, 5–23. Washington, DC: NAEYC.

University of Maryland. 2018. *Children Study Their World*. College Park: University of Maryland, Center for Early Childhood Education and Intervention.

6.2 **It Started with a Friendship Parade**

Angela Vargas

Connections to *Developmentally Appropriate Practice*

- Chapter 6: Creating a Caring, Equitable Community of Learners
- Chapter 7: Engaging in Reciprocal Partnerships with Families and Fostering Community Connections
- Chapter 10: Planning and Implementing an Engaging Curriculum to Achieve Meaningful Goals
- Chapter 11: Demonstrating Professionalism as an Early Childhood Educator

Case Overview

Professional educators integrate and use guidelines for developmentally appropriate practice to support early childhood learning and development. Professional practice requires a flexible and varied repertoire of teaching skills and strategies (NAEYC 2020). This case describes a group of second graders who, with their teacher, set about creating a school friendship parade. It is a story of making space for children, following their interests, offering invitations to nurture thinking, engaging family members, growing a caring community of learners, and realizing learning goals associated with school expectations and standards.

This case articulates multiple elements of developmentally appropriate practice, realized through the professionalism of a classroom teacher committed to regular reflection, intentional planning and practices, and advocacy on behalf of authentic learning opportunities for children.

Learning Objectives

1. Explore the role of practitioner reflection and conscious intention to guide the development and evolution of integrative primary grade experiences.
2. Examine ways in which informed advocacy for children includes authentically connecting the voices of children and families to stakeholders and decision makers, advocating in partnership with children.

Case Narrative

I see some of my second graders running through the playing field holding hands. The chain grows longer and longer. Back in the classroom, they tell me about their play outside. One child says, "I wonder how long we could make the chain if we invited kids from the other classes." I ask how she might try out her idea. The following day, the air is alive with excitement about the chain. One child explains, "It was like a parade!" Another adds, "A friendship parade! We should have a friendship parade with the whole school!" I ask them, "What do you think about that? What would it entail?" As they share, I start documenting.

In my classroom tenure, I regularly experience the rich social and academic learning that awakens when children are encouraged to follow their interests. Each year, I maintain a photo-documentation record of how the classroom community has met grade-level standards across domains. I regularly review previous years' documentation to inspire and align my teaching. As a result, I do not explicitly follow the sequence of grade 2 standards or strictly adhere to the district's pacing guide. I view the collaborative and complex learning opportunities that emerge from my relationships with children as a quilt of knowledge in which the children's perspectives, experiences, and our class resources are the threads that connect each square of ideas of the finished community quilt. This quilt includes all the instructional standards while honoring the uniqueness of each year's community of children.

In reflecting on the suggested friendship parade, I wonder how I might support children in connecting their parade ideas and current understandings to other relevant content, skills, and habits of mind. For example, we had been learning about goods and services, a required standard in second grade. I decide to tie this learning to the parade idea.

The children define *goods* as items to be paid for and wonder where money for items for floats and favors for the parade would come from. One child recalls a Parents and Teachers Association (PTA) visit, remembering that the PTA provides money for events. The children are excited to create a proposal. However, before going to the PTA, we will need the principal's permission to hold the parade at school.

As I observe the children's drawings and preparations for the proposal, I notice two girls working together to map out the parade. The next day, I share the girls' idea of creating a parade map and present the children with a school diagram. I challenge them to find a parade route that includes everyone and will pass by each classroom only once.

The parade planning filters through the entire instructional day. During math, children develop a budget, researching the cost of each item and number needed. In writing, we begin a persuasive writing unit. Each child writes an opinion piece on why the parade will be valuable to the community and why it should be funded. The class is engaging in profound and purposeful learning motivated by schoolwide friendship.

I reflect on how the children are evolving as individuals and as a unit. Children, some vastly different from each other, are working in harmony. For me, this rich collaboration is the realization of my commitment to a fully inclusive community where *every* learner is intrinsically motivated to engage and is supported and scaffolded to realize that engagement. I remember earlier in the year when working as a community created challenges for the children, with many big feelings. I had modeled questions during moments of misunderstanding: "What do you need?" and "Do you want a check-in, or do you want space?" We had held community circles to explore big feelings. Slowly, the children had begun to respond in ways that supported their friends instead of making assumptions about how they felt.

Now, seeing children immersed in collaboration on the parade, I wonder if creating space to reflect on their growth over time will enrich our parade discussions and collaboration. During community circle, I invite them to reflect using a yarn-tossing activity in which the speaker holds the yarn and then tosses it to another child to speak. I choose yarn to give them tangible insight into connections among our choices, actions, and feelings.

Ms. Angela: How have you become stronger at navigating your feelings?

Ricardo: When I used to get mad, I would stay in the problem. Now, I walk away.

Royce: Before I would get out of control. Now I grab my journal.

Ramón: Instead of getting mad when people are fighting, I ask people what they need.

Julieta: I used to think I could always help people. That did not always feel helpful to them. Now I ask: Do you need space?

The physical aspects of this reflection are more challenging than I imagined—think many yarn tangles. Yet the tangles engage the community. The next day I share a photo of our yarn work; the pattern it makes, as Prince notes in our discussion that follows, resembles a state or map. I reflect with the children again on what it feels like to be physically connected through the yarn.

Julieta: As we threw the yarn, some people weren't getting enough yarn or space.

Amir: Some people scooted back, which took [yarn] from the other people. If people pull on it, there is less for others.

Adonis: (*Refers to the photo of our yarn work.*) What it became, looks kind of like a state. Our community, it's the State of Love.

Aiko: Even though the yarn is not even, the friendship still grows.

Julieta: Maybe somebody will share a little string when you need it. Like when you share a little love, you get a little back. We give people what they need.

Adonis: There is a path, like on a map. You make places that mean love.

The children begin to map their emotional identities—the ways they understand their emotional responses and community relationships and how these have evolved over time—on what becomes known as a map of the "Love State." I am thrilled to see the children using the concrete image of a map from their parade planning as a metaphor to reflect their growing understanding of emotions and relationships. I am reminded that the most vibrant learning connections are those the children make themselves reflecting their lives, their interests, and their motivations. We are not only developing the skills to organize a parade but also developing the skills to organize ourselves.

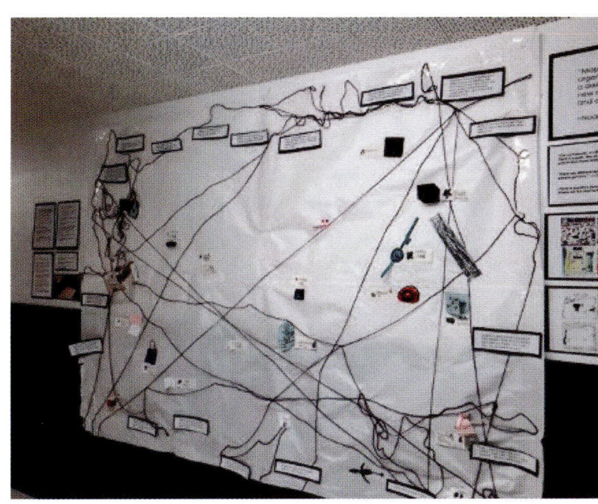

When we turn back to discussing the parade, the children decide that one group will present their proposal to the principal and another group will present to the PTA. After the first group practices their persuasive speeches, they head into the school boardroom. The principal asks some clarifying questions, which the children confidently answer, and then gives the green light. Next, we prepare for the PTA board presentation. While only one group of children is going to present, all the children want to be there, and they decide to create invitations for their families so they can attend.

From the comments on our social media page, I know parents have been actively following the children's work. I follow up on the children's invitations with an online event invitation, calling families to invite them personally and reminding them that all are welcome. I help families connect to arrange carpools to the pizza parlor. We have 100 percent family participation at the PTA presentation. The families enjoy pizza together (paid for by Title 1 school funds) and make new connections. When the moment arrives for the presentation, the children share their speeches, everyone listening intently. The PTA agrees to fully fund the parade. Everyone cheers and hugs. Then, children run off to play while the parents share their excitement and pride.

Once the parade goods arrive, the children form committees. With the help of their families, they get to work. They create banners so that all five second grade classrooms have one to carry and organize 600 paw-print charm bracelets to hand out as they walk the hall. Last, the children learn a multilingual friendship song to sing as they parade.

To maximize the chances that families can attend the parade, I advocate to hold the parade during the end-of-year field day. On that day, every class lines the wall by their classroom door. The five second grade classes fill the hallway with their banners, floats, and balloons, our class guiding the way. As we walk by each classroom, it signals that class to head out to field day. With all 600 students outside, the parade makes one lap around the track, spectators cheering.

The Love Parade project fills me with joy. I witness the children experience how powerful they are and to use that power for collective purpose and action. In collaboration, they organize themselves physically, emotionally, and mentally––asking questions, reflecting, empathizing, reading, writing, budgeting, speaking publicly, and advocating. I am delighted that families connect with the project and, as a result, experience a new relationship with the school and their child's education.

Takeaways and Next Steps

It may feel nebulous and overwhelming to consider bringing all the elements of developmentally appropriate practice to life in programs and classrooms. Intentionally attending to the key elements of professionalism can support the integration of developmentally appropriate practice into educators' professional practice.

For example, as illustrated in this case, viewing the children as a source of continuous learning informs educators' practice. *All* elements of a child's day influence learning—including recess and lunch, arrival and departure, in the hallway, or during specials (for example, physical education). When children share their important moments, teachers can listen and reflect, then shape instructional connections around those experiences.

Further, educators examine their own beliefs on children and their role in a learning community. Thinking of children as underdeveloped or emerging learners can lead to bias and inequity. Instead, teachers believe in children as brilliant, capable, and fully present members of the community. Children's creativity, curiosity, funds of family knowledge, and individual waves of development are authentically valuable to classroom collaboration and inquiry.

Also, effective educators research and internalize the instructional standards for their grade level. Standards then become tools to realize community learning efforts rather than firm descriptions that limit possibilities. For instance, when teachers design a classroom event, they can employ the academic skills and standards related to mathematics, personal finance, social science, and written and oral communication to realize the event.

Case Discussion Questions

1. Intentional educators sew a quilt of developmentally appropriate practices. What aspects of professionalism supported this teacher's quilt of learning?
2. How did the teacher advocate within the institution to ensure connection to children's educational interests and authentically engage families in their children's school lives?

General Discussion Question

1. In what ways are reflection and intentional practice essential to realizing learning communities that simultaneously "engage children's curiosity, interest, and motivation" (Masterson 2022, 217) and align with institutional standards and expectations?

References

Masterson, M. 2022. "Planning and Implementing an Engaging Curriculum to Achieve Meaningful Goals." In *Developmentally Appropriate Practice in Early Childhood Programs Serving Children from Birth Through Age 8*, 4th ed., NAEYC, 215–51. Washington, DC: NAEYC.

NAEYC. 2020. "Developmentally Appropriate Practice." Position statement. Washington, DC: NAEYC. www.naeyc.org/resources/position-statements/dap/contents.

6.3 The World Outside of the Classroom: Letting Your Voice Be Heard

Meghann Hickey

Connections to *Developmentally Appropriate Practice*

- Chapter 1: Intentional Teaching: Complex Decision Making and the Core Considerations
- Chapter 11: Demonstrating Professionalism as an Early Childhood Educator

Case Overview

Early childhood educators do not always recognize the importance of their role in the field. They face the challenge of facilitating children's development and learning while adhering to strict rules and regulations and, often, receiving minimal respect and earning low salaries and benefits. Yet research shows the critical role of educators in the development of young children and in their later success (Phillips et al., 2017). This case explores the experiences of an early childhood professional who uses a deep understanding of and engagement with developmentally appropriate practice to grow into her role as an advocate for the field and with policymakers.

Learning Objectives

1. Examine practitioner advocacy both for developmentally appropriate practice and for the workforce, supporting policy makers' understanding of field-wide challenges.
2. Explain the importance of knowledge of effective practices and policy for improving educational practice in the classroom and for supporting advocacy for the field.

Case Narrative

I began my career in the classroom because I had a love for spending time with young children and understanding why they acted the way they did. I was drawn to their authenticity and often underrated capabilities—while adults tend to doubt what young children know or can do, I loved watching them explore and figure their world out for themselves. When considering college, I wanted to study psychology to understand why children thought the way they did, but my dance teacher, who had observed me working with groups of younger dancers, steered me toward education by convincing me that I had a talent for teaching children by meeting them where they were and naturally scaffolding for them. In college, I attended a teacher education program intending to be an elementary school teacher but found a passion for work with children from birth to 5. The program at my university engaged students early in their studies in its lab school with observation and interaction and then increased responsibility over the four years through observation, curriculum planning, and program implementation steeped in theory and developmentally appropriate practice. Following a college career at an NAEYC-accredited university and after completing practicum in an NAEYC-accredited preschool, I entered the "real world."

The local preschool I worked in after graduating was very different from the university lab school. This program was like many other programs across the country, working to ensure that staff had autonomy in their settings, honoring their knowledge of child development, and promoting staff work as much more than "babysitting." However, the program was challenged by issues common to the field, such as recruiting and retaining diverse, qualified staff; meeting teacher training requirements; and responding to high staff turnover. I and my fellow educators struggled to meet the needs of the children without sufficient resources, knowledge, training, and support. For example, like most preschools, we met state-required ratios. However, the ratio-determined number of children assigned to adults did not account for the diversity of children's needs. Some children needed more teacher time and attention to be successful. In addition, if a staff member needed a day off, it became a chaotic shuffle of the other staff to make sure all the classrooms were covered. The program did ensure staff could have vacations and days off, but cold and flu season made maintaining ratios stressful. Feeling like you could not take a sick day because of the strain it would put on your coworkers was taxing and contributed to staff leaving to find jobs where they could better care for themselves. Although *Developmentally Appropriate Practice* emphasizes that "intentional educators are purposeful, reflective, and responsive" (Bredekamp & Willer 2022, 16), I found myself wondering how it was possible for educators to meet the complex needs of the children in the program with only minimal guidance and support.

Through an internship from an alumnus at my university, I had the opportunity to venture outside of the classroom to work in policy, advocating for the needs of educators. This was a big opportunity; teachers are typically taught that the only path following a degree program is to enter the classroom, and they are rarely exposed to additional opportunities in the profession. My decision to leave the classroom was complicated. I loved working directly with children, supporting their development and learning with "support and challenge[s] based on moment-by-moment interactions" (Masterson 2022, 182), but I wanted to make a larger impact. I was motivated by the struggles of my colleagues and by the low wages in the field. I did not feel I was being fairly compensated for the work I was doing and the passion I brought to my practice. I believed that public policy work might allow me to continue to identify with and participate as a member of the early childhood profession (NAEYC 2020) though serving in a different role.

In my first days as an advocate, I felt like an impostor because I had no formal policy experience; however, I was driven by the work of the organization and by the opportunity to improve the field for early educators. I discovered that I actually had a big advantage in the policy role because I understood the challenges of being an educator and how policy decisions affected the day-to-day work of educators, something that most of those making the policy decisions did not understand. I began my policy work with a project centered on the reauthorization of the Child Care and Development Block Grant Act (CCDBG). The US Department of Health and Human Services and the Administration for Children and Families proposed to amend the Child Care and Development Fund regulations to protect the health and safety of children in child care programs; to help parents make informed consumer choices and access information to support child development; to provide equal access to stable, high-quality child care for children from families with low income; and to enhance the overall quality of child care and the early childhood workforce. As one of the few people recently in a classroom, I was assigned to interview educators in the field about the proposed changes and to help ensure their voices remained authentic when translated into policy recommendations.

I could see that while the policymakers proposed important improvements, they had not considered the day-to-day impacts of the changes on programs. For example, improving inspections and criminal background checks for potential staff is a positive enhancement and would likely increase child safety. However, the policymakers did not recognize the delays that would result as state offices processed all the extra paperwork, thereby pushing back the date when a new educator was cleared to work, potentially resulting in programs being short-staffed. Policymakers also did not always consider the resource implications of their proposals. In the CCDBG plan, there were several components that would likely force providers to increase family tuition rates to meet the quality requirements and be eligible to receive public funding.

While the providers I spoke with believed that the proposed quality improvements were great ideas, they were extremely concerned about how to meet the quality levels without affecting tuition. Furthermore, if programs needed to increase tuition to meet the quality levels, families were likely to choose a lower-quality program because it would be lower cost as well. Providers asked that it be emphasized that helping families understand why quality early education matters and how to find high-quality programs would be critical to the stability of the early childhood field. Overwhelmingly, the educators I spoke with felt as though they did not have a seat at the table and their voices were not being heard. I was proud to give voice to their concerns and experiences, especially as I was one of only a few who truly understood the issues from their point of view.

Classrooms should be led by our strongest, most passionate educators. While I know that change in our field seems slow and it can feel challenging to keep advocating with seemingly minor progress, growing support for the professional status of the field can be done in ways that encourage skilled educators to stay in the classroom. When I accepted a position supporting early learning programs that were pursuing NAEYC accreditation, my passion centered around helping the programs work toward the key competencies of standard 6 of the professional standards and competencies (NAEYC 2019). As they pursue mastery of this standard, educators discover what resources are available to them and how they can be strong advocates. The voices of teachers are vital to policy decision making. Forming strong partnerships between those in the classroom and decision makers outside of the classroom is one way for these authentic voices to be heard.

Takeaways and Next Steps

To be a professional "means being part of something larger than oneself, united in an effort to effectively promote the development, learning, and well-being of all young children through a profession that is diverse, equitable, effective, well-prepared, and well-compensated for the complex and valuable work that they do" (Huang et al. 2022, 268). It is important for educators to remember that they are valuable and critically important both to the development of our youngest learners and to the evolution of the profession.

Early childhood educators do not have to leave the classroom, as I did, to help improve the field. All teachers can become advocates for themselves, families, children, and more effective policies while they are still teaching. Here are a few ways to do so:

- As you understand and recognize the value and importance of your work, begin sharing that information with others. Talk up your work at family gatherings. Share the importance of what you do with others in your life. Take to social media to share information. Strike up a conversation with someone in line at the grocery store.
- Seek opportunities to contribute your thoughts and opinions on the field and decision making that affects the field. Some opportunities require a minimal time commitment, such as submitting a comment or opinion at the website for a proposed rule change, and others involve more intensive experience, such as serving on a committee or participating in your local NAEYC Affiliate.
- Look for ways to build strong partnerships between those in the classroom and those in the education field outside of the classroom. Organizations like NAEYC are taking steps to stay connected to the field and seeking perspective and influence from classroom voices directly. Follow up on opportunities to share a story about a challenge you are facing so advocates know how to ask for support.
- Stay connected. It is easier to handle disappointment and continue to take action when you are in collaboration with others.

Remember that policy changes don't happen overnight. Try not to get discouraged when change doesn't happen immediately. Find advocacy opportunities that work for you and continue to speak out even when your voice feels small. The more we all speak together, the louder we become and the stronger the impact we can have over time.

Case Discussion Questions

1. How did this educator's training and experience contribute to her understanding of the profession?
2. It can be challenging to teach and advocate at the same time. Educators may feel that to be heard, they must leave the classroom. Do you agree? Why or why not? What are the effects of strong, passionate educators leaving the classroom to make a difference for the field in other ways? What impact can teachers have by remaining in the classroom while advocating in their roles as practitioners?

General Discussion Questions

1. Where might educator voices be recognized and respected as professionals?
2. How can early educators use their knowledge of developmentally appropriate practice to help legislators understand the role of educators in the development of children and the societal benefits of that role?
3. What are some additional ways for an educator to begin to engage in conversations about their role and the value of their work in settings outside of the classroom?

References

Bredekamp, S., & B. Willer. 2022. "Intentional Teaching: Complex Decision Making and the Core Considerations." In *Developmentally Appropriate Practice in Early Childhood Programs Serving Children from Birth Through Age 8*, 4th ed., NAEYC, 5–23. Washington, DC: NAEYC.

Huang, L., S. Loh, & A. Simpson. With L. Hogan, L. Recio, & M. Harrill. 2022. "Demonstrating Professionalism as an Early Childhood Educator." In *Developmentally Appropriate Practice in Early Childhood Programs Serving Children from Birth Through Age 8,* 4th ed., NAEYC, 253–68. Washington, DC: NAEYC.

Masterson, M. 2022. "Teaching to Enhance Each Child's Development and Learning." In *Developmentally Appropriate Practice in Early Childhood Programs Serving Children from Birth Through Age 8,* 4th ed., NAEYC, 181–214. Washington, DC: NAEYC.

NAEYC. 2019. "Professional Standards and Competencies for Early Childhood Educators." Position statement. Washington, DC: NAEYC. www.naeyc.org/resources/position-statements/professional-standards-competencies.

NAEYC. 2020. "Developmentally Appropriate Practice." Position statement. Washington, DC: NAEYC. www.naeyc.org/resources/position-statements/dap.

Phillips, D.A., M.W. Lipsey, K.A. Dodge, R. Haskins, D. Bassok, M.R. Burchinal, G.J. Duncan, M. Dynarski, K.A. Magnuson, & C. Weiland. 2017. *The Current State of Scientific Knowledge on Pre-Kindergarten Effects.* Brookings Institution and the Duke Center for Child and Family Policy. www.brookings.edu/wp-content/uploads/2017/04/duke_prekstudy_final_4-4-17_hires.pdf.

PART 7

Supporting Children with Disabilities and Implementing Inclusive Practices

Pamela Brillante

Disability is a natural part of the human experience and impacts individuals of all ages, ethnicities, genders, races, religions, and other identities. Unfortunately, it is still common for individuals with disabilities to be seen as different or "other," and as a result they are often still marginalized in their societies.

Every early childhood educator is likely to have taught or will teach a child with a disability, even if that disability has not been identified yet. As stated throughout the fourth edition of *Developmentally Appropriate Practice*, teachers need to be aware of their unspoken assumptions or biases about the academic capability or developmental progress of a child with a disability, which may impact how they teach or include the child within the classroom.

The case studies in Part 7 address the needs of children with both identified and potential disabilities and their families. Specifically, the cases present scenarios and questions regarding the following:

- Working with families of very young children with identified disabilities
- Determining a child's strengths as well as their specific needs to be independent and engaged learners
- Including children with disabilities, including autism, alongside same-age peers who are developing skills in a more traditional timeline
- Addressing behaviors that challenge educators
- Providing classroom supports and embedded intervention using a coteaching model
- Designing academic instruction, including adaptations, accommodations, and modifications, in the early grades

This chapter's content is aligned to *Developmentally Appropriate Practice* as well as to the 2009 joint position statement on inclusion from DEC (Division for Early Childhood) of the Council for Exceptional Children and NAEYC.

The writers of these cases have a wide variety of experiences and training in the area of early childhood special education. Some have academic training in special education and early childhood special education; others have no formal training in this field but draw on practical experience identifying and including young children with disabilities into their classrooms and communities. In length and level of professional experience, the authors range from those with fewer than 10 years in early childhood education to those who are master's and doctoral candidates to those who are veteran researchers and higher education faculty members. The authors represent many but not all of the roles found in the profession. They represent a variety of ages, ethnicities, gender identities, abilities, and disabilities. Residing and working in different states, the authors implement the regulations of the Individuals with Disabilities Education Act (IDEA) based on their individual states' administrative codes.

The one commonality is that each of the cases has been written by an author who has direct experience working with young children with disabilities, either as a teacher in an early childhood classroom that includes children with disabilities or as an early intervention provider for children with disabilities from birth to age 3.

Reference

DEC (Division for Early Childhood of the Council for Exceptional Children) & NAEYC. 2009. "Early Childhood Inclusion: A Joint Position Statement of the Division for Early Childhood (DEC) and the National Association for the Education of Young Children (NAEYC)." Position statement. Chapel Hill: The University of North Carolina, FPG Child Development Institute. www.naeyc.org/resources/position-statements.

7.1 Communication as a Two-Way Street? Creating Opportunities for Engagement During Meaningful Language Routines

Kameron C. Carden

Connections to *Developmentally Appropriate Practice*

- Chapter 7: Engaging in Reciprocal Partnerships with Families and Fostering Community Connections

Case Overview

Richie is 20-month-old toddler with a severe to profound sensorineural hearing loss. He received bilateral cochlear implants just before his first birthday. Cochlear implants, which often look like hearing aids, are small electronic devices that provide sound information to individuals with severe to profound deafness. With his cochlear implants, Richie is responding to sounds in his environment and is beginning to babble when playing independently with his toys. Richie's mom knows that she needs to provide a language-rich environment to support Richie's language development, but she is beginning to feel like she talks to Richie nonstop throughout the day to help him catch up to his peers. At the recommendation of a neighbor, she has also begun using picture flash cards with Richie to try to teach him new words. Despite her efforts, Richie has not said his first word yet, and his mom is frustrated and concerned.

Because of Richie's diagnosis of deafness, he is at risk for developmental language delay. Infants and toddlers who are at risk for developmental delays and their families may qualify for early intervention services from birth to 3 years of age. Early interventionists are trained professionals who provide services in the natural environment to develop parents' capacity for meeting their child's unique needs. This case example focuses on a typical parent concern during a session with an early interventionist, particularly for a child who is deaf or hard of hearing. During the exchange, the early interventionist employs a routines-based model that emphasizes supporting the family by fostering the child's independence, engagement, and social relationships in the context of daily routines (McWilliam 2010; McWilliam 2012; McWilliam 2016). The early interventionist and Richie's mom work together to discover opportunities throughout the day to create meaningful language routines that will engage Richie as well as his mom.

Learning Objectives

1. Describe the importance of creating opportunities for family participation and input into children's education, specifically children with disabilities.
2. Examine the role of educators in providing information about child development while creating opportunities for a parent to share information about their child's unique development.
3. Explain strategies for creating language-rich opportunities within daily routines.

Case Narrative

Chris, a speech-language pathologist, arrives at Richie's home on a sunny afternoon in late spring for an early intervention session. Despite the lovely weather, when she opens the door, Richie's mom, Caroline, seems clouded with worry. Caroline welcomes Chris in, and they sit down on the couch in the living room. Richie is playing with blocks at their feet, stacking the blocks in a tall tower, knocking them down, and starting over again. As he stacks the blocks, Richie babbles, "Buh, buh, buh, buh, buh," and he squeals when they fall. Caroline responds, "Yes, Richie, you're stacking wooden blocks? Can you say 'blocks'? You love to stack blocks over and over in the living room!" Chris has only been working with Richie and Caroline for a month, and she starts the session by asking, "Tell me about how things have been going since the last time we met." Caroline's lip begins to quiver as she answers.

Caroline: I feel like a terrible mother, and I don't know what else I can do. Richie was implanted nine months ago, and he's still not said a true word. He babbles all the time when he's playing by himself, but he doesn't respond when I talk to him! And I talk all day long. I talk about what washing the clothes, cooking dinner, taking out the trash, all the time. Sometimes, when I go to bed at night, I am hoarse from talking nonstop. I'm in a Facebook group for cochlear implant moms, and most of the other kids Richie's age are already saying four or five words! I shared my concerns with a friend down the street—her kid can hear—and she said she used vocabulary flash cards with her baby every morning after breakfast. He's 5 now, and he's so smart.

Chris: It sounds like you're feeling really defeated today, Caroline.

Caroline: I'm doing all the things I've been told to do, and he's just not giving anything back.

Chris: I hear you saying that it seems like Richie communicates to himself through babbling, but he's not saying any words to you yet. You mentioned that you talk about what you're doing when you wash the clothes, cook dinner, and take out the trash. What is Richie doing while you're talking about those things?

Caroline: He's normally playing with blocks or cars or trains near me, and I narrate what I'm doing. Like, when I load the washing machine, I might say, "I'm putting in the clothes. This is daddy's blue shirt that he wears to work. I'm putting it in the washing machine. Now, I'm putting in a pair of pajamas that you wear to bed. Look, they are blue and gray and have buttons all the way down the front." See? I'm talking and talking.

Chris: Wow! It sounds like you're providing a lot of great language to describe what you're doing! Because Richie's only been able to hear for nine months, we would expect him to have the language of a nine-month-old. At that age, most babies haven't said their first word yet, and they are just starting to babble new and different sounds. In our last session together, we discussed that Richie is listening and babbling like a twelve-month-old. I think it's reasonable to expect that he would begin to say his first words soon. Does Richie ever try to help you when you're loading the washing machine?

Caroline: Yeah, he likes to help me around the house, but he usually just throws all the clothes in the washer at one time, and I don't have time to talk about it as much as I'd like. So I usually end up loading it myself one item at a time while he runs around the laundry room.

Chris: Well, that sounds about like how a toddler would want to do laundry! Do you happen to have any loads of laundry that need to be done?

Caroline: Yeah, several.

Chris: I wonder what would happen if we gave Richie one piece of clothing at a time from the laundry basket to put in the washing machine. Then, maybe we can brainstorm how to talk *with* Richie about loading the washing machine together.

Caroline: We can try it, but I don't know if he will participate. I'll try anything at this point.

Chris: Why don't we go ahead and clean up these blocks? Let's head to the laundry room and see if we can think of some ways to engage Richie in loading the washing machine with a meaningful language routine that provides opportunities for both of you to participate.

Caroline: Let's do it.

Chris collects the blocks Richie is stacking in a bucket while Caroline picks Richie up and puts him on her hip. "Let's wash some clothes together, Richie!" she says. Chris follows Caroline and Richie into the laundry room, where a basket of dirty clothes is already waiting to be loaded.

Takeaways and Next Steps

A family-centered service at its best, early intervention should always be conducted in partnership with the parent or other home caregiver rather than as a direct service to the child. In this case, the early interventionist uses a series of reflective questions to gain more information about Caroline's specific concerns to "seek ways to promote and support" Caroline's goals *prior* to offering any suggestions (Mancilla & Blanco 2022, 153). Through reflective questioning, the early interventionist learns more about what Caroline is already doing to support Richie's language development as well as specific routines already occurring throughout their day where Caroline might incorporate additional strategies that promote language development. The importance of family-centered support is not unique to early intervention. Teachers and interventionists serving children with disabilities of all ages can work to create partnerships with families by inquiring about the goals for their child, listening reflectively, and responsively promoting and supporting those goals.

Selecting a routine—in this case, washing a load of laundry—is just the beginning. Now that Caroline and Chris are in the laundry room, Chris must guide the discussion through another round of reflective questions so that she and Caroline can select a language strategy to incorporate into the routine together. Caroline and Chris could select one of several evidence-based strategies used to accelerate the development of spoken language in children who are deaf or hard of hearing. For example, Chris may model acoustic highlighting of key words and phrases throughout the routine. Acoustic highlighting focuses the child's attention on key words and sounds by using a singsong speech pattern, pausing before the key word or phrase, and emphasizing the key word or phrase (Brooks 2002; Hearing First 2021). Chris and Caroline could work together to identify key words or phrases for a laundry routine, such as the names of clothing items, or routines-based actions, such as "put it in."

Case Discussion Questions

1. How do Chris's questions during this exchange reflect guideline 2C of the position statement on developmentally appropriate practice (welcoming family members in the setting and creating multiple opportunities for their participation)? Why is it important for educators to develop opportunities for family participation in their child's education?
2. What other information could Chris have provided to Caroline about language development in toddlers? Could she have said anything in a different way?
3. Should Caroline and Chris focus on first words during the laundry routine? What prerequisite skills or strategies that support the development of communication might Chris explore and model with Caroline? Consider developmental skills like imitation, joint attention, and turn taking.
4. Considering guideline 4D.5 (creating language-rich environments that focus on the diversity and complexity of language in children's communities), what other routines could Caroline and Chris have engaged Richie in during the session to provide a language-rich routine?
5. Before Caroline and Chris begin the laundry routine with Richie, what are some strategies that Chris might consider modeling for Caroline to create a language-rich routine?

General Discussion Question

1. How might an educator in a toddler program create language-rich classroom routines to create opportunities for communication and foster language development?

References

Brooks, B.M. 2002. *My Baby and Me: A Book About Teaching Your Child to Talk.* St. Louis, MO: The Moog Center for Deaf Education.

Hearing First. 2021. *LSL Strategies and Techniques.* Philadelphia, PA: Hearing First. www.hearingfirst.org/m/resources/176.

Mancilla, L., & P. Blanco. 2022. "Engaging in Reciprocal Partnerships with Families and Fostering Community Connections." In *Developmentally Appropriate Practice in Early Childhood Programs Serving Children from Birth Through Age 8,* 4th ed., NAEYC, 145–57. Washington, DC: NAEYC.

McWilliam, R.A. 2010. *Routines-Based Early Intervention: Supporting Young Children and Their Families.* Baltimore, MD: P.H. Brookes.

McWilliam, R.A. 2012. "Implementing and Preparing for Home Visits." *Topics in Early Childhood Special Education* 31 (4): 224–31. https://doi.org/10.1177%2F0271121411426488.

McWilliam, R.A. 2016. "The Routines-Based Model for Supporting Speech and Language." *Revista de logopedia, foniatría y audiología* 36 (4): 178–84.

7.2 Eli Goes to Preschool: Inclusion for a Child with Autism Spectrum Disorder

Abby Hodges

Connections to *Developmentally Appropriate Practice*

- Chapter 9: Teaching to Enhance Each Child's Development and Learning
- Chapter 10: Planning and Implementing an Engaging Curriculum to Achieve Meaningful Goals

Case Overview

This case study is about a preschool child with autism spectrum disorder (ASD) with limited play and language skills who is attending a new general education classroom. The teacher, Ms. Ramesh, makes accommodations and modifications to support this child's engagement in the classroom routines and activities. In addition, the case involves teaching strategies that both address the individual child's goals and objectives and provide opportunities for peers to engage and interact with their classmates with ASD in a developmentally appropriate way to model an inclusive approach.

Learning Objectives

1. Explain ways to modify an individual's environment to provide enriched learning opportunities.
2. Identify ways to embed social opportunities for peers with diverse abilities into their play.
3. Describe examples of how to make learning experiences more meaningful for children by building on their interests, knowledge, and skills.

Case Narrative

Eli is a 5-year-old boy who has a diagnosis of ASD. Eli primarily uses single words to communicate. He engages in behaviors such as repetitive hand and body movements (for example, flapping hands, walking on his toes, jumping up and down) as well as making repetitive sounds. Eli's favorite things to play with are figures and Matchbox cars, and he likes to line them up in rows and sort them by color. He prefers to play alone. When other children approach him, he does not engage with them but remains very object focused. If someone interrupts his play routine, he will become upset and begin to throw things or cry. Eli struggles with many fine motor tasks and becomes very frustrated when doing art activities at the table. He does not like to get his hands dirty or wet. He is a sweet, affectionate boy who enjoys giving and receiving hugs; he also loves music.

Eli's parents have struggled to find a good school for him. At his previous early learning program, the staff claimed they did not have a good understanding of autism and that they "had tried everything to get him engaged" and were only successful when they provided one-on-one support, which they could not sustain. One year later at a new school, his parents express their desire for Eli to communicate his wants and needs verbally and would like him to develop friendships.

Today is Eli's first day at his new school in a public half-day preschool class. The room has 15 children and two adults. Children are ages 4–5 and will be entering kindergarten next fall. Two other children in the class have also been diagnosed with ASD.

The classroom is well organized and arranged in centers, and there is a large group area with a carpet. All cubbies, shelving, and tables feature visuals that coincide with what belongs in each space. When children arrive for the day, they hang up their coats and bags and find a spot on the carpet. Once everyone has arrived, one teacher leads the class in large group time, which includes calendar, weather, and two children sharing for show-and-tell. Next, a song or two is sung and the teacher describes which centers are open for the day. Centers might include dramatic play, art, literacy, and math. The children are dismissed in small groups to centers and rotate when they hear a bell followed by the "Rotate Song." After center time, the children go outside for recess. Once back inside from recess, the class eats snack and then returns to the carpet for the "Goodbye Song."

The classroom teachers are diligent to organize and maintain their classroom in an attractive manner, keep an organized and consistent daily schedule, arrange the environment and daily schedule to support all children's independence, plan activities around easily recognized preplanned themes (for example, transportation, farm, community helpers), and encourage teamwork throughout the day.

Eli arrives for his first day of school and is timid at first. He puts his backpack away and then immediately runs over to the shelf with the basket of Matchbox cars and begins to line them up in a row. When prompted by Ms. Ramesh to transition to large group time, he begins to cry. This continues for several minutes until Ms. Ramesh begins the first song, at which point Eli timidly walks toward large group time and sits with the other children. Ms. Ramesh notices that Eli is moving his hands rapidly in a flapping motion. She decides to provide instruments to the children in the circle, and Eli begins to play with the instrument instead.

When large group time is over, it is time to transition to centers. All children are paired up to increase opportunities for social engagement and provide a peer model. Eli is paired with a neurotypical peer, Bella, and they transition between activities together. The children select from a choice board with visuals of the centers. Bella chooses that she and Eli will go to the art center first, where sponge shapes are placed in various colors of paint. Eli cries loudly when paint touches his hands. Bella offers Eli a paper towel, and Ms. Ramesh comes over to assist. She decides it might be best for Eli to use clothespins to pick up the sponges so his hands can stay dry.

Next, Eli and Bella go to the dramatic play center. The class is learning all about transportation and so there are various replicas of traffic signals (stop signs, traffic lights), lots of toy vehicles, and a life-size train made of boxes with dolls in it. Bella offers Eli a police officer hat, but Eli is immediately drawn to the

Matchbox cars. He begins to line them up. Bella gets in the train and pretends to be the conductor. When it is time to transition to the next center, Eli does not want to leave the cars. Understanding the power of providing choice to mitigate problem behavior, Ms. Ramesh invites Eli to bring a car with him. "Would you like to bring the red car or the blue car with you?" she asks. Eli chooses the blue car and walks to the math center alongside Ms. Ramesh. She provides positive descriptive praise to Eli, saying, "Great job coming to the table so nicely, Eli." For the tracing number activity in the math center, she opts to have Eli use the Matchbox car instead of a crayon to trace the number.

At recess, Eli pulls Ms. Ramesh by the hand over to the swing set to communicate that he wants to be pushed on the swing. When it is time to go inside, Eli cries and runs away from the other children. Ms. Ramesh persuades him to go back inside by reminding him of what is next and offering him a choice, saying "First, we are going inside, then it is snack time. Would you like to be the line leader or the caboose?" Eli chooses to be the line leader and heads toward the door.

Once back inside, a teacher hands out the snack for the day. She provides each child the option of single-portion size bags of cheese crackers or pretzels and places a few apple slices in front of every child. Some children have a hard time opening the bag, but the teacher notices that Eli opens his right away. Rather than help each child herself, she suggests to a few of the children that they could ask Eli for help, which they do, and he readily assists. She acknowledges Eli for being such a good helper. After snack, the class transitions to the carpet. This time, Eli takes one car with him and transitions with ease. The class sings the "Goodbye Song," and the children line up to go home.

Once the children have gone home for the day, the teachers come together and discuss what went well and what did not go well. They would like for Eli to transition without problem behavior, attend during large group, and initiate tasks within a few seconds of being prompted or ask for help. They decide that it might be helpful for Eli to have a visual schedule of his own for transitions, at least until he becomes more accustomed to the daily routine. They also discuss using different visuals, such as a photo or social story that represents "how to sit in circle," so that all the children have multiple ways to understand the expectations. For Eli in particular, they determine that they will slowly and systematically increase the amount of time he is expected to remain at large group time. At first they will have him remain in large group for three minutes and once he is consistently successful for that amount of time—minimal to no crying, minimal to no attempts to leave large group time—increase the duration. The teachers strategize options for how to incorporate more social opportunities for all the children, particularly the children with ASD.

Takeaways and Next Steps

Eli's teachers are committed to supporting the diverse abilities of the children in their classroom. They understand the importance of structuring the classroom (for example, use of visuals, physical layout) and organizing activities (for example, include multisensory components, balance of child- and teacher-directed, use of peer modeling, incorporating choice) to support learning and interplay between the children and their environment, shaping patterns of growth.

In their end-of-day team meeting, the teachers strategize ways in which they can continue to incorporate meaningful, accessible, and responsive learning opportunities so that all of the children can participate and benefit from multiple interactions with their peers across many contexts. The teachers may even seek additional consultation to individualize their teaching strategies further to meet Eli's specific needs and will continue to use his interests to encourage his participation in various activities. They know that it is important to prioritize goals, and those affecting the safety and well-being of all should be first.

Case Discussion Questions

1. How do the activities reflect principle 1 of the position statement on developmentally appropriate practice?
2. How does the case illustrate core consideration 2—individuality—of the position statement?
3. What more might be done to increase opportunities for Eli to socialize with his peers?
4. How might Ms. Ramesh involve Eli's parents in his learning?
5. What challenges in implementing various activities with Eli might come up for the teachers, and how could they address these challenges?
6. What challenges might come up during unstructured child-directed activities (for example, center time, outdoor play) for Eli, and how could the adults in the classroom address these challenges?
7. How do the activities support all the children and the children with autism in particular? In what ways might the activities hinder development?

General Discussion Questions

1. What benefits and drawbacks might there be to pairing a child with a disability and a child without a disability, as is the practice in this classroom? How might you promote inclusion in other ways and in other contexts, such as on the playground?
2. What can the teachers do to partner with families in their children's learning?

7.3 Preschool Classroom Supports and Embedded Interventions with Coteaching

Racheal Kuperus and Desarae Orgo

Connections to *Developmentally Appropriate Practice*

- Chapter 8: Observing, Documenting, and Assessing Children's Development and Learning
- Chapter 10: Planning and Implementing an Engaging Curriculum to Achieve Meaningful Goals

Case Overview

This case study portrays a 4-year-old preschooler, Kyle, who has been identified by both medical doctors and the school's Individualized Education Program (IEP) team as having a global developmental disability with specific difficulties with fine and visual motor coordination. For example, he often walks into furniture and peers, trips over his own feet, and uses impulsive full-body movements. These difficulties are causing delayed readiness skills and inhibit Kyle's access, participation, and progress in the general education curriculum. Kyle has an IEP and is being educated in a general education preschool classroom that is cotaught by a general education teacher (Mrs. Komel) and a special education teacher (Ms. Orzano).

This case study focuses on the use of observations and the collaboration between the two classroom teachers in providing key adaptations to materials, instruction, and assessment to assist all learners to succeed in an inclusive classroom.

Learning Objectives

1. Identify ways to observe, document, and assess young children's progress and achievements through purposeful coteaching implementations.
2. Demonstrate differentiated instructional strategies learned from the coteaching model in an inclusion classroom.

Case Narrative

Kyle is a 4-year-old child in an inclusive preschool classroom of 3- and 4-year-olds. The class uses a full-time coteaching model where the class is taught by one general education pre-K teacher (Mrs. Komel) and one special education pre-K teacher (Ms. Orzano). As coteachers, both Mrs. Komel and Ms. Orzano assess the children, most often by taking anecdotal notes from observations (noting both the time and day) as well as discussing changes in children's learning, behaviors, and actions. Through assessing Kyle, they identify that he has difficulty with transitions.

Mrs. Komel and Ms. Orzano have common planning time each day because the school administration believes that each teacher brings important knowledge to the table for planning and assessment. The following conversation between the teachers focuses on Kyle's need for redirection and prompting to follow the daily routine.

Mrs. Komel: I am not sure if you realize how hard of a time Kyle gave us the other day when you were at your inclusion conference! He would not transition for your substitute teacher at all!

Ms. Orzano: Oh no! What happened? He was doing so well with his transitions.

Mrs. Komel: He does well when you are here, but he didn't want to sit next to the substitute, and he was running into other children and colliding into centers and furniture! It was a nightmare. I dread the days when you are not here for your students!

Ms. Orzano: I understand you might have felt a little frustrated with him, but they are all "our" students, and you do well with him when I am the one leading the lesson to the whole group. I think he takes redirection very well from you.

Mrs. Komel: Yes, they are "our" students, but we are only coteaching because he is in the room and there is no space in the building for you to have your own special education preschool classroom like you should. I am just saying that he knows the routine when you are here, but when you are not here, he falls apart. You are the one who "gets" him and knows what to do with him.

Ms. Orzano: Well, you know I believe in inclusion for every child, and I think it makes teaching and learning better for everyone. I know it's not easy, but we can continue to come up with strategies for Kyle to help him with his difficulties. We both know plenty of children without developmental delays who have trouble with transitions and routines too. Let's not think about the labels we have for Kyle, but let's think about what Kyle's needs are.

Mrs. Komel: Kyle needs to have someone with him at all times so he does not interrupt the learning for the other children. Sitting next to one of us at whole group is beneficial because we can redirect him immediately. That works.

Ms. Orzano: It does work, but I just don't think that is realistic for the future. It doesn't really teach him what to do during transitions, so he needs another kind of support now. What about the visual schedule we use with the class to teach them the routine? Do you think it works for Kyle? How could we make that work better for him?

Mrs. Komel: I don't even know if he realizes the visual schedule is there or what it means. He is better when an adult is next to him teaching him what comes next.

Ms. Orzano: Let's do some observations and data collection and see what we can find out how and when Kyle uses the visual schedule.

The classroom visual schedule comprises actual photos of each activity scheduled for the day along with words describing the activity. After collecting some data, the teachers realize that Kyle does use the visual schedule, but he seems to pay attention to and use only the first few segments of it. Ms. Orzano moves the visual schedule lower on the wall, close to the floor, so that it is at eye level when Kyle is sitting during whole group time. The data does not change. After the fourth segment, Kyle has a difficult time finding the next segment within the sequence. At the next planning time, the teachers talk about what they have discovered from their observations and plan what they will do.

Ms. Orzano: I think our visual schedule is overwhelming to Kyle. Maybe we can shorten it and chunk the schedule into bigger parts of the day?

Mrs. Komel: I don't think that is fair to the other children. They are learning from the visual schedule just fine. It is not fair to them to make it so much easier, so they have nothing to learn.

Ms. Orzano: So what can we do to make sure that Kyle is still part of the classroom routines and activities, but that it is adapted to be more manageable for Kyle? I recognize how you want the whole class to benefit, but I do feel that Kyle needs stronger guidance throughout our day.

Mrs. Komel: Can you make Kyle his own schedule to use? The adult with him can keep it and use it with him.

Ms. Orzano: That is one idea, but I really want Kyle to be a full member of the classroom and to use the same materials everyone else uses as much as we can. Just like I don't want Kyle to become dependent on an adult to help him transition, I don't want him to become dependent on having his own visual schedule that is different from the one everyone else uses. I don't want to do something different for Kyle until we exhaust all the ways we can modify what we have.

Mrs. Komel: Okay, but how? What did you learn at your inclusion conference the other day that we can do?

Ms. Orzano: Well, my inclusion conference was really about the philosophy of inclusion and how it benefits all students by raising the quality of education for everyone. I know I am going offtrack here, but I still think it is a waste of time to keep sending me to these conferences alone. I love to go to them, but until we all get on the same page with inclusion, I am not sure we can make real change.

Mrs. Komel: Well, we know that is never going to happen around here, so just be happy you still get to go! Anyway, back to Kyle, we know he is very interested in numerals and lists of things. Maybe we could incorporate numerals and a list into the visual schedule?

Ms. Orzano: Oh, I love that! Maybe we can just make a board with four spaces on it and label them *1*, *2*, *3*, and *4*. We can have the schedule assistant put up four segments of the schedule at one time; they can do this after snack, after playground, and after lunch. I will continue to check in with Kyle during each schedule change so he is prepared for upcoming activities.

Mrs. Komel: It may even be a great activity for some of the other children to oversee deciding what the next four segments are in the sequence. I could make that a classroom job and use it as an assessment each day for our math standards.

Ms. Orzano: We could even design some supports for children at different levels, so while we could have different expectations for children, we can still use the same visual schedule for everyone!

Takeaways and Next Steps

Ms. Orzano makes the new visual schedule and helps teach everyone how they will use it. It takes a little time for many children in the class to get used to it, but the teachers gain some insight on many children's ability to sequence using this new assessment data. Kyle responds to the new visual schedule technique with ease after a week of consistency. He even enjoys being the schedule assistant when he is assigned the job. Both teachers agree that this was a win-win solution for everyone and that having the opportunity to use their combined knowledge and skills to co-plan and coteach really can benefit every child.

Case Discussion Questions

1. Inclusion is more than just a practice; it is a philosophy. How different do you believe Mrs. Komel's and Ms. Orzano's philosophies on inclusion are? Cite your evidence.
2. How does Ms. Orzano try to advocate for Kyle and inclusion in general to her coteacher? What else could she do?
3. The Joint Position Statement of the Division for Early Childhood (DEC) and NAEYC on inclusion (DEC & NAEYC 2009) identifies the defining features of inclusion as access, participation, and supports. How did Mrs. Komel and Ms. Orzano provide access, participation, and support for Kyle within this routine?
4. What evidence do you see in the case that the teachers used a strengths-based approach with Kyle? In what ways could they do more of this?
5. Chapter 8 of *Developmentally Appropriate Practice* reviews using assessment data to determine whether a program is having the intended impact on children. How did Mrs. Komel and Ms. Orzano's observations and data inform them on the progress of every child?
6. What key adaptations to materials and instruction were made by Ms. Orzano and Mrs. Komel? What other strategies can Ms. Orzano and Mrs. Komel use if the visual schedule plan doesn't have a long-lasting positive impact on Kyle?

General Discussion Questions

1. Discuss elements of a strong coteaching partnership. What supports might teachers need?
2. Based on Chapter 10 of *Developmentally Appropriate Practice*, give some examples of how curriculum and standards are used to anchor the planning and decision-making process to make a learning activity individualized to meet the needs of a child with a disability as well as appropriately challenging for a whole class.

Reference

DEC (Division for Early Childhood) & NAEYC. 2009. "Early Childhood Inclusion: A Joint Position Statement of the Division for Early Childhood (DEC) and the National Association for the Education of Young Children (NAEYC)." Position statement. Chapel Hill: The University of North Carolina, FPG Child Development Institute. www.naeyc.org/resources/position-statements.

7.4 Addressing Challenging Behavior Using the Pyramid Model

Ellie Bold

Connections to *Developmentally Appropriate Practice*

- Chapter 6: Creating a Caring, Equitable Community of Learners
- Chapter 7: Engaging in Reciprocal Partnerships with Families and Fostering Community Connections
- Chapter 8: Observing, Documenting, and Assessing Children's Development and Learning
- Chapter 9: Teaching to Enhance Each Child's Development and Learning

Case Overview

This case explores several guidelines of developmentally appropriate practice that highlight the importance of early childhood educators supporting children with disabilities. The case discusses a 4-year-old child with autism spectrum disorder (ASD) who exhibits challenging behavior, which describes "any repeated pattern of behavior, or perception of behavior, that interferes with or is at risk of interfering with optimal learning or engagement in pro-social interactions with peers and adults" (Smith & Fox 2003, 6). Understanding the reason a child is engaging in challenging behavior (known as the *function* of the behavior) is essential for the teacher to both prevent the behavior and teach and reinforce more appropriate replacement behaviors.

Jackson persistently has tantrums (screaming, crying, and hitting peers) when he transitions between activities throughout the day. His teacher, Ms. Evans, collaborates with her teaching assistant, Mr. Davis, and Jackson's family to understand the function of the behavior and to develop a plan to teach and reinforce a routine that will support Jackson during transitions (Dunlap et al. 2022). The intervention aims to facilitate smoother transitions throughout the day for Jackson by incorporating visual supports for him to communicate his needs and providing differential reinforcement for the desired behaviors (Masterson 2022).

Learning Objectives

1. List some strategies for teaching self-regulation skills to children using direct verbal and nonverbal techniques.
2. Articulate the value of strong family partnerships when supporting children with challenging behavior in the classroom.
3. Describe the importance of utilizing observation and data collection to inform the development and monitoring of behavioral interventions.
4. Explain how to individualize teaching strategies for children with needs in language acquisition and expression, particularly during daily transitions in the classroom.

Case Narrative

Jackson, who is 4 years old, attends an inclusive pre-K class and was diagnosed with ASD a year ago. Jackson lives at home with his mother and older sister (who is in second grade). This is Jackson's first experience in school, and his mother has shared with Ms. Evans her concerns about his behaviors at home when asked to do something he doesn't want to do. She shares her hopes for Jackson to have more peer interactions in the classroom, as he prefers to play alone and has a hard time sharing toys with his sister.

The classroom uses the Pyramid Model as a framework to promote children's social and emotional competence. This framework is a tiered system of supports for children, beginning with universal components of high-quality environments and nurturing and responsive relationships. Working up the Pyramid, more targeted supports are provided to children as needed (for example, extra practice and small group instruction); individualized interventions are utilized at the top tier.

The Pyramid Model also provides opportunities to teach emotional literacy—the ability to identify, understand, and respond to one's emotions in a healthy manner (Head Start Early Childhood Learning & Knowledge Center [ECLKC] 2021)—and self-regulation across naturally occurring routines and activities. For example, every day during circle time, the children in Ms. Evans's class identify how they are feeling, and they read stories about managing difficult emotions or interactions with peers. They discuss these situations and practice a variety of problem-solving skills together, such as how to ask for a turn. The classroom also has a cozy corner (a calm-down area) with self-regulation tools, such as pinwheels to help the children take deep breaths and a photobook of each child's family. The children practice using the cozy corner, and only one child uses it at any one time.

Perhaps most important, the daily schedule is consistent day to day; Ms. Evans and Mr. Davis review it each morning with the children upon arrival and highlight any changes. The predictability of routines helps children know what is expected of them and helps them develop emotional literacy. When children understand what is expected of them, they are less likely to experience frustration or demonstrate challenging behavior.

Jackson begins in the classroom at the start of the year. Before the first day of school, Jackson and his mom visit the classroom to introduce Jackson to Ms. Evans and Mr. Davis and give him time to explore the room. Jackson's mom has told Ms. Evans that Jackson's favorite toys are LEGOs, so she ensures that a box of them is available to him during his visit. Jackson speaks only a few words, and he signs for some of his needs, like "more" and "all done." Jackson rarely interacts with his peers, but he will play near a peer without difficulty if he has his own toys. During the first few weeks of school, Jackson does well. He enters the classroom without incident, follows directions with visual supports, and navigates between activities with minimal prompting.

A few weeks into the school year, Jackson demonstrates more difficulty making transitions during the school day. Ms. Evans provides one-minute verbal and visual warnings before activity transitions in addition to the official transition signal. When prompted to transition from center time to small group time, Jackson starts to tantrum. He screams, cries, and if a peer is in reach, he sometimes hits them. Ms. Evans knows that Jackson's mom has experienced some difficulty with his behaviors at home, so she talks with her at drop-off to see if she has any recommendations. Jackson's mom shares that she sometimes supports him through transitions at home, helping to clean up and guiding him to the next activity. Ms. Evans and Mr. Davis decide to increase their support of Jackson during this time and begin to label how he is feeling, provide extra warnings for transitions with an individualized visual schedule, and reward him upon transitioning to the table with praise. However, these strategies have little success; his behavior steadily increases in intensity and duration, with Jackson unable to communicate his desires through speech.

After several weeks, Ms. Evans asks Jackson's mom to join her and Mr. Davis for a meeting after school to discuss next steps. Given the lack of success in reducing Jackson's behaviors and the safety risk presented by his aggression with peers even with the implementation of targeted supports, Ms. Evans feels that it would be most beneficial to Jackson to develop an individualized behavior intervention plan. The Pyramid Model includes a step-by-step process for development of such a plan, and Ms. Evans presents the option to Jackson's mom. Incorporating Jackson's mom into the process is a necessary component, particularly as she can use the same strategies at home.

Together, they work through the process to identify the function of Jackson's behavior—to gain a desired object or attention, avoid a person or task, or reduce or increase the level of stimulation—through targeted observation of Jackson's transitions from center time to small group time. Using an antecedent-behavior-consequence observation strategy, Ms. Evans identifies the function of Jackson's behavior to be his desire to avoid or escape a task (changing activities from what he wants to do to what he doesn't want to do), as his tantrums most often result in Jackson not participating in the activity during small group time. Ms. Evans and Mr. Davis have observed Jackson struggling to transition when it requires him to discontinue playing with his preferred LEGOs, and Jackson's mom indicates she experiences similar difficulties at home when she asks Jackson to stop playing to eat dinner.

Next, Ms. Evans develops a replacement behavior—a way for Jackson to communicate his desire to escape from the small group activity. She gives Jackson a visual cue card to ask for extra time in his chosen center (blocks) and teaches him that presenting the card will allow him to stay for three more minutes. In addition, Jackson's mom uses a similar card at home to support his behaviors transitioning to dinner and bedtime. Finally, Ms. Evans and Mr. Davis implement a reinforcement system for Jackson. His mom shares that Jackson's favorite food is Annie's Cheddar Bunnies, which he rarely eats at school. She provides Ms. Evans with a box, and Jackson earns five cheddar bunnies when he joins the small group activity. Similarly, Jackson's mom offers them to Jackson upon joining the dinner table. Besides the cheddar bunnies, the teachers and Jackson's mom also provide praise and other social feedback (big smiles, positive attention) as part of the reinforcement. This is an important aspect of a reinforcement system so that the tangible or edible reinforcers can be reduced and removed over time.

Ms. Evans tracks Jackson's progress by measuring the duration of his tantrums before and after these intervention strategies. Jackson's tantrums quickly decrease as he learns to use the cue card requesting more playtime. After a few weeks, Ms. Evans and his mom are able to reduce the extra time to two minutes. After his extra time, Jackson transitions easily to the table and accepts his cheddar bunnies and social reinforcements. This dual intervention strategy—teaching Jackson a replacement behavior and rewarding his participation—supports Jackson's behavior and increases the time he willingly and productively engages in a small group activity.

Takeaways and Next Steps

Using the two-pronged intervention approach in this case enables Ms. Evans and Mr. Davis to learn more about Jackson and how to provide him more effective support. Jackson's mother is an essential team member throughout this process and provides valuable recommendations and support that enables Jackson's success in the classroom. The teachers find it rewarding to track Jackson's progress and see both a reduction in challenging behavior and an increase in the time he spends engaged in small group activities. Though time consuming to plan, the return on time invested in the form of Jackson's improved engagement and communication and the decrease in stress to the classroom team is well worth it.

Case Discussion Questions

1. How does the Ms. Evans and Mr. Davis's collaboration with Jackson's mom illustrate guideline 2F of the position statement on developmentally appropriate practice?
2. How might the teachers begin to fade or reduce Jackson's use of the cue card for more playtime and cheddar bunnies to increase his time spent in the small group activity?
3. How did teachers incorporate guideline 4B.4 into Jackson's intervention?

4. What could Ms. Evans and Mr. Davis do to encourage Jackson to interact with his peers over the course of the intervention?
5. What challenges in implementing this intervention might come up for the teachers or for some of the other children, and how could the teachers address these challenges?

General Discussion Questions

1. What are additional ways to individualize teaching strategies for children with language needs?
2. What role could a child's peers play in an intervention such as described in this case?

References

Dunlap, G., K. Wilson, P. Strain, & J. Lee. 2022. *Prevent-Teach-Reinforce for Young Children: The Early Childhood Model of Individualized Positive Behavior Support*. 2nd ed. Baltimore, MD: Brookes.

Head Start ECLKC (Early Childhood Learning & Knowledge Center). 2021. "Fostering Emotional Literacy in Young Children: Labeling Emotions." *What Works Brief*, no. 21. https://eclkc.ohs.acf.hhs.gov/mental-health/article/fostering-emotional-literacy-young-children-labeling-emotions.

Masterson, M. 2022. "Planning and Implementing an Engaging Curriculum to Achieve Meaningful Goals." In *Developmentally Appropriate Practice in Early Childhood Programs Serving Children from Birth Through Age 8*, 4th ed., NAEYC, 215–51. Washington, DC: NAEYC.

Smith, B.J., & L. Fox. 2003. *Systems of Service Delivery: A Synthesis of Evidence Relevant to Young Children at Risk of or Who Have Challenging Behavior*. Tampa: University of South Florida, Center for Evidence-Based Practice: Young Children with Challenging Behavior. https://ohiofamilyrights.com/Reports/Special-Reports-Page-4/Systems-of-Service-Delivery-A-Synthesis-of-Evidence-Relevant-to-Young.pdf.

7.5 Is There a Disability? How Teachers Can Be the First to Help

Alyssa Brillante

Connections to *Developmentally Appropriate Practice*

- Chapter 7: Engaging in Reciprocal Partnerships with Families and Fostering Community Connections
- Chapter 8: Observing, Documenting, and Assessing Children's Development and Learning
- Chapter 9: Teaching to Enhance Each Child's Development and Learning

Case Overview

Alex, a kindergarten student and a dual language learner (DLL), is not speaking much in class in either English or his home language of Spanish. His teacher, Mrs. Gorman, had hoped to see progress as the school year continued, but after several months, she is concerned and begins to seek out help from others on how to help him.

Mrs. Gorman collects some anecdotal data on Alex that concern her, and she shares these concerns with his mother. Alex's mother is not convinced there is anything to be concerned about, believing that he is "just quiet."

Through a discussion with a colleague, the teacher realizes that she needs to rethink her approach to teaching and assessing this child as well as to building a relationship with his family. This case study provides an example of a teacher collecting anecdotal observations and seeking assistance to understand what the child's needs really are so she can develop interventions in the classroom that can help him now.

Learning Objectives

1. Explain both the purpose and the process of ongoing assessment to determine children's learning through different lenses, including identifying dual language needs and/or determining if further information is needed to identify developmental or learning disabilities.
2. Demonstrate an understanding of the role of families as an important source of information about their children as well as the educator's responsibility for establishing respectful, reciprocal relationships with families.

Case Narrative

Alex is a kindergarten student who most people at the school think of as reserved since he doesn't talk much to his peers or his teachers. His classroom teacher, Mrs. Gorman, knows a little bit about Alex and his family. His kindergarten registration form indicates that he speaks both English and Spanish at home with his family. The form also says that his grandmother speaks Spanish at home, but his mother and sisters are all listed as bilingual.

Five other students in Alex's classroom also speak both English and Spanish at home. Mrs. Gorman does not speak Spanish herself, but she has made sure there are many books, labels, and other classroom materials in both languages available to everyone. During informal observations, Mrs. Gorman has documented that many times Alex is often unoccupied or seems to not know what to do. Several months into the school year, Mrs. Gorman sees Mr. Garima, her mentor who is also a kindergarten teacher, in the hallway and asks him some questions about Alex.

Mrs. Gorman: Hi, Andy. I was wondering if you had any time to give me some suggestions or advice on how I can help one of the boys in my class, Alex. I worry about his language. I think he speaks Spanish and English at home, but he doesn't speak much in school. Who do I see about getting someone to help him?

Mr. Garima: Okay, so before I can give any advice, I need to know more about Alex. Does he speak Spanish to any of his classmates? Do you know how much Spanish he speaks at home? I had Alex's older sisters when they were in kindergarten, and I remember that their mother, Mrs. Torres, feels it is very important for her children to be fluent in English. What has she said to you when you talked to her about this?

Mrs. Gorman: I haven't met with her about this yet; I thought the specialist would do that. I really haven't gotten to know his mom yet this year. I see her when she drops Alex off and picks him up.

Mr. Garima: I've found it helpful to develop a relationship with families early on so we can talk informally throughout the school year. That relationship helps me get to know the child so much better and the community too. Knowing what's relevant to the children in my class supports me in knowing what and how to teach them.

Mrs. Gorman: I didn't realize there was a problem until now.

Mr. Garima: You really don't need a reason or wait for there to be a problem to meet with a family. I would suggest that you meet with Alex's mom very soon and get to know her better. Ask her some specific questions about how both his Spanish and English are developing and how he is using them at home and if she has any concerns.

Mrs. Gorman: Thanks, Andy, I will ask Mrs. Torres this afternoon at pickup if a meeting tomorrow after school will work.

Mr. Garima: She was very helpful to me in the classroom. She read stories on tape for our classroom and brought in some great information about their culture that I still use. There are some other families in your class who will be great resources for you.

Mrs. Gorman plans a meeting with Mrs. Torres for the next day at pickup, and she writes down what she has observed Alex doing in class to share with his mother—things like not following oral directions right away, watching what the other children do first before responding, and repeating questions he is asked but not giving an answer.

At her after-school meeting with Alex's mother, Mrs. Gorman begins with a concern.

Mrs. Gorman: I am very concerned that Alex isn't talking much in class.

Mrs. Torres: He's just quiet. He is a boy. It's all girls at home . . . he has no boys to play with.

Mrs. Gorman: Is Alex speaking English or Spanish at home? Do you speak in Spanish to him?

Mrs. Torres: We speak English. He is just quiet, always playing by himself, but he is fine, no problems.

Mrs. Gorman: Is there anything you are concerned about with Alex?

Mrs. Torres: No, he is a good boy, he is fine.

The next morning Mrs. Gorman meets with Mr. Garima to let him know how the meeting with Mrs. Torres went.

Mrs. Gorman: So, Andy, Mrs. Torres didn't give me much information, but I think I didn't ask the right questions. I was nervous. Do I ask the ESL teacher for advice? What about the speech therapist or someone from the special education department? Maybe there is a disability they haven't uncovered yet?

Mr. Garima: He is in your class right now, so trust your instincts. I am sure you know what his strengths are and what he likes to do. Use that as a starting point.

Mrs. Gorman: But I'm not an ESL or special education specialist. I don't want to do something that will be harmful to him.

Mr. Garima: First things first—he is a kindergarten student, and you know all about kindergartners. Your instincts are telling you to look more closely at this child to get more information on him, which is great. Let's go back to what your assessments already tell you about him. What does he like to play with?

Mrs. Gorman: He loves the trucks in the block area! Sometimes he is so loud that I have to take them away.

Mr. Garima: Don't take the trucks away! You can use his love of trucks to engage him with you and his peers and that will help you assess and teach him. What else does he like?

Mrs. Gorman: Recess.

Mr. Garima: Whom does he play with at recess? How does he communicate with them?

Mrs. Gorman: He runs around and plays soccer with some of the other boys in the classroom. But honestly, I don't really know how he communicates with them.

Mr. Garima: Well, let's go back and look at Alex through that lens too. Establish a relationship with him. Focus on what he can do, and then use trucks and recess time to gather more information about him. Watch specifically for how he communicates with peers. Take lots of anecdotal notes and even record some videos you can upload into our secure school assessment system. Use that information to adapt and modify what you are already doing. The observations and assessments will help you see the progress he makes, and they will also be helpful in analyzing the data to see if what you are observing is related to Alex learning two languages or a potential developmental or learning disability or both.

Mrs. Gorman: I guess I have few big tasks ahead of me now, but you are right, I do know what our curriculum and standards say he should be able to do before first grade. I just need to get to know him better and how he communicates and uses language. I should also reach out to the ESL and special education specialist to see if they have any good suggestions for me about teaching and assessing Alex in my classroom right now.

Mr. Garima: Those are great ideas! Getting to know Alex may also help you think of more specific questions the next time you see his mom that would be more helpful to you. Let's also plan an activity our classrooms can do together where we can invite parents like Mrs. Torres. That will be a great way for you to get to know each other.

Takeaways and Next Steps

Mrs. Gorman gets advice and assistance from Mr. Garima on collecting specific data and using different methods to assess Alex formally and informally. Following his advice, she looks for ways in which Alex can communicate with the skills that he does have while using his specific interests as tools to help her collect more information about him and build their relationship. She also researches ways to help children use language and modifies her instruction to support Alex's participation during activities and communicate with his peers. Mrs. Gorman seeks guidance from Mr. Garima and other colleagues on ways to communicate more effectively and appropriately with families to help build relationships with them.

Case Discussion Questions

1. Based on the information presented in the case and in Chapter 8 of *Developmentally Appropriate Practice,* what additional data might Mrs. Gorman want to collect about Alex, and why?
2. What could Mrs. Gorman have done differently during the family meeting with Mrs. Torres? What are some ways the teacher can improve her relationship with Mrs. Torres so they can work more collaboratively?
3. Based on what Alex can do at present, how can Mrs. Gorman provide multiple ways for Alex to demonstrate the communication skills he does have?
4. Describe ways in which Mrs. Gorman can improve her understanding of language development. Who at the school might be able to help her?
5. Mrs. Gorman notes that Alex is often unoccupied in class or doesn't seem to know what to do. How might the daily routine or environment be contributing to this? What steps could Mrs. Gorman take to find out?
6. Guideline 4H in the position statement on developmentally appropriate practice states that "educators differentiate instructional approaches to match each child's interest, knowledge, and skills" (NAEYC 2020, 24). What can Mrs. Gorman do right now to individualize, adapt, and modify her classroom and her instruction to help Alex participate in classroom activities and communicate with peers? Why is it important that she take these steps?

General Discussion Question

1. What are some valid and reliable assessment tools that can be used with students who have similar characteristics as Alex? Research a few and report back to the group what you have found.

Reference

NAEYC. 2020. "Developmentally Appropriate Practice." Position statement. Washington, DC: NAEYC. www.naeyc.org/resources/position-statements/dap/contents.

7.6 Adapting and Modifying Instruction Using Reader's Theater

Michelle Gonzalez

Connections to *Developmentally Appropriate Practice*

- Chapter 6: Creating a Caring, Equitable Community of Learners
- Chapter 9: Teaching to Enhance Each Child's Development and Learning

Case Overview

This case study explores the planning and instruction of a small group reading activity for second grade students. The teacher, Mr. Perez, works to individually accommodate students with and without reading disabilities in the same lesson with the appropriate use of scaffolds to maximize the children's participation and learning. His efforts to use the Reader's Theater strategy to adapt reading materials to meet the abilities of all the students and promote fluency are not entirely successful.

Learning Objectives

1. Identify opportunities for scaffolding learning with strategies that support children's reading fluency.
2. Identify and evaluate the effectiveness of using differentiated instructional approaches to match each child's interests, knowledge, and skills.

Case Narrative

Mr. Perez teaches a second grade class of diverse students with a range of abilities, including students with identified disabilities who have Individualized Education Programs (IEPs) that specify goals for reading. One of the grade-level Common Core standards that Mr. Perez needs to address for all children in second grade pertains to reading fluency.

In a recent professional development session, Mr. Perez learns about the Reader's Theater strategy, which has students do repeated readings of a text in a script format. This is an effective way to build fluency. The class has recently read *A Bad Case of Stripes* by David Shannon. Mr. Perez's students enjoy this book, and he feels that its playful dialogue and dynamic narration will make for a good Reader's Theater script.

Mr. Perez is not a reading specialist or a special education specialist, and he feels he needs some additional coaching to adapt and differentiate for the different instructional levels of the students in his class. He consults with the school's reading specialist, who recommends that he create a heterogeneous group of five students who have varying abilities in reading. Mr. Perez chooses the following students:

- Bethany is diagnosed with dyslexia and uses individualized strategies for decoding and word recognition. Her independent reading level is a bit more than one year below grade level.
- Noelle is reading about a half year below grade level, but she does not have an identified disability that affects her reading.
- Alexander is reading on grade level.
- Joseph is reading on grade level.
- Hunter loves reading, and both her independent and instructional levels in reading are about one year above grade level.

Mr. Perez assigns the roles for each character of the book *A Bad Case of Stripes*. For Bethany's character, he rewrites the script to make the lines shorter and to the point. He thinks this will be easier for Bethany and help her with her fluency. To meet Hunter's needs, Mr. Perez decides to have her write parts of the script on her own.

Mr. Perez is ready to start! He tells the small group of students that they will be doing something called Reader's Theater, which is like putting on a play by reading a script, and that it is a fun way to practice reading fluency. They will put on this play for the rest of the class and Dr. Anderson, the school principal. Mr. Perez shows the students the script and asks if anyone can read the title. All five hands go up.

Hunter: *A Bad Case of Stripes*. I know this book! This is the book we read last week!

Noelle: I love this book! It really helped me see how I should change for me and not for others!

Alexander: This book was so funny, with Camilla changing throughout the whole book! It was hilarious when her face changed to a pill, but I really liked the end when she didn't care anymore what the other kids said about her. I can't wait! What part will each of us have?

Mr. Perez tells his students that everyone will have a part, and they will practice reading their parts together today. They are eager to start.

Mr. Perez reads a few lines of the script to provide a fluency model. He then hands out the script and tells the students which parts they will have. He gives them highlighters so they can highlight their parts. He tells them that they will practice reading their roles until the timer goes off, then come back together and practice as a group. Alexander and Joseph ask if they can practice in the class library area. After Mr. Perez's agreement, they skip away.

Mr. Perez asks Bethany and Noelle to go to the back table to highlight and read the script together and says that he will join them in a few minutes. He then pulls Hunter aside and asks if she wants to read two characters for the play and write additional lines for her assigned characters. Mr. Perez suggests that she try adding interesting vocabulary words to her lines. He then asks if she has any suggestions. Hunter ponders for a bit.

Hunter: Hmm, I remember that Camilla does not say a lot in the book, and I was always wondering how she was feeling. I can add more lines for her and feeling words.

Mr. Perez: What a great idea! By adding more dialogue and feeling words, you can help us understand Camilla more as a character. This goes along with what we've been learning about character traits. I can't wait to see what you come up with!

Hunter walks back to her desk, and Mr. Perez heads back to the table, where he sees Bethany and Noelle finishing their highlighting. He takes a quick peek at their scripts and notes they have both highlighted their parts correctly. Then he asks them to read their lines. Bethany reads her first line in a slow, monotone voice.

Bethany: You are covered in stripes!

Mr. Perez is concerned that she replaced the words "you're" with "you are" and substituted "in" for "with." Bethany also struggles to sound out the words "covered" and "stripes." He decides that it may be easier for her to read if she hears the sentence out loud and uses her index finger to follow along.

Mr. Perez: Let's stop here a minute and practice again. Let's use your fingers to track the words when I read the sentence out loud.

Mr. Perez reads the sentence several more times, and Bethany takes several turns reading the sentence. She is now reading the sentences correctly but still in a monotone voice.

Mr. Perez: Bethany, do you notice what type of punctuation mark is in the line you just read?

Bethany: An exclamation mark?

Mr. Perez: Yes, and what should we do when we see exclamation marks?

Noelle: Change our voice to sound excited or even loud!

Mr. Perez: Yes, Noelle, that is correct. Bethany, how do you think Camilla's mom would feel if she came into the room and saw her daughter covered in stripes?

Bethany: Surprised or mad.

Mr. Perez: Okay! Now reread the sentence, sounding surprised or mad.

They continue to read the script together, and Bethany succeeds in reading her lines fluently and with expression. Mr. Perez calls Hunter, Joseph, and Alexander to join the rest of the group at the back table, where they practice the script together until they are ready for the performance. When it comes time for them to read their parts as a group and present for the rest of the class, the principal, Dr. Anderson, comes in to watch.

During the performance, Hunter does an amazing job, and Joseph, Alexander, and Noelle all do a fine job too. To Mr. Perez's surprise, Bethany struggles with her lines and does not read with expression as she had done during the practice. She is standing apart from her group during the performance with a scowl on her face. Not only does she not seem engaged with her reading, it appears that she is struggling to fit into this group.

At the end of the performance, Mr. Perez has all the students comment and give compliments to their peers like they always do to recognize each one's hard work.

Later, Mr. Perez meets with Dr. Anderson, and while she is complimentary of the lesson, she does have some observations. To her, it seems like Hunter was the star of the show, with the most lines and the most sophisticated dialogue of anyone. Most of the class had comments and compliments for Hunter, but none had comments or compliments for Bethany. It also seems to her that Mr. Perez is modeling low expectations for Bethany to the rest of the group and that she didn't seem to enjoy this activity. Mr. Perez is initially surprised by this feedback. He believes that he has carefully considered each child's abilities and needs.

Takeaways and Next Steps

Mr. Perez used the Reader's Theater strategy to engage readers of varying levels to improve their fluency and foster a community of learners. This strategy allows him to use scaffolding and address their reading needs and abilities. However, Mr. Perez's success in using techniques and individual modifications based on students' needs is mixed, which leaves Mr. Perez with a lot to think and reflect about.

He decided to rewrite part of the script for Bethany to be easier to read because he is aware that "as children begin new challenges, they may need some support from teachers so they can manage the challenge" (Masterson 2022, 185). Also, the small group format allowed him to "give each child more attention and . . . provide support and challenges tailored to children's individual levels" (187).

Since Mr. Perez has worked hard to differentiate his instruction for the students and wants Bethany to feel included in the activity with the rest of the class, he is discouraged by her performance and concerned that she did not seem to enjoy the activity. He had believed that, although reading is a struggle for her, helping her to participate on her level with her peers would be a positive thing for her.

Mr. Perez also struggles with his supervisor's feedback and isn't sure what to make of it. He wonders if adapting the materials is just lowering his expectations for Bethany, which is apparent to the other students in the group and inhibiting the development of a truly equitable community of learners. He just isn't sure what else he can do.

Case Discussion Questions

1. What assumptions does Mr. Perez appear to have made about Bethany and Hunter? How did these assumptions influence his choice of strategies and, eventually, the outcome of the experience for each student?
2. How was Bethany supported by Mr. Perez's adaptation of the materials for her? What are some reasons this did not help her to be successful?
3. Adaptations can be made to instruction, the social environment, and the level of personal assistance as well as to materials. How could Mr. Perez have adapted his instruction, the social environment, or the level of personal assistance for Bethany that might have been more successful than adapting only the materials? What factors besides Bethany's reading level should Mr. Perez consider when making adaptations?
4. How did Mr. Perez ensure that each member in the small group felt valued? What else could he have done?

General Discussion Questions

1. How can educators meet students' academic needs while helping students feel valued in the classroom?
2. How might the Reader's Theater strategy be used in subject-matter areas beyond reading?

Reference

Masterson, M. 2022. "Teaching to Enhance Each Child's Development and Learning." In *Developmentally Appropriate Practice in Early Childhood Programs Serving Children from Birth Through Age 8,* 4th ed., NAEYC, 181–214. Washington, DC: NAEYC.

7.7 Supporting Children with Learning Disabilities in Mathematics: The Importance of Observation, Content Knowledge, and Context

Renee B. Whelan

Connections to *Developmentally Appropriate Practice*

- Chapter 3: Context Matters: Reframing Teaching in Early Childhood Education
- Chapter 4: Teaching Content in Early Childhood Education
- Chapter 8: Observing, Documenting, and Assessing Children's Development and Learning
- Chapter 9: Teaching to Enhance Each Child's Development and Learning
- Chapter 10: Planning and Implementing an Engaging Curriculum to Achieve Meaningful Goals

Case Overview

This case explores the importance of using developmental trajectories to effectively gauge students' understanding of mathematical concepts and scaffold their learning appropriately. There is a variable progression in early childhood development; development occurs at different rates for different children. Some children may quickly move up levels in the trajectory and learn concepts simultaneously while other children may slide back on the trajectory, needing further reinforcement in understanding a specific concept or gaining a mathematical skill. Learning trajectories help teachers determine how to support the children within their zone of proximal development. This pathway may not always be straightforward; however, teachers can still determine where each child is developmentally and scaffold accordingly.

In this case, a third grade teacher is using a concrete approach in working with a small group of students, including students with math-related learning disabilities, to support their understanding of multiplication in math story problems. He uses culturally relevant terminology and examples in his math story problems to engage students. As the teacher has the students solve problems on their own, he formatively assesses by observing and documenting each student's understanding of this concept in relation to the developmental trajectory for multiplying.

Learning Objectives

1. Explore the use of developmental learning trajectories to gauge understanding of mathematical concepts.
2. Identify opportunities to scaffold learning opportunities that support children's understanding of mathematical concepts.
3. Describe the importance of using culturally relevant examples to engage students in math instruction.

Case Narrative

Agnes is a student in Mr. Golda's third grade class who speaks Polish and English at home with her parents. She is quiet in class yet is becoming more talkative during small group instruction. Agnes has an identified math-related learning disability that has affected her math performance. Numerical problem solving as well as representation of quantity information is difficult for Agnes. Her working memory also affects her ability to easily remember basic arithmetic facts and solve multiple-step word problems. She has an Individualized Education Program (IEP) in place.

Enrique's family is from Mexico. Like Agnes, Enrique, speaks two languages at home—Spanish and English. Enrique also has an identified learning disability and an IEP; however, his disability affects his ability to solve math word problems rather than solve equations. He also struggles with reading, which has affected his performance in mathematical problem solving.

Both Agnes and Enrique meet with their teacher, Mr. Golda, every day during small group math instruction. They typically meet with a couple of other peers who may or may not need extra support. The rest of the students are at their math stations doing hands-on work, independently or collaboratively, in the areas of multiplication/division, fractions, rectangular arrays/area, and two-dimensional shapes. Small group time today involves Agnes, Enrique, Paul, and Maria.

Mr. Golda: Today we will be working on solving a math story problem using multiplication. I have some materials that we can use. Let's see if we can solve our problem!

Paul: You mean we are going to use these sticks and cubes for the multiplication problem?

Mr. Golda: Good observation Paul, yes, we are! I heard that Agnes is having her cousins over for Międzynarodowy Dzień Dziecka [which is Children's Day in Poland that the family still celebrates in the United States]. Agnes's mother told me she is putting Agnes in charge of telling her how many sandwiches she needs for her four cousins.

Maria: We need to get that number right, Mr. Golda. We don't want Agnes to run out of snacks for everyone!

Mr. Golda: That is right, Maria, we don't want to run out of snacks! So, if Agnes needs to make two mini kielbasa sandwiches for each of her cousins, how many will she have to make?

Agnes is now smiling from ear to ear at the teacher's mention of Międzynarodowy Dzień Dziecka and the need to make mini kielbasa sandwiches. Mr. Golda writes the story on his whiteboard and gestures to the craft sticks and cubes.

Mr. Golda: How would you solve this story problem using the craft sticks to represent the people and the cubes to represent the sandwiches?

Mr. Golda guides Agnes in this physical demonstration with manipulatives by repeating the question slowly a couple of times and then using his whiteboard to underline key considerations, such as four cousins and two sandwiches for each cousin.

Agnes: I need to make eight sandwiches, $4 \times 2 = 8$.

Mr. Golda: Okay, that was great, Agnes, but do you think you will feel left out when your cousins are eating your mother's delicious mini kielbasa sandwiches? You didn't make enough for yourself too.

Enrique: What is kielbasa?

Maria: Isn't kielbasa like chorizo, Mr. Golda?

Mr. Golda: Yes, Maria, kielbasa is a bit similar to chorizo.

Enrique: I love chorizo, and I think Agnes needs to make enough for all of us, Mr. Golda!

Mr. Golda: Enrique, I agree, that is an excellent idea! Why don't we first pair up and find out how many sandwiches would be needed if Agnes wanted two sandwiches for herself too.

All the children are engaged in the math problem presented. Some are using the manipulatives available while others use the whiteboards to represent the problem. After a few minutes, Mr. Golda refers to $4 \times 2 = 8$ on the board and asks how he should represent the equation to include the additional child (Agnes) who wants a couple of sandwiches.

Agnes: $6 \times 2 = 12$. I need 12 sandwiches.

Mr. Golda: How did you solve that problem, Agnes?

Agnes: I added two more craft sticks.

Mr. Golda: Okay, let's look at this again. The craft sticks represent the number of people. If we need sandwiches for Agnes and four of her cousins, how many do we need all together? Everyone, show me your answer using your whiteboard or your manipulatives.

Paul: It is five.

Mr. Golda: Okay, so everyone please show me five craft sticks or five marks on your whiteboards. Enrique, do you remember how many people needed sandwiches? Let's do that together out loud so we know if we have the right answer.

Enrique: Agnes and her cousins.

Mr. Golda: How many cousins?

Enrique: Four.

Mr. Golda: So let's count Agnes and her four cousins to see how many altogether. Is everyone ready?

Children: One, two, three, four, five. They have five people.

Mr. Golda: How many sandwiches are we making for each of them?

Children: Two!

Mr. Golda: So what is our math problem?

Children: 5 × 2! Agnes needs to make 10 sandwiches.

Mr. Golda: Great job. Let's see how we do with more math problems.

Mr. Golda displays another math story problem. This time he incorporates Enrique's and Paul's interest in playing soccer into the story. Mr. Golda also incorporates both English and Spanish numbers in this story problem and asks the children to pair up to solve it. There are other manipulatives available on the table and whiteboards with markers for the students to choose and use to support their answers. He demonstrates highlighting the critical information in the word problem as he repeats the question out loud using Spanish for some of the words in addition to English. The children succeed and share how they solved the problem. Mr. Golda gives them all a high five and tells them he is proud of their problem-solving work.

For the final part of small group, the students each get a problem to solve independently. As the students work, Mr. Golda jots down notes on his clipboard. The notes are specific to each child's performance and are entered into an area on the sheet that is based on the learning trajectory for multiplication. These notes provide Mr. Golda with a formative assessment of each student's independent and instructional levels on the trajectory of learning math. By understanding this, he can determine how to scaffold the child to the next level in multiplication.

Mr. Golda's teaching practices in this situation focus on the Concrete Modeler benchmark on the trajectory from Dr. Doug Clements and Dr. Julie Sarama's learningtrajectories.org, which is one example of a trajectory specific to early childhood mathematics ([LT]2, n.d.). The Concrete Modeler definition is "Solves small-number multiplying problems by grouping—making each group and counting all. Solves division/sharing problems with informal strategies, using concrete objects; up to 20 objects and 2–5 people. May justify results by equipartitioning using counting, arrays, or patterns." Mr. Golda's next goal for Agnes and Enrique and the rest of the group is to work on related problems independently with some peer check-ins to reinforce understanding of multiplication at this level. Afterward, Mr. Golda has plans to introduce the students to lessons in the Parts and Wholes level on the trajectory. The definition of Parts and Wholes is "predicts qualitatively the inverse relation between divisor and quotient in simple, concrete situations. Can re-assemble equal groups or parts to make the collection of the single whole as '*n* times as many (much)'" ([LT]2, n.d.).

Takeaways and Next Steps

Mr. Golda knows the importance of understanding the developmental pathway in learning various mathematical concepts as well as goals and examples of activities at each level of development. By using the learning trajectories as a formative assessment, Mr. Golda has become more skillful in differentiating his instruction for each learner with and without IEPs. After using these trajectories for some time, Mr. Golda has a better understanding of how children develop various mathematical skills and can more effectively scaffold instruction for children to progress to the next level on the trajectory, even if they fall back a level. Understanding the learning trajectories have complemented his math curriculum and math workshop approach.

Because Mr. Golda has established reciprocal relationships with his students' families, they have openly shared about family experiences and traditions that they celebrate. Mr. Golda has seen that when he incorporates those personal elements into his instruction and classroom environment, the children become more attentive and motivated as they see themselves reflected in these ways. He strives to include culturally responsive components, as well as the children's interests, in his daily instruction because of the positive impact on the students' learning. This has also had a positive effect on how the children view each other.

Case Discussion Questions

1. What effective strategies did Mr. Golda use to engage the students during small group math?
2. Mr. Golda intentionally incorporated the children's families and customs in his lesson. By doing this for both Enrique and Agnes, how is Mr. Golda supporting their learning?
3. Mr. Golda used a very intentional formative assessment at the end of his lesson. What other ways can teachers know what children are learning, and how can they use that information to make informed and meaningful decisions about teaching?

General Discussion Questions

1. What knowledge, skills, and understanding should teachers have to effectively support children's content learning? What other information and understanding would you want if you were tasked with designing a math activity for a small group?
2. Locate developmental trajectories for several areas of your curriculum, including mathematics and literacy instruction. Compare them to the written curriculum that you use, or one that you can examine if you are not currently working with children, to see if they follow a similar pattern of skill development.

Suggested Resource

Multiplying/dividing: www.learningtrajectories.org/index.php/math/learning-trajectories/multiplying-dividing.

Reference

[LT]2. n.d. "Learning and Teaching with Learning Trajectories." Accessed August 12, 2022. www.learningtrajectories.org.

PART 8

Supporting Dual Language Learners and Respecting Cultural and Linguistic Diversity

Jennifer J. Chen

INFANT

Facilitating a Child's Transition from Home to Group Care Through the Use of Cultural Caring Routines

Josephine Ahmadein

PRESCHOOL

Engaging Dual Language Learners in Conversation to Support Translanguaging During a Small Group Activity

Valeria Erdosi and Jennifer J. Chen

KINDERGARTEN

Incorporating Children's Cultures and Languages in Learning Activities

Eleni Zgourou

GRADE 1

Adapting Teaching Materials for Dual Language Learners to Reflect Their Home Languages and Cultures in a Math Lesson

Karen Nemeth

GRADE 2

Studying Celestial Bodies: Science and Cultural Stories

Zeynep Isik-Ercan

GRADE 3

Respecting Diverse Cultures and Languages by Sharing and Learning About Cultural Poems, Songs, or Stories from Others

Janis Strasser

Part 8 is devoted to analyzing and reflecting on developmentally appropriate practices that support the learning of dual language learners (DLLs) and foster respect for cultural and linguistic diversity among all children. Reflecting the understanding that children's development and learning are influenced by their cultural and linguistic experiences, Part 8 demonstrates that responsive teaching practices involve leveraging the cultural and linguistic repertoires of children and their families as assets in learning activities. The focus on DLLs is particularly exigent because they constitute a fast-growing child population across the United States and, thus, contribute to increased cultural and linguistic diversity in early childhood classrooms nationwide. Teachers working with DLLs are presented with both the challenge and opportunity of addressing DLLs' diverse developmental and learning needs responsively as well as fostering a culturally and linguistically respectful classroom dynamic for all children. The question is *how*.

The six cases in Part 8 allow readers to explore possible insights into this question by considering examples of teachers' implementation of and reflection on their pedagogical practices. The cases also encourage readers to analyze other ways in which these teachers' practices might be culturally and linguistically responsive to the specific developmental and learning needs of children. Each case study focuses on children of a particular age group (infants, preschoolers, kindergartners, first-graders, second-graders, or third-graders) and involves a specific learning format (working with children one-on-one, in a small group, or in a large group).

Collectively, the case studies feature two main themes:

- Valuing and incorporating the diverse cultural and linguistic characteristics of DLLs and their families as strengths for learning
- Providing opportunities for children to learn about one another's home languages and cultures to cultivate respect for cultural and linguistic diversity

Within these themes, common threads weave through the case studies. One such thread is that the teachers are intentional in developing, applying, and deepening their own cultural and linguistic responsiveness to children's diverse developmental and learning needs. They are also intentional in promoting and modeling understanding of and respect for the diverse home languages and cultures of others. These teachers' efforts reflect intentionality in decision making as foundational to developmentally appropriate practice. Another common thread is that the case studies demonstrate how teachers support children's language or bilingual development not in isolation but in conjunction with other areas of learning, especially the social, emotional, and cognitive domains. This approach is based on the recognition that language learning is one of the key domains of child development—one that facilitates and is facilitated by the other developmental domains.

In addition to sharing some common threads, the case studies reflect the coverage of four different topics:

- Collaborating with a family to scaffold a bilingual infant's social and emotional development
- Supporting translanguaging by engaging DLLs in bilingual conversation
- Promoting respect for cultural and linguistic diversity among children
- Designing linguistically and culturally meaningful teaching materials and activities to enhance children's content learning

The seven writers for Part 8 are all dedicated early childhood educators or teacher educators whose contributions to the field of early childhood education span at least a decade in various capacities, including as educators, researchers, leaders, and program coordinators. They have also contributed to the field through their professional/research publications on a variety of topics, especially those focusing on the development and learning of DLLs as well as pedagogical practices with these learners. Individually and collectively, these writers demonstrate a steadfast commitment to fostering multicultural and multilingual knowledge as well as respect for linguistic and cultural diversity. Most are from bilingual and bicultural or multilingual and multicultural backgrounds, representing a rich tapestry of diverse cultures and languages, including Castilian Spanish, Catalàn, Chinese, Greek, Hungarian, and Turkish. While all of the writers are situated in the northeastern United States, their professional contributions, leveraging the breadth and depth of their expertise, extend into the national and, for some, the international realm.

8.1 Facilitating a Child's Transition from Home to Group Care Through the Use of Cultural Caring Routines

Josephine Ahmadein

Connections to *Developmentally Appropriate Practice*

- Chapter 1: Intentional Teaching: Complex Decision Making and the Core Considerations
- Chapter 3: Context Matters: Reframing Teaching in Early Childhood Education
- Chapter 7: Engaging in Reciprocal Partnerships with Families and Fostering Community Connections

Case Overview

This case examines a basic component of a child's physical environment, namely the educator, as the most consequential in either providing or inhibiting a continuous, comprehensive, and responsive learning experience for the child. It unveils the critical connections between all of the adults involved in a child's life that are necessary to generate a unique learning context that can influence the child's successful development and learning. In this case, Ms. Jackie, an infant and toddler teacher, relies on understanding and adopting the family's cultural caring routines to provide a safe, smooth transition from home to group care for Pooja, a 10-month-old girl. This teacher not only understands that there must be a coexistence between commonality and context (two core considerations in the position statement on developmentally appropriate practice) to facilitate the growth and well-being of the infants in her care but also shows her understanding of the third core consideration, individuality, as she provides experiences for young children based on each one's unique characteristics and experiences.

Learning Objectives

1. Identify the critical interconnections among a child's family context, the community, and the early learning program and their impact on the child's overall learning and development.
2. Demonstrate ways a teacher can facilitate a child's ability to thrive by using attachment-building techniques with both the child and family.
3. Articulate developmentally appropriate strategies for supporting a young child's transition from home to group care.

Case Narrative

Before the Transition: The Introduction Meeting

Two weeks before Pooja starts her first day at the center, Ms. Jackie (a White, monolingual teacher) contacts Pooja's parents, Mr. and Mrs. Gupta, to schedule an introduction meeting with them.

Ms. Jackie wants to learn as much as she can about Pooja and her family, but she is also respectful of what Mr. and Mrs. Gupta are comfortable sharing regarding their cultural background, home language, Pooja's daily routines, and other important facts about Pooja. Ms. Jackie learns that Pooja has been taken care of at home since she was born and has not spent time with anyone outside the home. Pooja's parents speak Bengali to Pooja, her family's home language. Ms. Jackie also learns that being held as much as possible is an essential part of her daily routine. Pooja only drinks liquefied foods fed to her in a bottle, almost always while being held by her mother. She has never been offered solid food, nor has she been introduced to a spoon.

Knowing Pooja has only heard Bengali, Ms. Jackie asks Pooja's parents to provide a list of words and short phrases in Bengali that she can use in the classroom to help Pooja adjust to her new environment. Mr. and Mrs. Gupta quickly agree to the suggestion and include on the list one of Pooja's favorite games, "Tai, tai, tai" (which means *clap, clap, clap*), as well as some of her favorite songs.

During the Transition: The Development of Trusting Relationships

As Mrs. Gupta is dropping off Pooja on the first day, Pooja emits loud, piercing cries and arches her back in protest. Though this makes it hard for Ms. Jackie to offer Mrs. Gupta reassuring words, she endeavors to do so in a positive, calm tone amid Pooja's inconsolable sadness. For instance, as Pooja's mother is leaving, Ms. Jackie says, "It's going to be okay, Mrs. Gupta. I will call you in a couple of hours to give you an update on Pooja." As Ms. Jackie comforts Pooja, she starts singing a fragment of a reassurance separation song that will become a daily, consistent element in forming the crucial trust that Pooja needs to thrive in her new environment:

> . . . 'cause my mommy comes back,
>
> She always comes back,
>
> Mommy comes back to get me.
>
> My mommy comes back,
>
> She always comes back.
>
> She never will forget me.

As the day goes on, Pooja occasionally looks around curiously at the children and toys around her, but she frequently cries and tries to pull away from Ms. Jackie to go toward the entrance door, where she last saw her mother. Ms. Jackie calmly acknowledges Pooja's emotions with familiar, reassuring words and songs.

During feeding time, sitting next to other infants in high chairs, Ms. Jackie holds Pooja on her lap and offers Pooja her bottle from home. She recalls the words and routines Pooja's mother shared with her during their introduction meeting and starts using them, like singing Pooja's favorite songs: "Twinkle, Twinkle, Little Star," "Snowflakes, Snowflakes," and "The Wheels on the Bus."

Ms. Jackie says, "Let's do some tai, tai, tai," as she claps her hands in one of Pooja's favorite games in an attempt to keep Pooja motivated to keep feeding. This game elicits some happy laughter before Pooja yawns. Ms. Jackie says, "Ghumu korbe!" (Time to sleep!) and prepares Pooja for her nap.

Each day, Ms. Jackie remains patient and empathetic. Slowly but consistently, Pooja makes progress. Ms. Jackie continues to invest time and thought in helping Pooja adjust to the program. She understands and practices what Chen and Ahmadein (2018) describe: "By incorporating the native cultures and languages of infants and toddlers into their authentic daily routines and activities, the caregivers naturally help to create necessary continuity and familiarity between the home and the childcare setting" (9).

For three weeks, Ms. Jackie feeds Pooja on her lap alongside the other infants who are sitting in high chairs. Then, one day, Pooja points to a chair next to other infants. No longer is she pushing back and turning her head forcefully around to avoid the spoon as she had done before.

Ms. Jackie asks, "Do you want to sit next to Jake and Ali?" Pooja smiles and lunges toward the high chair. Ms. Jackie happily sits Pooja down. Pooja begins to accept some table food too, though not yet from a spoon. She still prefers the food to be given to her by hand into her mouth. Watching Pooja eat her food, Ms. Jackie exclaims, "Ummmm, so good!"

Ms. Jackie shares Pooja's progress with Mrs. Gupta, who is very pleased to hear about it. However, at home, Mrs. Gupta continues to feed Pooja liquefied foods in her bottle whenever Pooja refuses solid foods. Ms. Jackie is concerned that in doing so, Pooja might take longer to accept finger foods and self-feed, both at home and at school. However, she continues to remain patient as she monitors Pooja's all-around progress and updates Mr. and Mrs. Gupta accordingly, gathering further data in case it is needed for future discussions.

While continuing to concentrate on consistent routines, Ms. Jackie has also started using sign language during the daily sing-alongs. She does the same during reading time. Imitating Ms. Jackie, Pooja begins to use some signs while singing along. Signing gradually becomes an additional tool of comfort and attachment for Pooja. Ms. Jackie suggests that Mr. and Mrs. Gupta use sign language with Pooja at home to facilitate the continuity of practice, and they both gladly accept this suggestion. Ms. Jackie also suggests letting Pooja hold her own spoon during solid feedings and singing her favorite songs to encourage Pooja to try table foods more.

Takeaways and Next Steps

This case illustrates the crucial role an early childhood educator plays in the development and learning of very young children from culturally and linguistically diverse backgrounds. It reinforces the importance of the continuity of learning between home and early childhood settings as well as a strong family–teacher partnership to benefit the child's development and learning. It also highlights Ms. Jackie's intentional efforts to incorporate cultural and linguistic values and behaviors that are different from her own, thus demonstrating that she stands committed to "recognizing differences as variations in strength, not deficits" (Bredekamp & Willer, 2022, 12).

After three months, Ms. Jackie's hard work has paid off as she witnesses Pooja's physical, social, and emotional growth. For example, Pooja smiles and lunges forward to Ms. Jackie at drop-off times. Pooja has also learned to use her hands to hold food. Ms. Jackie has gained the trust of not only Pooja but also her parents. Her intentional effort to form a positive partnership with Pooja's parents around Pooja's daily care and learning demonstrates what Chen and Ahmadein (2018) describe as "[seeking] to engage them in a collaborative endeavor to promote their child's language development and multicultural learning" (8). Importantly, Pooja's many positive interactions with Ms. Jackie have helped foster a growing secure attachment between infant and teacher.

Despite the encouraging progress made by Pooja, Ms. Jackie realizes that the work continues. Ms. Jackie intentionally plans to continue introducing new words in English while integrating words that Pooja already knows in her home language. Ms. Jackie demonstrates the value of embracing the whole child, including her home language and culture, in facilitating a smooth transition from home to group care for the child.

Furthermore, this case demonstrates that all learning occurs within a child's social, cultural, and linguistic contexts. Effective educators view these contextual factors as strengths and intentionally incorporate them throughout their daily interactions with children (core consideration 3 and guideline 2 of the position statement on developmentally appropriate practice).

Case Discussion Questions

1. How does this case demonstrate the crucial role of intentional teaching and the teacher's respectful strategies in facilitating an infant's transition from home to group care? If the teacher had not been as responsive to the family, how might this have affected her relationship with the family and the child? How might the child's development have been affected?
2. How does Ms. Jackie begin to establish a trusting relationship with Pooja and her family?

3. How does the teacher incorporate the knowledge she gains from the introduction meeting with Pooja's parents to facilitate a smooth transition for Pooja?
4. When Ms. Jackie realizes that Pooja's mother continues to feed Pooja her bottle at home, she chooses to wait and monitor Pooja's progress with self-feeding rather than bring her concerns to Mrs. Gupta. What might have been her reasoning for this decision? What do you see as the benefits and drawbacks of these two approaches?
5. How does Ms. Jackie incorporate Pooja's cultural and linguistic backgrounds and routines from home to better facilitate her social and emotional development?

General Discussion Questions

1. Why is it important for educators to capitalize on cultural and linguistic differences as valuable resources and strengths in promoting young children's development and learning?
2. How else might teachers support young children whose language, culture, and daily routines differ from their own or from those of the early learning program?

References

Bredekamp, S., & B. Willer. 2022. "Intentional Teaching: Complex Decision Making and the Core Considerations." In *Developmentally Appropriate Practice in Early Childhood Programs Serving Children from Birth Through Age 8*, 4th ed., NAEYC, 5–23. Washington, DC: NAEYC.

Chen, J.J., & J. Ahmadein. 2018. "Respectful Practices with Infants and Toddlers: Educating and Caring for the Youngest Children from Culturally and Linguistically Diverse Backgrounds." *Dimensions of Early Childhood* 46 (3): 7–12 [Spanish version, 13–18].

8.2 Engaging Dual Language Learners in Conversation to Support Translanguaging During a Small Group Activity

Valeria Erdosi and Jennifer J. Chen

Connections to *Developmentally Appropriate Practice*

- Chapter 1: Intentional Teaching: Complex Decision Making and the Core Considerations
- Chapter 2: The Principles in Practice: Understanding Child Development and Learning in Context
- Chapter 9: Teaching to Enhance Each Child's Development and Learning
- Chapter 10: Planning and Implementing an Engaging Curriculum to Achieve Meaningful Goals

Case Overview

Ms. Bentley teaches dual language learners (DLLs) in an English-Spanish bilingual preschool. This preschool follows the child-centered HighScope educational approach. Ms. Bentley's preschool classroom serves a multiage group of eleven 3- and 4-year-olds. Although Ms. Bentley is a monolingual English speaker, she has made a concerted effort to learn Spanish from Ms. Yanive, her bilingual teaching assistant, and the children during the last three years of her teaching at this preschool. As a result, she can now communicate with the children in some Spanish.

Ms. Bentley is supported by Ms. Yanive, who helps to translate key concepts used in all learning activities. Both Ms. Bentley and Ms. Yanive plan lessons together as well as share ideas and observations of each other's teaching and the children's learning.

One component of the daily routine in the HighScope educational approach is small group time. At this preschool, daily small group time lasts about 15 minutes, during which children engage in different learning activities. Understanding that language learning is most effectively facilitated through social interaction and meaningful conversation with others, Ms. Bentley and Ms. Yanive intentionally leverage small group activities to engage children in translanguaging practices that respect and value their dual language repertoire and potential. According to García (2009), "Translanguaging is the act performed by bilinguals of accessing different linguistic features or various modes of what are described as autonomous languages, in order to maximize communicative potential" (140). Baker (2011) defines translanguaging as "the process of making meaning, shaping experiences, gaining understanding and knowledge through the use of two languages" (288).

During this small group activity, Ms. Bentley engages five boys in conversations related to painting and understanding circular objects. This case serves as an example of how Ms. Bentley supports multimodal communication and the children's meaning making. It also demonstrates the fluidity of translanguaging in action.

Learning Objectives

1. Identify effective strategies for respecting and facilitating DLLs' diverse ways of communicating their ideas and needs.
2. Analyze ways to design and implement learning activities that can promote social interaction and conversation between the educator and DLLs.
3. Explain ways in which translanguaging is beneficial to fostering dual language competence in children.

Case Narrative

During a field trip to the pumpkin patch in October, Rolando was fascinated by the roundness of pumpkins. Ms. Bentley and Ms. Yanive have also consistently observed children creating or building circular representations during play. In response, they intentionally design a meaningful activity of painting circles as a context for engaging children in supportive conversations, which aligns with NAEYC's (2020) position statement on developmentally appropriate practice.

For the painting activity, Ms. Bentley is working with five boys with varying language abilities. Lorenzo and Derick (both age 4) and Evan (age 3) communicate in both English and Spanish; Rolando (age 4) speaks only English and is learning Spanish; and Macario (age 3) is learning English and currently responds mostly in Spanish.

Ms. Bentley is more knowledgeable about the bilingual development of Lorenzo and Derick because they were 3-years-olds in her multiage class the previous year. She has been teaching the other three boys for just two months at this point.

Before the Painting Activity

To prepare for the activity, Ms. Bentley has chosen a hollow cylinder tube with a round bottom as the tool for children to dip and tap paint onto a paper to show a circle. The choice of the cylinder offers children a concrete and tactile object with which to associate and create a representation of roundness. Learning about circles is an emerging focus that reflects Ms. Bentley's respect for children's interests. The concepts of circles and roundness are subsequently reinforced through other naturally occurring learning opportunities in the classroom, such as identifying circular objects.

During the Painting Activity

In preparation for painting, the children in Ms. Bentley's group put on their smocks. Ms. Bentley announces that today they are going to use paint to make circles. Each prepared tray contains a piece of paper, a cup of orange paint, and a cylinder. Along the side of the trays, Ms. Bentley has placed a paper towel for cleaning needs.

The following verbal and nonverbal exchanges between Ms. Bentley and individual children represent only part of the happenings during the activity.

Rolando: (*Sees the trays.*) We are going to do orange.

The other boys: Me too.

Ms. Bentley: Why do you think we are going to use the color orange?

Rolando: Pumpkin!

All five boys: Orange!

Ms. Bentley: Yes, orange pumpkins. Naranja para calabaza.

Ms. Bentley: Watch this—mire! I'm going to go dip. (*Dips the cylinder into the paint and holds up the tube.*) What do you see, Lorenzo?

Lorenzo: A bubble.

Ms. Bentley: A round bubble. And now I'm going to tap. I'm going to dip and tap. Now you are going to do this on your own.

Ms. Bentley: (*Points to her paper.*) You are going to make circles.

All five boys: (*Say in chorus.*) Bubbles!

Ms. Bentley: (*Gives each child their tray.*)

Derick: I made a big circle.

Ms. Bentley: (*Affirms what Derick said by saying it in Spanish to support the children's Spanish learning.*) Sí, un grande círculo.

Lorenzo: I made a big bubble.

Ms. Bentley: You are so excited about that. You both made big round objects!

Ms. Bentley: (*Sits next to Macario and gestures.*) You are dipping and tapping.

Macario: Sí.

Evan: (*Uses his hands to get more paint out of his cup.*)

Ms. Bentley: What's happening, Evan?

Evan: (*Shows Ms. Bentley his hands.*)

Ms. Bentley: You're making hands?

Evan: Yeah, give me more colors.

Ms. Bentley: Necesitas más naranjo?

Evan: (*Shakes his hands in the air to indicate he wants more paint.*) Yeah!

Ms. Bentley: (*Gives Evan more orange paint.*)

Ms. Bentley: (*Goes over to Lorenzo.*) Are you going to paint some more? You have lots of round shapes on your paper. I wonder how many you have.

Lorenzo: (*Holds up three fingers.*)

Ms. Bentley: You have three. (*Counts with Lorenzo in Spanish.*) Uno, dos, tres.

Lorenzo: (*Points to the paint on his hands.*)

Ms. Bentley: I know you don't like paint on your hands. How can we solve that problem?

Lorenzo: (*Shrugs.*)

Ms. Bentley: You can wipe it on the towel.

Lorenzo: (*Shakes his head.*)

Ms. Bentley: Would you like gloves?

Lorenzo: (*Nods.*)

Takeaways and Next Steps

Children articulate their knowledge in diverse ways, reflecting their language abilities and communication skills (Chen 2016; Chen & Shire 2011). This case demonstrates Ms. Bentley's understanding that language learning occurs meaningfully in context, as reflected in her concerted efforts to initiate and sustain conversations with children about things that interest them and what they are doing. During these interactive dialogues, Ms. Bentley intentionally applies what Rinaldi (2001) calls "pedagogy of listening." She does so by listening actively to the children's sharing of ideas to better understand how they think and how they engage in multimodal communication to convey their thinking. This practice helps both Ms. Bentley and children make meaning of what they experience and is particularly important for supporting language learning and communication skills in these DLLs. Ms. Bentley is also intentional in engaging children in two-way communication to build a positive rapport with each child (Nemeth 2022).

Besides encouraging verbal communication, this case illustrates Ms. Bentley's ability to understand and encourage children's nonverbal means of communicating their knowledge and needs. Ms. Bentley is drawing on her personal experience of having lived in a foreign country where she didn't understand the language. She became particularly sensitive to observing the nuances of people's facial expressions and body language and regularly using miming as a strategy to get her point across. In working with DLLs, she intentionally observes their nonverbal cues to get a clearer understanding of what they are trying to convey and then engages them in conversation to confirm or reaffirm their attempts at communicating. Ms. Bentley also draws on her knowledge of each DLL to provide developmentally appropriate language support, including respecting and making efforts to interpret each individual child's multiple means of communication. By applying these strategies, Ms. Bentley seeks to establish positive interactions with the children to make them feel safe and valued to voice their ideas, questions, and needs in whatever communicative modality and language they feel comfortable.

In a typically occurring post-activity discussion between Ms. Bentley and Ms. Yanive, Ms. Bentley reflects on her teaching practice during this activity. She discovers that she initiated nearly all of the conversations and did most of the talking. Ms. Yanive observes that perhaps because it has only been two months of school, the DLLs are still learning how to communicate and might not feel comfortable talking much. Encouraged by Ms. Yanive's observation, Ms. Bentley decides that as time progresses and the children's language skills advance, she will gradually assume a more facilitative role in conversing with the DLLs and engage them more frequently in child-centered dialogues and learning activities.

Upon reflecting with Ms. Yanive, Ms. Bentley also recognizes that the activity itself is mostly teacher directed, which may have limited the children's active learning. They discuss ways to offer more opportunities for creative expression and more varied, enriched teacher–child and child–child conversations.

Case Discussion Questions

1. High-quality language-promoting strategies are particularly important for advancing children's language development (Chen & de Groot Kim 2014). What additional strategies might Ms. Bentley have used to support the DLLs' emerging communicative and translanguaging abilities in a small group learning context?
2. In what ways did the conversations during the learning activity demonstrate the teacher's knowledge of each child's dual language abilities?
3. How might the teacher-led conversation in this case have supported or detracted from the children's bilingual development?
4. How might the teacher adjust the small group painting activity in ways that reflect a more child-centered approach? What opportunities might this practice provide for children's bilingual learning?

General Discussion Questions

1. How might a monolingual educator and a bilingual educator in the same classroom collaborate effectively to make good use of each other's skills and knowledge to optimize DLLs' translanguaging repertoire and potential?
2. How might teachers design and conduct small group learning activities to maximize DLLs' bilingual development?

References

Baker, C. 2011. *Foundations of Bilingual Education and Bilingualism*. 5th ed. Clevedon, UK: Multilingual Matters.

Chen, J.J. 2016. *Connecting Right from the Start: Fostering Effective Communication with Dual Language Learners*. Lewisville, NC: Gryphon House.

Chen, J.J., & S. de Groot Kim. 2014. "The Quality of Teachers' Interactive Conversations with Preschool Children from Low-income Families During Small-Group and Large-Group Activities." *Early Years: An International Research Journal* 34 (3): 271–88.

Chen, J.J., & S.H. Shire. 2011. "Strategic Teaching: Fostering Communication Skills in Diverse Young Learners." *Young Children* 66 (2): 20–27.

García, O. 2009. "Education, Multilingualism and Translanguaging in the 21st Century." In *Social Justice Through Multilingual Education*, eds. T. Skutnabb-Kangas, R. Phillipson, A.K. Mohanty, & M. Panda, 140–58. Clevedon, UK: Multilingual Matters.

NAEYC. 2020. "Developmentally Appropriate Practice." Position statement. Washington, DC: NAEYC. www.naeyc.org/resources/position-statements/dap/contents.

Nemeth, K. 2022. *Educating Young Children with Diverse Languages and Cultures*. New York: Routledge.

Rinaldi, C. 2001. "The Pedagogy of Listening: The Listening Perspective from Reggio Emilia." *Innovations* 8 (4): 14.

8.3 Incorporating Children's Cultures and Languages in the Classroom

Eleni Zgourou

Connections to *Developmentally Appropriate Practice*

- Chapter 2: The Principles in Practice: Understanding Child Development and Learning in Context
- Chapter 3: Context Matters: Reframing Teaching in Early Childhood Education
- Chapter 4: Teaching Content in Early Childhood Education
- Chapter 6: Creating a Caring, Equitable Community of Learners
- Chapter 7: Engaging in Reciprocal Partnerships with Families and Fostering Community Connections

Case Overview

This case study focuses on a key factor in the implementation of developmentally appropriate practice, "recognizing the multiple assets all young children bring to the early learning program as unique individuals and as members of families and communities" (NAEYC 2020, 5). After identifying a few of each family's cultural assets, Ms. Thompson invites a member of each child's family to her kindergarten classroom to engage the children in activities related to their linguistic and cultural backgrounds. In this way, she gets to know the children's individual experiences within their cultural context, which will help her understand the impact those experiences have on the children's development and learning. Depending on the learning experiences involved in each family's presentation, Ms. Thompson uses them as opportunities to build content knowledge (for example, math, literacy, science).

This case focuses on a Greek grandmother's bread-baking activity with the children in the classroom. The activity presents a valuable opportunity for Ms. Thompson to intentionally introduce math and science concepts, engage children in rich language interactions, and incorporate literacy tools that promote language and literacy competencies.

Learning Objectives

1. Analyze the types of strengths and funds of knowledge families from diverse linguistic and cultural backgrounds bring to the classroom.
2. Discuss (1) ways that children's responsibilities (for example, translating for a family member) as members of their cultural group may also be seen as strengths and (2) ways that these strengths and responsibilities shape child development.
3. Identify ways to support and sustain children's connection with their families, cultures, and languages.
4. Analyze culturally and linguistically meaningful ways to promote children's engagement with learning content in the classroom (for example, math, science, and literacy).

Case Narrative

Before the Learning Activity: Identifying Each Family's Cultural and Linguistic Assets

Ms. Thompson's class is ethnically, culturally, and linguistically diverse, with families coming from Argentina, Guatemala, Mexico, Colombia, Turkey, Greece, Portugal, and the United States. Some families are recent immigrants, but most of them have been living in the United States for at least one or two generations. Ms. Thompson contacts each family and invites them to her classroom to engage the children in an activity drawn from their own linguistic and cultural backgrounds. Ms. Thompson emphasizes that all families, regardless of their backgrounds, can contribute unique linguistic and cultural practices, and she helps families view those practices as assets. Ms. Thompson's invitation is well received, and she schedules the families to come on different days throughout the school year. For example, Konstantinos's grandmother from Greece will make homemade olive bread with the children, Eduardo's father from Argentina will play his bandoneón in the classroom, Laura's mother from Colombia will teach a few Spanish words to the children, and Mary's aunt from the United States will read a storybook to the children.

During the Learning Activity: Baking Olive Bread from the Greek Culture

Konstantinos's grandmother, Mrs. Economou, is the first to visit Ms. Thompson's kindergarten classroom. She speaks Greek fluently and some English. Because the teacher does not speak Greek, Konstantinos translates a few words from Greek to English for his teacher. Konstantinos introduces his grandmother: "This is my grandmother from Greece. She will make eliopsomo (Greek olive bread) with us."

Irene: What is eliopsomo?

Konstantinos: It is a kind of bread with olives.

Jackson: I have never had bread with olives before.

Konstantinos: Really? We have eliopsomo every week.

Ms. Thompson: I am so excited to learn about eliopsomo, which is a special food common in Konstantinos's Greek culture. We have to keep in mind that eliopsomo may not be common in another culture. Can we all say "eliopsomo"?

Children: Eliopsomo!

Konstantinos smiles, showing a sense of pride when his peers loudly repeat the word "eliopsomo" in Greek.

Konstantinos's grandmother begins unpacking her measuring cups, spoons, and other kitchen equipment as well as the ingredients for the bread, including flour, sugar, yeast, pitted olives, and herbs. As she unpacks each ingredient, she shows it to the children and tells them how it is called in her language. Ms. Thompson recognizes some of the ingredients and helps Konstantinos name them in English: "This is flour, this is sugar, and this is yeast, which makes bread rise." The children look with curiosity. Some children indicate how some of the ingredients are called in their home language. A child makes a connection with how her family uses flour.

Mary: We have flour at home too. We make cookies with my mom and my sister.

Ms. Thompson: That's wonderful, Mary. I bet the cookies you are making at home are delicious. What else can we make with flour?

Paul: My dad makes chocolate chip pancakes.

Sophia: My mom makes cake.

As the conversation continues, Mrs. Economou displays the olive bread recipe in Greek and in English that she had prepared ahead of time with the help of Ms. Thompson. On a piece of paper, Mrs. Economou and Ms. Thompson have glued a picture of each ingredient, its label in English and Greek, and the quantity of each ingredient needed for the bread. Mrs. Economou shows it to the children, and Ms. Thompson explains what a recipe is and how it is used. Next, the grandmother assigns a task to each child. For example, Mary will help measure the flour using a measuring cup. Each child takes turns measuring their assigned ingredient and adding it to a big mixing bowl.

The bread-making activity quickly turns into a science and math lesson. Children learn about the importance of precision, and they practice counting and measuring. Konstantinos's grandmother prepares the yeast with Valentina's help, and Ms. Thompson explains how yeast works, showing a brief YouTube demonstration video. She emphasizes that the water can't be too hot. A group of children assist with chopping the olives, using plastic knives. Mrs. Economou describes how olives are handpicked from their trees in her country and highlights that this is a social activity in which the entire extended family and sometimes neighbors gather to harvest olives. When all ingredients are placed in a big mixing bowl, Mrs. Economou mixes them, turning them into a dough. Then, she cuts the dough into pieces and gives one piece to each child. Each child then kneads the dough. After a few minutes, Konstantinos's grandmother encourages the children to let the dough sit in a warm place to rise until it doubles in volume. Just then, Ms. Thompson announces that it is time to get ready to go to lunch.

Later in the afternoon, Ms. Thompson brings the children back to the bread-making activity to complete the final part, which is to bake their bread doughs. The activity concludes with the children enjoying their homemade olive bread.

Ms. Thompson announces that next week, Mark's father from the United States will visit the classroom and teach the children how to play baseball.

Takeaways and Next Steps

The case example shows how a kindergarten teacher capitalizes on one family's funds of knowledge (Moll et al. 1992) to encourage family engagement, support deeper cultural understanding, and provide content teaching, all of which help promote the children's development and learning across domains. It also highlights the importance of building family–teacher partnerships to benefit the children's development and learning (Chen 2016).

Ms. Thompson reflects on the strategies she can further implement to identify families' additional funds of knowledge. For instance, family interviews may be appropriate, but supplemental strategies, such as home visits to observe family rituals, may also be effective (Iruka, Curenton, & Eke 2014). The teacher understands that this process requires building trust, respect, and rapport with the families. However, working with the families of dual language learners may present additional challenges due to "language barriers, immigrant status, and limited knowledge about the US education system that prevent them from actively participating in school activities" (Chen & Shire 2011, 21). Ms. Thompson plans to intentionally consider the potential barriers the families of the children in her classroom face and develop strategies to overcome them. For example, she can "ensure appropriate communication [with the family members], including providing translated material" (Chen 2016, 126).

Besides identifying families' funds of knowledge, Ms. Thompson reflects on how she can expand on the baking activity to incorporate additional experiences that promote children's learning. Instead of using it as an isolated activity, she could integrate it into a broader set of activities drawn from other families' backgrounds. For example, she could initiate a discussion during a mealtime about the kinds of bread or other types of food children eat at home (Chen & Shire 2011).

As Ms. Thompson reflects on the activities and the families' participation, she also considers the sociocultural contexts in which the children develop and learn. As Mrs. Economou had explained to the class, in the Greek culture, harvesting olives is often a social activity that involves the entire family and community members. This suggests strong family and community ties. Ms. Thompson wonders how this social context influences development and learning for children raised in such cultures. Furthermore, the bread-making experience uncovers a role of some children who live in homes where a language other than English is spoken—that of translator for some family members. Ms. Thompson considers the implications that this role might have in a child's cognitive, social, emotional, and language development.

Case Discussion Questions

1. How is the importance of family–teacher relationships reflected in this case study (guideline 2 of the position statement on developmentally appropriate practice)?
2. In what ways does Ms. Thompson utilize the families' funds of knowledge to help make the children and families feel included in her classroom? As she further identifies the families' funds of knowledge, how might she expand on this knowledge?
3. In what ways does the bread-making experience influence the children's development in various developmental domains (principle 2)?
4. How does the teacher support content learning in the bread-making activity?
5. How might Mrs. Economou's interaction with the children in the classroom impact their learning?
6. How might the teacher use the families' visits to facilitate respect for language differences and encourage the use of home languages at home and school? How would this benefit the children?

General Discussion Questions

1. How might teachers identify and incorporate families' funds of knowledge in their classrooms?
2. How else might teachers capitalize on children's cultural and linguistic assets to encourage learning across content areas throughout the school year?
3. How might teachers overcome language barriers when inviting family members to engage children in learning experiences related to their own cultures?

References

Chen, J.J. 2016. *Connecting Right from the Start: Fostering Effective Communication with Dual Language Learners*. Lewisville, NC: Gryphon House

Chen, J.J., & S.H. Shire. 2011. "Strategic Teaching: Fostering Communication Skills in Diverse Young Learners." *Young Children* 66 (2): 20–27.

Iruka, I.U., S.M. Curenton, & W.A.I. Eke. 2014. *The CRAF-E4 Family Engagement Model: Building Practitioners' Competence to Work with Diverse Families*. Waltham, MA: Academic Press.

Moll, L.C., C. Amanti, D. Neff, & N. Gonzalez. 1992. "Funds of Knowledge for Teaching: Using a Qualitative Approach to Connect Homes and Classrooms." *Theory into Practice* 31 (2): 132–41.

NAEYC. 2020. "Developmentally Appropriate Practice." Position statement. Washington, DC: NAEYC. www.naeyc.org/resources/position-statements/dap/contents.

8.4 Adapting Teaching Materials for Dual Language Learners to Reflect Their Home Languages and Cultures in a Math Lesson

Karen Nemeth

Connections to *Developmentally Appropriate Practice*

- Chapter 1: Intentional Teaching: Complex Decision Making and the Core Considerations
- Chapter 4: Teaching Content in Early Childhood Education
- Chapter 7: Engaging in Reciprocal Partnerships with Families and Fostering Community Connections
- Chapter 9: Teaching to Enhance Each Child's Development and Learning
- Chapter 10: Planning and Implementing an Engaging Curriculum to Achieve Meaningful Goals

Case Overview

This case describes the adaptations a teacher makes to help first-graders who are dual language learners (DLLs) learn about addition. These practices reflect the framework on developmentally appropriate practice, including the understanding that "each child reflects a complex mosaic of knowledge and experiences that contributes to the considerable diversity among any group of young children . . . including family languages, dialects, and vernaculars" (NAEYC 2020, 7).

Ms. Mazzeo's first grade class includes four children who are DLLs. One of them speaks Polish and three speak Spanish. In the first month of first grade, Ms. Mazzeo introduces simple addition to her class by explaining and providing plastic blocks for counting and adding. The Spanish and Polish speakers are not showing signs of meeting this learning goal, and Ms. Mazzeo realizes that her lessons might depend too heavily on her spoken explanations, making it difficult for children who are DLLs to fully comprehend them. After reading portions of Chapter 6 of *Developmentally Appropriate Practice* (Wright 2022), Ms. Mazzeo plans adaptations appropriate for the DLLs in her class that support their home languages.

Learning Objectives

1. Describe how educators can address the core considerations of individuality and context when using culturally and linguistically relevant materials to plan math lessons.
2. Describe ways to make math lessons meaningful and accessible to each child by using familiar items as manipulatives.
3. Analyze and describe ways to adapt math content-specific aspects of the curriculum to meet children's specific interests and learning needs.

Case Narrative

Before the Learning Activity

Ms. Mazzeo works with the small group of four children who are DLLs. She asks their families to send to school empty, cleaned food packages and/or photos of food packages that are culturally relevant and familiar to their child. She gathers these pictures, along with pictures from magazines and the internet chosen by the children, and glues them to small boxes to simulate food packages.

Ms. Mazzeo also prepares a poster with key vocabulary words in each of the languages spoken by the children: *plus, more, sum, answer, add, equals, same,* and the number names for 1–10. She gathers books with related content, such as *Too Many Tamales* by Gary Soto and *Stone Soup* by Ann McGovern.

During the Learning Activity

Ms. Mazzeo engages the children who are DLLs in a small group to identify the materials that will help them learn about addition in meaningful ways. Manipulatives that look like familiar, culturally relevant objects have intrinsic meaning for the students as they learn the vocabulary needed to acquire new skills in English and their home languages (Clements et al. 2018; Erikson Math Collaborative 2017; NASEM [National Academies of Sciences, Engineering, and Medicine] 2017; Nemeth 2017). These materials make it possible for the DLLs to build vocabulary learning in both English and their home languages while also learning math skills.

Ms. Mazzeo demonstrates the concept of addition, encouraging each child in the group to count and move their manipulatives to show the appropriate sum. As they work on these demonstrations together, Ms. Mazzeo frequently refers to the vocabulary poster to help children make connections between familiar number and operation words in their home languages and the new words in English.

Ms. Mazzeo: (*Holds up three "foods" and gestures/asks each child to put three of their own "foods" on their desk.*) In English, I say, "Foods—three foods." En Español, decimos alimentos—tres alimentos. (*Uses her translation app to say the same phrase in Polish to help the DLLs get oriented to the demonstration. Counts 1–3 in English and then counts 1–3 with the children in Spanish.*)

Maja: один два три ("jeden, dwa, trzy").

Ms. Mazzeo: Thank you, Maja. Let's all count to three in Polish with Maja: *jeden, dwa, trzy*. One, two, three.

Group: Jeden, dwa, trzy. One, two, three.

Ms. Mazzeo: You are counting in two languages, Polish and English! Now, let's add together: one plus two equals three. In Polish, we say, "Jeden plus dwa równa się trzy." (*Demonstrates by having the children move their foods accordingly.*)

Ms. Mazzeo then engages the children in talking about the types of foods depicted on their manipulatives and expands the dialogue to include the food items: one box of rice plus two cans of beans equals three foods.

Lucia: I like those beans. I want more beans!

Ms. Mazzeo: Who else likes to eat beans? Who cooks the beans in your family?

Luis: My dad cooks beans and mi abuelita.

Ms. Mazzeo: Oh! Your dad and your grandmother cook the beans! Should we add more? (*Shows the children how to add another can of beans to their display and add.*) 2 plus 2 equals 4 foods. Now let's point to the numbers on our vocabulary poster in English, Spanish, and Polish.

The group continues for a few more minutes until Ms. Mazzeo observes each child demonstrate basic comprehension of addition. She then stows the materials to be ready for repeating and expanding the lesson in the coming days. Later that day, Ms. Mazzeo reads the book *Too Many Tamales* to the whole class and highlights key words that she repeats in English, Spanish, and Polish.

Takeaways and Next Steps

This case example demonstrates the value of a coordinated approach to lesson planning that allows the teacher to focus on a particular skill—in this case addition—while including content and context that support each individual child's learning in ways that are culturally, linguistically, and ability responsive across multiple learning domains. The teacher includes active learning with manipulatives that connect learning with familiar items from home. The role of family members is empowering for the adults and children as the lesson uses culturally meaningful items provided from each child's home. The teacher provides multiple activities for the DLLs to learn and practice the vocabulary and skills that are the target of this lesson and multiple means of expressing what they are learning.

Planning this lesson gives Ms. Mazzeo her own food for thought:

1. What are some meaningful items the children can bring or make that represent their home life and culture other than food?
2. What other learning experiences could I provide that use this framework by including vocabulary in both English and the DLLs' home languages, meaningful hands-on materials, and other STEM content?
3. What next steps can I take to examine the manipulatives that I have in my classroom and replace them with items that are culturally and linguistically meaningful to each child? (A child who is learning English might not understand why they are counting dots on a page, but counting glue pots for everyone in the class or counting the number of blocks they need to complete a tower would be more concrete.)
4. What other strategies can I use to build language and learning for the DLLs in my class?

Case Discussion Questions

1. How did Ms. Mazzeo address the core considerations of individuality and context in planning the materials and activities for this intentional math lesson?
2. How did the components of this lesson plan support principle 5 of the position statement on developmentally appropriate practice?
3. To extend the lesson and make the most use of the culturally familiar materials, what other activities could the teacher do with the DLLs to further implement guideline 1E of the position statement on developmentally appropriate practice?

General Discussion Questions

1. Consider how you would teach the skill of addition to a child who doesn't understand your language. How do meaningful materials play a role in making sense of the learning activity in connection with guideline 1B of the position statement on developmentally appropriate practice?
2. How might you communicate with families about providing meaningful items from home to demonstrate addition in connection with guideline 2B of the position statement on developmentally appropriate practice?

References

Clements, D., J. Sarama, T.S. Kutaka, & H. Banse. 2018. *Supporting Dual Language Learners and English Language Learners in Early Math: Research-Based Tips for Teachers.* Denver, CO: Marsico Institute. www.learningtrajectories.org/documents/1571674858177.pdf.

Erikson Math Collaborative. 2017. "Promising Math 2017." Proceedings of the Conference on Access to Math for Young English Language Learners. Erikson Institute: Chicago, IL.

NAEYC. 2020. "Developmentally Appropriate Practice." Position statement. Washington, DC: NAEYC. www.naeyc.org/resources/position-statements.dap.

NASEM (National Academies of Sciences, Engineering, and Medicine). 2017. *Promoting the Education Success of Children and Youth Learning English: Promising Futures.* Washington, DC: National Academies Press. www.nap.edu/catalog/24677/promoting-the-educational-success-of-children-and-youth-learning-english.

Nemeth, K. 2017. "Make Math Meaningful for Diverse Learners." *Teaching Young Children* 11 (1): 4–6. www.naeyc.org/resources/pubs/tyc/oct2017/make-math-meaningful-diverse-learners.

Wright, B.L. 2022. "Creating a Caring, Equitable Community of Learners." In *Developmentally Appropriate Practice in Early Childhood Programs Serving Children from Birth Through Age 8*, 4th ed., NAEYC, 111–44. Washington, DC: NAEYC.

8.5 **Studying Celestial Bodies: Science and Cultural Stories**

Zeynep Isik-Ercan

Connections to *Developmentally Appropriate Practice*

- Chapter 4: Teaching Content in Early Childhood Education
- Chapter 6: Creating a Caring, Equitable Community of Learners
- Chapter 7: Engaging in Reciprocal Partnerships with Families and Fostering Community Connections
- Chapter 10: Planning and Implementing an Engaging Curriculum to Achieve Meaningful Goals

Case Overview

This case focuses on engaging families in children's learning by sharing and honoring their cultural traditions and heritages and on fostering children's understanding of and appreciation for cultural differences. Ms. Alissa's second grade class undertakes a science and literacy project focused on astronomy. In addition to experiences in which the class explores the scientific nature of the moon, earth, and sun, Ms. Alissa plans a literacy project around families' cultural stories about the moon, sun, and other celestial bodies. Families are invited to share these stories by sending videos, songs, and pictures. The children take turns sharing these cultural stories with the class each day during the last week of the project.

Learning Objectives

1. Articulate ways that early childhood educators can design learning experiences across multiple developmental domains and subject areas.
2. Analyze ways that early childhood educators can collaborate with and learn about culturally and linguistically diverse families as well as engage them in classroom learning.
3. Identify ways educators can acknowledge, promote, and honor children's identities to help create an equitable classroom.
4. Identify ways to introduce learners to multiple ways of being, learning, speaking, and thinking.

Case Narrative

Before the Learning Experience: An Interdisciplinary Unit on Astronomy

Ms. Alissa has 21 learners in her urban second grade classroom in a midwestern city. Seven of these learners are dual language learners (DLLs) of Spanish and English and attended kindergarten and first grade in the same school. Three children are recent refugees from Burma and are just beginning to learn English, supported by the English as a Second Language (ESL) program. The rest of the learners speak only English. They consist of five African American learners and six White learners. Ms. Alissa does not have formal training on teaching DLLs, but she is enthusiastic about the hands-on science content and potential opportunities for furthering language learning for all of her students.

Ms. Alissa, in collaboration with a researcher from the nearby university, creates an interdisciplinary, interactive science and literacy astronomy project that purposefully focuses on content that may be considered advanced for second-graders. Ms. Alissa and the researcher wish to engage children's intellectual skills in learning higher-level content through developmentally appropriate learning experiences. The content goals for the children include understanding how day and night occur, analyzing why the moon appears to change shape, and investigating how seasons occur.

During the Learning Activity: Students Sharing Cultural Stories

The project is conducted during an entire afternoon each school day for three weeks. The researcher supports the classroom teacher with a three-dimensional technology component: on a mobile computer, children take turns using keyboard commands and moving the mouse to simulate the movements of the earth and moon in a 3D module. The other children can watch the movements on a large screen. Children also engage in hands-on experiments, such as rotating a globe while shining a flashlight on it to demonstrate how the earth's rotation results in day and night and playing sequencing games to show the phases of the moon.

Throughout the project, children explore nonfiction and fiction books on astronomy; write responses to what they read; read aloud to their partners; and work in groups to present a topic to the class about the relationships between the sun, moon, and earth. The children choose how they will represent their ideas, including by drawing, writing in either English or their home language, or acting them out.

As a way to engage all the families, particularly those speaking languages other than English, Ms. Alissa tells the children that they are going to collect and write down any cultural stories that their families can share about the sun, moon, and earth. Subsequently, all families receive a written invitation over email (translation is embedded through an app for those who need it) to participate by sending videos, songs, and pictures along with their cultural stories about the moon, sun, and earth. After a few technology issues, all families are able to participate and do so eagerly. They share their videos on a cloud drive created for the class. During each afternoon in the third week, the children present their cultural stories to the class.

The videos are played in the families' original language, and Ms. Alissa distributes copies of the translations for the children to follow along. Ms. Alissa purposefully asks the children beforehand to see if they can guess the English translation of any of the words that they hear from the family members speaking in the video.

Jesus is the first one to share. Ms. Alissa helps him play the video of his grandmother sharing in Spanish the famous ancient Rabbit Moon story from Mexico:

> It was a long time ago. God was still on the earth, walking, eating, and living his life like a human. After a long walk, God got so tired and hungry and could not move anymore. He was worried that this was the end of his life. He laid down and almost lost consciousness. Just at that moment, a rabbit came running toward him. He said, "I can help you. Because you gave me all of my food before, I can become your food, so you continue to feed my friends." God got up and got his energy back. He needed this kindness. He was so pleased with Rabbit's generosity that he engraved his image on the moon. Still, if people look carefully at the moon, they can see the reflection of a rabbit.

This story fascinates the children. They begin talking about the moon's craters and all of the possible tracings they can do to imagine different things along with the rabbit engraved on moon. After hearing the story, Ms. Alissa asks children to pick up the Spanish words they have heard repeatedly in the video and try to guess what they are in English. Children identify the words *dios*, *la luna*, and *conejo* in the video and match them to their English counterparts (*God*, *the moon*, and *rabbit*, respectively).

Nay Chi's Burmese family recently moved to the United States from a refugee camp in Thailand. He shares a video of his parents telling a famous moon story from Burma, with the help of Ms. Alissa, who distributes the written translation:

> There was a very big dog in the forest, always fighting with large animals and trying to take their food. One day the big animals like the tiger, the lion, and the rhino came together and offered a challenge to him: "Only if you can catch the moon we will accept you as our leader and give you our food." Then the big dog chased the moon for a long time, until one day he bit the moon. That moment, the moon went dark. People say it is the eclipse when you see the moon going dark, but for ancient people in Burma, it was actually the dog biting the moon.

The children are very intrigued and begin asking Nay Chi questions. Nay Chi keeps quiet while nodding and smiling during most of the discussion. Ms. Alissa notices that he has drawn "∞"—the infinity symbol in English that is the written word for *moon* in Burmese.

Takeaways and Next Steps

Ms. Alissa is always passionate and excited about providing opportunities for interdisciplinary learning through engaging topics. Although she admits that this three-week project was overwhelming and might not have been possible without the assistance of the researcher and a supportive school principal, Ms.

Alissa is quite energized by the cultural stories component. She had been unsure how willing the parents would be to share them. Now, she plans to leverage the families' enthusiasm to encourage greater participation in family–teacher conferences by inviting them to share their expertise on their children.

Ms. Alissa anticipated that it would be interesting for the children to hear different languages, but by the end of the project she gains a new appreciation of the rich heritage that all of the children, not just those who are DLLs, bring to the classroom. She feels that her students have also become more curious about other languages and cultural experiences.

Through this cultural story-sharing experience, Ms. Alissa intentionally provides opportunities for monolingual learners to learn from their multilingual peers. For example, she asks all her learners to see if they can identify a few words in Spanish and Burmese during the presentations, which helps to elevate the status of second language learning and honors the DLLs for their skill in speaking two languages. By doing so, she does not label her learners only as English language learners (which may imply a deficit-based view, as if their home language is not important). Instead, she identifies them and their families as valuable learning resources and emerging bilinguals (a strengths-based view). Ms. Alissa thinks about other ways she could have supported Nay Chi as she noticed that he did not have a good opportunity to talk about his cultural story and interact with his classmates.

Besides elevating the value of second language learning, Ms. Alissa does not single out DLLs as children with "different" cultures. Instead, by asking *each* child for their cultural stories, Ms. Alissa demonstrates her intentional effort to include all children's diverse family heritages in the learning experience (Isik-Ercan 2017). Ms. Alissa next plans to begin a discussion with other teachers to share her experience and organize a multicultural night as an end-of-the-year event so that all the children in the school can participate in a cultural sharing experience.

Case Discussion Questions

1. Ms. Alissa requests cultural stories from *all* of her learners. How does that support the creation of a caring, equitable community of learners?
2. How do you think Ms. Alissa helped the children discern similarities and differences between cultural beliefs and scientific evidence about phenomena?
3. How else might Ms. Alissa have moderated Nay Chi's video presentations given that he was not ready to verbalize additional information in English? What other support might Ms. Alissa provide to facilitate a conversation?
4. How does the project as a whole meet some of the expectations stated in guideline 4 of the position statement on developmentally appropriate practice, particularly 4C?

General Discussion Questions

1. In what other ways can teachers incorporate the strengths of DLLs and families into classroom learning experiences?
2. How else can teachers help foster children's understanding of and respect for all cultural identities and expressions?
3. Immigrant families, regardless of socioeconomic status, usually are well equipped with internet technologies as they must communicate with family and friends across continents (Isik-Ercan 2012). Still, what could a teacher do if a student's family is unable to record a cultural story or otherwise participate in a technology-centered activity?
4. Ms. Alissa admits that this learning experience was complex and she was able to accomplish it with the support of a researcher. How might a teacher create similar experiences, or accomplish similar goals, with more limited resources?

References

Isik-Ercan, Z. 2012. "In Pursuit of a New Perspective in the Education of Children of the Refugees: Advocacy for the 'Family.'" *Educational Sciences: Theory and Practice* 12 (4): 3025–38.

Isik-Ercan, Z. 2017. "Culturally Appropriate Positive Guidance with Young Children." *Young Children* 72 (1): 15–21.

8.6 **Respecting Diverse Cultures and Languages: Sharing a Favorite Poem, Song, or Story of an Individual from Another Culture and Language**

Janis Strasser

Connections to *Developmentally Appropriate Practice*

- Chapter 6: Creating a Caring, Equitable Community of Learners
- Chapter 7: Engaging in Reciprocal Partnerships with Families and Fostering Community Connections
- Chapter 10: Planning and Implementing an Engaging Curriculum to Achieve Meaningful Goals

Case Overview

This case focuses on the importance of early childhood educators' actions to engage and collaborate with young children and their culturally and linguistically diverse families in the educational process, including "getting to know each child well, understanding each child as an individual and as a family and community member, . . . seeking information from the family," and understanding that each child's differences include their "various social identities . . . cultural experiences, [and] . . . family languages" (NAEYC 2020, 7).

Ms. McNeal's third grade class consists of 20 students. Among them are four children whose families are from China, Latin America, and Poland. To help her students become a community of learners, in the beginning of the school year, Ms. McNeal gives her students a homework assignment in which they will record and share aspects of their families' unique languages, cultures, and funds of knowledge. She has read and reflected on the examples to consider for primary grades in Chapter 6 of *Developmentally Appropriate Practice* (Wright 2022) and knows that each child's home language "embodies valuable cultural capital and is an integral part of a child's identity; it mirrors who she is, where she came from, and where she is headed" (Nemeth 2014, 64).

Learning Objectives

1. Articulate ways that early childhood educators can design classroom activities and discussions that include opportunities for sharing and learning about diverse family backgrounds.
2. Analyze ways that early childhood educators can collaborate with and learn about culturally and linguistically diverse families.
3. Identify opportunities for learning experiences that reflect children's and families' lives and cultures.
4. Describe opportunities for students to listen to a variety of languages and learn about diverse customs and cultures that are represented in the community.

Case Narrative

Before the Learning Activity: The Interview Assignment

One of Ms. McNeal's students, Michelle, speaks Chinese with her grandparents and both Chinese and English with her parents. In addition, two students in Ms. McNeal's class speak mostly Spanish at home and another student speaks Polish and English at home. To find authentic ways to share with the class the languages and cultures of these children's families as well as those of the other families, Ms. McNeal creates a homework assignment in which all the students interview someone they know (a member of their family, a family friend, a neighbor, or a member of the community) who speaks a language other than English.

For the assignment, students ask the individual to share a poem, story, or song in their language and explain the significance of it. Ms. McNeal discusses the assignment with families at Back to School Night and posts the assignment on the school website. Additionally, she compiles and posts a list of people from the neighborhood and the school community who speak other languages for students who don't have access to anyone to interview. The students previously learned how to interview and record an interview using a phone, an iPad, or other electronic device.

After interviewing the individual in English or in a mutually understandable non-English language about their favorite poem, song, or story, the students ask about the meaning and significance of it to, in turn, share it in their own words. Ms. McNeal suggests that the students use note cards during their presentations to help them remember the important points to share. To respect differences in the students' pace and ability to communicate information orally, Ms. McNeal does not set a time limit for each presentation.

During the Learning Activity: Students Sharing Interviews

Michelle is the first to share her interview with the class. She says, "My grandma shared her favorite story with me. In English, it's called 'The Frog in the Well.' It's about a frog who lives in the bottom of the well and has never been outside it. One day, a sea turtle passes by and the frog wants to show off his well, so he tells the sea turtle how happy and comfortable he is living at the bottom of his well and invites the turtle to see it. The sea turtle goes in and sees the bottom of the well. He then tells the frog about all the great things he has experienced while living in the ocean and how he is proud to live in such a magnificent place. The frog is shocked to hear about all the great things outside of his well that he's never seen before and gets embarrassed that he thought he knew everything about the world. Grandma said she picked this story because it was her favorite story growing up. She also said it teaches a very important lesson to never think that you know everything."

Michelle plays the recording of her grandma sharing the story in Chinese on her phone, which was allowed in this classroom for educational purposes. As the other students hear her grandmother speaking, a few start laughing. Michelle's smile fades and she blushes.

Ms. McNeal says, "Let's remember to be respectful to our classmates. Sometimes when we hear a language we have never heard before, it sounds new or different." This gentle reminder helps quiet the laughing. She refocuses the class on the discussion at hand by asking, "Who has a question or comment for Michelle about the story she shared?"

Kristin: That's cool. In first grade, we read *Frog and Toad.*

Jackson: Was the story in a book, or did someone make it up and tell it to her?

Michelle: I think it's a story everyone knows, and the grown-ups tell the children.

Devon: It sounds really complicated to speak Chinese. Is it hard?

Michelle: I don't think so. I just learned how to speak it when I was a baby before I learned how to speak English.

Mia: Can I go next? My Grandma Halinka shared her favorite song in Russian. It's called "Kalinka." She said there's a dance that goes with it. The words are "Little red berry. Little red berry of mine. In the garden is a little raspberry. My little raspberry." We found a YouTube video of it in Russian with the dancing. My grandma grew up in Poland, but she had to learn to speak Russian because in school, she was not allowed to speak her language, Polish. That's why the favorite song she picked was in Russian. I couldn't believe that her teachers wouldn't let her speak her language or she would get punished. But I don't like it when my grandma speaks Polish to me when we are in the supermarket or other places where no one else speaks Polish. I don't want people to think she doesn't know how to speak English.

Llaoli: My mom always wants to speak Spanish when we are at the mall. I hate that too. I ask her to only speak Spanish to me at home.

Olivio: I don't see what the big deal is. Sometimes my dad speaks Spanish and sometimes he speaks English. Who cares?

It is time to go to lunch, so Ms. McNeal explains that they will continue their discussion this afternoon and Mia will share the recording of her grandmother's song.

Takeaways and Next Steps

This case focuses on the teacher's commitment to supporting the home languages and cultures of the students in her class and the broader community. As her students begin to share their interview contents, Ms. McNeal realizes that there are sociopolitical nuances and personal struggles facing individuals who speak a different language other than English (for example, Mia's grandmother was prohibited from speaking her home language in school; two students express discomfort with having family members speaking their home languages in public). The teacher is demonstrating an "ongoing interest in each child's unique knowledge, skills, and cultural and linguistic experiences and recognize[s] these as assets for learning" (NAEYC 2020, 15).

Ms. McNeal realizes that she needs to think more about how to use and extend her students' family and cultural experiences to broaden the children's understandings about the world. She will contact Mia's family to explore the possibility of inviting her grandmother to come in and talk to the class about her feeling of not being allowed to speak her home language in school and its impact on her life.

Ms. McNeal also thinks about the comments Mia and Llaoli made about how they feel when family members speak their home language in public. She postulates that if she has more group discussions that honor and support the home languages of her students, maybe it will help them feel more positive and comfortable with their family members speaking their home languages. It will also help to prepare the students to listen respectfully to new, unfamiliar languages without making fun of them. In this connection, Ms. McNeal will talk with Michelle privately during lunch to make sure her feelings weren't hurt when the children laughed at how her grandmother sounded when she shared the story in Chinese. Reflecting on the complex issues that emerged during the classroom discussion, Ms. McNeal realizes that she needs to go beyond fostering students' respect for linguistic and cultural differences and help them appreciate the value of speaking more than one language.

Ms. McNeal's reflections demonstrate her understanding that "young children are developing multiple social identities that include race, language, culture . . ." (Wright 2022, 119), and she is committed to honoring "the perspectives, experiences, and realities of children and their families from culturally, linguistically, and economically diverse backgrounds" (119–20). Through intentional teaching, she wants to ensure that she avoids the types of stereotypical cultural sharing and assumptions that do not reflect the actual experiences of the students in her class.

Case Discussion Questions

1. How does the interview activity reflect guideline 1 of the position statement on developmentally appropriate practice?
2. How else might the teacher address, in developmentally appropriate ways, her concerns regarding Llaoli's and Mia's negative comments about their family members speaking their home languages in public?
3. Besides inviting Mia's grandmother to visit the class, how might Ms. McNeal incorporate elements of guideline 5D.2 of the position statement on developmentally appropriate practice?
4. How are this interview assignment, the teacher's reflections, and her next steps related to guideline 4B.2 of the position statement on developmentally appropriate practice?
5. Do you think Ms. McNeal's response to the laughter that occurred during Michelle's presentation was effective? Why or why not? Why might she have chosen to only briefly address the behavior rather than to have a deeper discussion with the whole class? How might she have used that teachable moment to build empathy, understanding, and awareness as a learning community? What are some ways she can follow up at a later time?
6. What might be a developmentally appropriate follow-up activity for the class to learn more about how children and adults who speak more than one language use those languages in different settings?

General Discussion Questions

1. What are other ways for educators to foster children's respect and appreciation for linguistic and cultural differences?
2. What are some ways educators can support cultural sharing without introducing or reinforcing stereotypes? What should they consider?
3. Considering the notion of "fair and equitable pedagogy" (Wright 2022, 119), how can a teacher avoid the tourist approach in inviting students to share their home experiences throughout the school year?

References

NAEYC. 2020. "Developmentally Appropriate Practice." Position statement. Washington, DC: NAEYC. www.naeyc.org/resources/position-statements/dap.

Nemeth, K. 2014. *Young Dual Language Learners: A Guide for PreK–3 Leaders*. Philadelphia, PA: Caslon.

Wright, B.L. 2022. "Creating a Caring, Equitable Community of Learners." In *Developmentally Appropriate Practice in Early Childhood Programs Serving Children from Birth Through Age 8*, 4th ed., NAEYC, 111–44. Washington, DC: NAEYC.

Index

Page numbers followed by *f* indicate figures.